Digital Futures
for Cultural and Media Studies

To Tina Horton

As they say, the message is in the song!

Digital Futures
for Cultural and Media Studies

John Hartley

WILEY-BLACKWELL

A John Wiley & Sons, Ltd., Publication

Library of Congress Cataloging-in-Publication Data is available

Hardback ISBN 9780470671009
Paperback ISBN 9780470671016

A catalogue record for this book is available from the British Library.

This book is published in the following electronic formats: ePDFs 9781118106693; Wiley Online Library 9781118106723; ePub 9781118106709; mobi 9781118106716

Set in 10.5/13 pt Minion by Toppan Best-set Premedia Limited
Printed in Malaysia by Ho Printing (M) Sdn Bhd

1   2012

Contents

1. The History and Future of Ideas   1

2. Cultural Studies, Creative Industries, and Cultural Science   27

3. Journalism and Popular Culture   59

4. The Distribution of Public Thought   94

5. Television Goes Online   117

6. Silly Citizenship   133

7. The Probability Archive   155

8. Messaging as Identity   176

9. Paradigm Shifters: Tricksters and Cultural Science   199

References   215

Acknowledgments   236

Index   238

1

The History and Future of Ideas

False facts are highly injurious to the progress of science, for they often endure long; but false views, if supported by some evidence, do little harm, for every one takes a salutary pleasure in proving their falseness: and when this is done, one path towards error is closed and the road to truth is often at the same time opened. (Charles Darwin 1871: xxi)

Part I: Reading Digits

Reading, which was in decline due to the growth of television, tripled from 1980 to 2008, because it is the overwhelmingly preferred way to receive words on the Internet. (Bohn and Short 2010: 7)

Media and cultural studies grew up in the era of the press, broadcasting, mass consumption, and national popular culture. Were these innocent novelties, harmless entertainments for suburbanizing workforces and their nucleating families? Early cultural and media studies thought not. Media consumption and everyday cultural practices were beset on all sides by darker forces that seemed to be exploiting the pleasure-seeking consumer for quite different ends, both political and corporate. Given that the mid twentieth century was the high water mark for totalitarianism in politics as well as capitalist monopolies in the media marketplace, it is no wonder that cultural and media studies were founded in suspicion of those who

---

Digital Futures for Cultural and Media Studies, First Edition. John Hartley.
© 2012 John Wiley & Sons, Ltd. Published 2012 by John Wiley & Sons, Ltd.

own and control the media. As a result, media and cultural studies readily took over from communication science and cybernetics a model of communication that seemed to express this structurally opposed and even antagonistic difference between producers and consumers. This was the linear 'sender → message → receiver' model, made famous by Claude Shannon (1948). It placed producers at one end, consumers at the other, and causation as an arrow going one way only, as 'information' is sent from active agent to passive receiver.

It is easy to see how this model can be used as a metaphor for communication through the media. The 'sender' may be a capitalist corporation or a state; the 'message' may be propaganda, for consumerism, capitalism, or communism; and the 'receiver' is a passive individual, often feminized as 'the housewife,' reduced to 'behavior' rather than self-motivated action. Thus, there is room for duplicity and deceit at each link in the process. The producer may have hidden motives; the message may have hidden meanings; and the recipient may be made to behave in ways that he or she would not otherwise have chosen (media effects). Although such a model of communication has been criticized and reworked many times over the years, it still has a commonsensical hold over much work in the field, and also across government policy, corporate strategy, and community engagement in relation to popular media and culture.

With the emergence of digital, interactive, and participatory media and of the 'user,' as opposed to the consumer, it is timely to rethink this underlying model of communication. An alternative is in fact readily to hand. The 'dialogic model of language' implies turn-taking, mutual productivity, context-specific uses, and an example of an almost infinitely complex system – namely language and its 'institutional forms' in textual systems such as literature, media, journalism, and science – that is nevertheless continuously produced by myriad unmanaged and self-organizing 'users' or speakers, whose agency is 'open' but not 'free-for-all.'

It is my hope that media and cultural studies can be reformed not only to take account of the technological consequences of digital media but also to take seriously the dialogic model of communication – where, you will note, 'the consumer' disappears entirely. Instead, 'meaningfulness,' 'social networks,' and 'relationships' surface as crucial components of the process. They replace 'content,' 'information,' or the 'message' with human interaction based on self-expression (albeit constrained by language and other systems of communication), description and argumentation ('truth-seeking' in Karl Popper's terms), as well as play, 'phatic' chatter, and imaginative invention. Of course, language can be used for exploitative, duplicitous, and hidden purposes just as much as any other medium, but a model of communication in which *everyone is a producer*, and where these constraints are continuously renegotiated in action, is surely preferable to one based on behaviorist assumptions that reduce human agency to the status of the lab rat.

A further implication of shifting our analytical lens from the linear model to a dialogic one is that we can extend the study of media and culture from its present fixation with a tiny minority of powerful *producers* (i.e. industry professionals) to a *population-wide* focus on how all the 'agents,' individual or institutional, in a given communication, media, or cultural system act and are acted upon as they use it (i.e. the 'people formerly known as the audience').

If media and cultural studies are to transform – from a linear to a dialogic mode; from producer to consumer; from powerful corporation and charismatic celebrity to *everybody* in the population; from representation to productivity; from structural opposition to dynamic systems; from cultural *studies* to cultural *science* – is there anything left that we might recognize *as* media and cultural studies? My answer takes the form of this book: it remains interested in the media, popular culture, and textual systems as the best evidence for sense-making practices at large scale, and it retains the familiar focus of cultural and media studies on questions of meaning, identity, power, and 'the human,' in the context of technology, the market economy, and global interaction among our dispersed and diverse but 'convergent' species (Jenkins 2006).

One thing that cultural and media studies do particularly well, in my view, is to study the situated and contextual process – both informal (in self-organizing networks) and formal (via institutional agency) – of the *emergence of ideas* in mediated networks. How that is done on a society-wide scale using the latest communications technologies is no longer a matter of interest to media and cultural scholars alone. It has also become a vital interest among economists, who seek to understand *innovation* as the process where new values, both cultural and economic, *emerge* from a complex open system. The contemporary digital media, which are dialogic, consumer co-created, population-wide, productive, and dynamic, may be just the place to study the *evolution of novelty*.

Each ensuing chapter takes these general issues forward in a specific context:

- Chapter 2 (CULTURAL STUDIES, CREATIVE INDUSTRIES, AND CULTURAL SCIENCE) maps out the changes that may be required in our disciplinary settings if we are to do justice to emergent meanings.
- Chapter 3 (JOURNALISM AND POPULAR CULTURE) subjects journalism – and journalism studies – to a comparative historical analysis that shows how modern 'mass' journalism was originally invented on a dialogic model of communication, only later falling prey to the linear model that dominates the domain today. The chapter argues that the dialogic model is re-emergent in the digital age.
- Similarly, Chapter 4 (THE DISTRIBUTION OF PUBLIC THOUGHT) shows how the public sphere itself has evolved in the global era, not only by going online but also through such self-organizing market mechanisms as the 'airport bestseller,' a hitherto neglected media form, which coordinates and distributes ideas in a way that may help us to understand how new ideas using new media may have evolved their own coordinating mechanisms, despite the fear of the amateur that currently preoccupies the minds of expert professionals who are used to 'representing' the population at large in the realm of ideas.
- Chapter 5 (TELEVISION GOES ONLINE) shifts the focus to television, exploring what happens when television opens out, from 'representative' broadcasting to 'productive' digital affordances.
- Chapter 6 (SILLY CITIZENSHIP) takes these ideas further to show how the agents 'formerly known as the audience,' especially those *not* counted as citizens, for example children, may be making up new forms of civic engagement even as they play with the digital media.
- Chapter 7 (THE PROBABILITY ARCHIVE) pursues online television into the archive – specifically YouTube – to show how that pursuit changes what we mean by archiving, and the very nature of the archive itself, in the process. Shifting from 'representative' to 'productive' status also changes the nature of the archive from 'essence' to 'probability' – a move that has profound implications for our disciplinary methodology.
- Chapter 8 (MESSAGING AS IDENTITY) throws caution to the wind and proposes the reclassification of our species – *Homo sapiens* – as *Homo sapiens nuntius*: 'messaging humanity.' Here the idea is that personal identity itself is a *product of*, rather than input into or affected by, our messaging interactions with one another, such that the very idea of 'the message' needs to be updated from noun to verb (thing to action), somewhat after the manner of the visionary architect Buckminster Fuller (Buckminster Fuller, Agel, and Fiore 1970), whose autobiography

was entitled *I Seem to be a Verb*. Well – we seem to be constituted by our messaging.

• Chapter 9 (PARADIGM SHIFTERS: TRICKSTERS AND CULTURAL SCIENCE) draws the themes of the book together by highlighting the extent to which *change* has been a constant 'problem situation' for the humanities just as it has been for economics. Thus, the tradition of the trickster in classical mythology and in anthropology, which has been investigated using the classic tools of textual analysis and 'thick description,' may be linked with that of the entrepreneur, the focus of evolutionary economics. Both the mythological trickster and the Schumpeterian entrepreneur are agents of system change or 'creative destruction,' the 'go-betweens' who link, disrupt, and renew different worlds to produce new meanings.

Thus, this book sets out on a path to reorient and reconceptualize media and cultural studies, while investigating some examples of digital futures along the way to see which way they are pointing.

My Media Studies

My involvement in what would eventually be called media studies started in the 1970s, on the trail of the 'active audience.' During the broadcast era, the idea of such a thing may have seemed perverse. At the time, media audiences were widely thought to be passive couch potatoes, exhibiting behavioral responses to psychological stimuli coming from powerful commercial and political agencies whose motives were far from pure. The pursuit was even more quixotic because I had no training in 'audience studies,' if by that was meant ethnographic description, sociological survey, or psychological experiment on the bodies of 'subjects.' I was trained in literary history and textual analysis, which are just as empirical and realist as the social sciences but are focused on discourse not agents. I had a very different model of the 'active audience' in my head, based on early modern popular culture in both of the major spheres of representation: imaginative (the audience for popular drama) and political (mass readership of the press).

• My exemplary *imaginative* audience was modeled on Shakespeare's own, the question being what Elizabethan popular drama could tell us about the ideas of its time. There was little talk of couch potatoes in relation to Shakespeare's audience, although some critics did make unflattering assumptions about what the 'groundlings' could understand compared to the courtiers in the audience. But that was simple class prejudice, because what made Shakespearean theatre fascinating was that groundlings and courtiers alike attended the plays, which were both commercial and critical blockbusters. I was interested in a popular dramatic tradition that linked the top of society with the bottom in mutually illuminating dialogue (Bethell 1944), and I approached television audiences in the same spirit.

- My model *political* audience was the first mass 'reading public,' produced by the democratic activists of the American, French, and Industrial Revolutions, and in particular by the 'pauper press' of the early nineteenth century – the first mass reading public of the industrial era. These audiences were 'active' to the point of insurrection.

It seemed that if audiences were considered as active agents, seeking enlightenment as well as entertainment, indeed seeking it *in* entertainment, then television would present itself as a completely different object of study compared with what the social sciences researched – psychologists looking for pathological behavior, pollsters looking for marketing opportunities, or political economists looking for capitalist influence. Instead, broadcast television presented itself as a means for extending imaginative and political representation to whole populations. So, my media studies says that the *most popular* media, from Shakespeare to *Big Brother* (Hartley 2008), are open, generative resources for growing popular self-realization and emancipation.

Once you set off down the path of equating popular media and popular emancipation (both imaginative and political), you will quickly be intercepted by those who say that the media are owned and controlled by vested interests in a power structure, with programming designed to keep the potatoes on the couch, watching the ads for neo-liberalism. Very well; but this is to see culture as confined to the intentions of the most cynical and exploitative producers, ignoring both positive potential and long-term unintended consequences. In the long run, do we care more about the motivations of capitalists or about the ideas that their energies put into circulation? For instance, do we remember Charles-Joseph Panckoucke or do we remember the ideas of the Enlightenment and revolutionary France? Panckoucke was the first French media mogul, but few remember him now. At this distance of time, the speed, efficiency, and scale of his operations, taking revolutionary newspapers and literature to the far reaches of France and beyond, look more impressive than his contemporary influence or fortune. These were but the means by which he was able to create a nation-sized 'social network' in which the struggle to implement the Enlightenment, or to resist it, could become a practical political endeavor for a whole population. Similarly, few recall that Shakespeare himself was a pioneer media entrepreneur, an investor and executive of a joint-stock company that produced popular entertainment for profit. And no-one accuses Shakespeare of downplaying the disruptive force of early capitalism in his plays even as he benefitted financially from it in his business.

As for audiences, treating them as lacking in the mental resources to deal with their own entertainment is not only demeaning but also a case of academic bad faith. For, if all the psychological experiments and sociological surveys *do* reveal an audience characterized by vulnerability to media effects, then what are media academics and researchers doing to help them to become independent? Teaching students to become expert in blaming the media for their effects on *other* people may produce the very things we rail against – disempowerment, disengagement, passivity, and risk aversion. In my view, media studies needs to teach both knowledge, including self-knowledge, and action, both critical and creative – together they constitute true digital literacy for an 'active audience.' The educative role of media studies does not pathologize the object of study. Instead, it propagates astute reading, adept navigation, contextual understanding, and creative productivity.

Studying the media as resources for popular imagination and emancipation means that their overall importance in the history of modernity has far outweighed their scale as a sector of the economy. They are an 'enabling social technology' – like the law, science, and markets, all of which are important as coordinating and regulating mechanisms that enable other kinds of creative productivity to flourish. We rarely assess the law or science by reference to their scale as 'industries' or markets by reference to the cost of maintaining them as markets. Their importance is that they coordinate intercourse and regulate trade in large-scale economies. They enable the growth of knowledge, as do the media.

The emergent 'creative industries' are in the twenty-first century taking over the position that 'the media' held in the twentieth. However, there is a major difference. The media were conceptualized as the 'enabling social technology' of *ideological control* for a mass society, but the creative sector may be regarded as the social technology of *distributed innovation*. As productivity migrates out of firms, organizations, and expert systems into the homes and heads of the population at large, media studies will need to attend to new sources of creative innovation and productivity. 'Ordinary' people may realistically pursue and publish their own imaginative, intellectual, or political emancipation, driving growth and change as they go.

It will be the recurrent theme of this book that the 'active audience' tradition has been given a powerful boost by the emergence of digital technologies, the internet, Web 2.0, and consumer-created content. During these developments, 'the audience' has transmogrified into 'the user,' and industrial-era, one-way, mass communication has added to its broad social reach a mode best described as dialogic, demotic, and DIY/DIWO (do it yourself/do it with others).

The industry-generated model of digital content shown in Figure 1.1, produced by the International Data Corporation (Gantz and Reinsel 2010), shows a 2010 estimate of the extent of user-generated content, compared with the previous monopoly of 'enterprise-generated content.' As the Venn

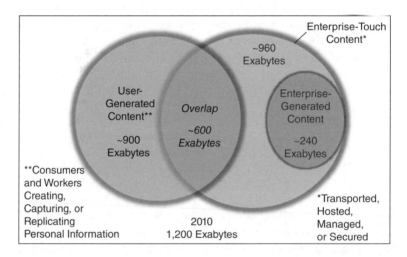

Figure 1.1 The Scale of the Problem: User-Generated Content. 'More than 70% of the Digital Universe [in 2010] will be generated by users – individuals at home, at work, and on the go. That's 880 billion gigabytes' (Gantz and Reinsel 2010: 11).[1] Source: Gantz and Reinsel (IDC Digital Universe Study, sponsored by EMC) (2010).

[1] 'Enterprise-touch' means information for which enterprises may be legally or managerially responsible but that they have not generated themselves, for example the videos on YouTube.

diagram makes clear, there is an unprecedented overlap between users and enterprises (typically commercial enterprises). For instance, an astonishing amount of content is uploaded by users, whether these are private individuals or workers for other enterprises, on YouTube and similar sites, such as Tudou in China (whose name, 'potato' in Mandarin, is a play on the English term 'couch potato').[2] But these sites themselves – their security, servers, legal status, design, and information architecture and management – are commercially owned and operated (in YouTube's case, by Google). Gantz and Reinsel use the expression 'Enterprise-Touch' content, a suggestive term for a phenomenon that radically undermines the traditional consumer/producer distinction.

This reconfiguration of media means the 'active' audience's own *actions*, not their behavioral *reactions*, now constitute the most important empirical field for the investigation of dynamic change. The mediated enterprise of self-directed creative interaction among all the agents in a system – for example in social network markets – can be investigated empirically. The scale of productivity escalates year by year, from gigabytes to petabytes to zettabytes – 2010 was the first year that this unit was reached (the '1200 exabytes' shown in Figure 1.1 is equal to 1.2 zettabytes; see also Bohn and Short 2010). As a result, the tools required to model and measure dynamic change in such systems must come from mathematics, complexity theory, evolutionary economics, and game theory. Media studies needs to develop expertise collaboratively with these fields.

The future is digital for media studies, and that will require new competencies, for instance in large-scale, computer-generated data; new horizons, for instance linking our interdisciplinary field with the natural sciences, bioscience, and 'science and technology studies'; and new problem situations, for instance moving beyond the familiar 'producer → text/commodity → consumer' chain to an evolving social-network model of the media. 'Digital futures' will pose serious questions for media studies as well as for media organizations and audiences.

Disciplinary Context

My disciplinary cluster is the humanities and creative arts, known in Australia as 'HCA.' One difference between HCA and other disciplines lies in the interface between the discipline and its object of study. Simply put,

---

[2] Source: Bulkley (2008). See http://www.tudou.com.

many disciplines *face out*: law, engineering, medicine (etc.) face an impersonal object (the law, mechanics, the body, etc.) that needs to be understood and manipulated by a defined profession or industry. But HCA *faces in*: traditionally the object and beneficiary of this kind of knowledge has not been 'the industry' or 'the profession' but *the student*, whose taste, judgment, comportment, and conduct are formed and shaped as the 'outcome' of knowledge practices. Thus, where an engineering or law student may practice engineering or the law, a humanities student practices ... being human. As a result, humanities-based research has developed a strongly values-based tradition of criticism and critique, rather than a 'science'-based tradition, either pure or applied. Further, the graduates of HCA programs, often the largest cohort in a university, don't face out towards a *profession* or industry entry scheme for their employment, but to a chaotic, global, dynamic, and uncertain set of *markets*. They qualify for no accredited point of entry other than the notorious 'swimming lesson' that most arts graduates must undertake before finding their niche in a complex open system – they sink or swim.

Immersed in uncertainty, always exposed to potential disutility, but heir to some universalist claims, those who study culture – especially in the domain of cultural studies – have come to see their own disciplinary situation as disruptive and their knowledge-forming practices as an intellectual version of Schumpeterian 'creative destruction' (Schumpeter 1942; Hartley 2003; Lee 2003). They work against the grain of both established knowledge systems and professional or industrial applications of such knowledge. The traditional mode of HCA 'research' was *criticism* – both various forms of literary and art criticism and 'critique' of the politico-economic or social status quo. This type of research is not easily oriented towards an industrial or professional 'end user' – it does not face out *towards* a paying customer, as research in, say, engineering or computer science may readily hope to do. For some HCA specialists, the 'end user' is another academic specialist, contributing to the deepening of a field of study; for others, it is no less than contemporary subjectivity and identity as such, a humanity and a creative capability that graduates will carry around with them in their heads and know via their relations with others. The humanities are split between in-close analytic specialism and a universalist-emancipationist agenda for intellectual and ethical/political reform. They are but weakly connected to commercial R&D (research and development) or public policy formation.

The so-called 'new humanities' – including communication and cultural and media studies – have proven much more willing than the 'old' humanities to engage with the markets their graduates will face. These markets are themselves chaotic, dynamic, and not always morally pure, so what they 'want' of a graduate or from a research collaboration is not at all clear in advance, and not always what universities are best at delivering. Thus, if the ideal qualifications for a journalist are foot-in-the-door tenacity, a street-fighter's will to win a story, and fearlessness in the face of uncertainty, not to mention a habit of being attracted to the worst districts in the worst countries to talk to the worst people about what makes them angry, fearful, or vengeful, then a traditional university's default ethical settings may be an impediment, and disciplinary or scholarly protocols a limiting preparation. The tension between the demands of the so-called 'real world' and the practices of institutionalized learning have been managed over a couple of generations in the 'new humanities,' often at new universities – former institutes of technology, polytechnics, and teacher training colleges – where 'doing' vies with 'knowing' both interpersonally and across pedagogy and the curriculum. No-one can claim to have solved the problem, but the new humanities do offer HCA researchers and graduates the chance to have a go at those difficult syntheses between knowing and doing, values and facts, criticism and utility, the formation of individual judgment and the productivity of organized investment.

Not having direct links to private firms or public departments can be a source of alienation for the HCA researcher, but it can also be a competitive advantage. The need for this kind of 'dispersion across difference' flows in HCA's lifeblood. Non-specialist polymath interdisciplinary homelessness can be turned to advantage. It produces problem-solving agility, the ability to deal with diversity (across time, space, form, and identity), and a 'method' that can apply to multiple problem situations in the form of the habit of in-close critical attention to documents, discourses, and power (in the context of individual creative imagination) that can see both the wood ('macro'-level systems, relationships, and cultures) and the trees ('micro'-level creative work in the here and now). In an era of hyper-specialization, it is increasingly unusual to work across such a wide range of concerns, especially in the sciences. But it is impossible to do justice to specialist domains without knowing how they fit together and how different national economic and cultural systems interconnect in a globalized economy and technologically networked culture.

From Industrial Consumption and Behavior to Networked Productivity and Dialogue

This book results from a sustained period of research into the uses of multimedia while I was a Federation Fellow of the Australian Research Council (see Hartley 2005, 2008, 2009). During that time it became clear that, despite their own contingency, uncertainty, and incomplete formation, the disciplinary foundations of cultural and media studies are as much in the process of fundamental transformation as are the media and cultures that these fields seek to explain. This book is therefore an account of the growth and transformation of ideas, both *in* and *about* media and culture, in a period of unprecedented technological and economic turbulence. Change is driven by technological invention and geopolitical shifts such as globalization and the rise of emergent economic powerhouse countries such as China. It has resulted in the rapid evolution and expansion of digital creativity, social networks, and media content, including what is often called 'consumer' co-creation – although what is meant by the very notion of the consumer has changed beyond recognition in the process.

At the same time, continuities can be discerned that require attention to cultural and media history and to the history of ideas. For instance, we can learn about digital media and journalism by recalling the development of print; or we can understand some of the functions of YouTube by comparing it with the archives of an earlier period. From this point of view, each chapter explains the new by reference to the old, showing how the creation and distribution of new ideas – and their uptake among very large populations – has become ever more distributed and productive during the shift from modernist media (print-based, broadcast, centralized) to the digital media of the coming period.

Within the detail of the specific situation or context relevant to each chapter that follows, some general lessons can be learned. Perhaps chief among these is the observation that ideas are not separable from the context or medium of their generation. A shift from broadcasting or print publishing to digital media changes the ideas. The very ideas of what counts as journalism, the public sphere, television, citizenship, a museum, and identity (i.e. the topics of Chapter 3, Chapter 4, Chapter 5, Chapter 6, Chapter 7, and Chapter 8) are all transformed as they migrate to new platforms, reinvented anew by myriad users until their previous form is scarcely recognizable. Thus I shall argue in succeeding chapters that:

- *Journalism*, like the magnetic sphere of the Earth, whose N/S geomagnetic polarity reverses every few tens of thousands of years (we're overdue for one now), is going through a reversal in the direction of its communicational causation in the digital era. When print was dominant (say, from the 1850s to the 1950s), popular culture was the object and destination of news media; the direction of communicational causation was top-down, *from* corporate or state agencies *to* the populace. In the interactive era the direction of causation has reversed; popular culture is the bottom-up origin and subject of journalism (the addresser, rather than addressee). Despite resistance by the industrial heavyweights, journalism is now displaying a trend towards peer-to-peer or user-generated content, although corporate enterprises continue to be responsible for content management, display formats, and legal liabilities. I shall argue further that this change in polarity (popular culture as cause not effect) reverts to the directionality that characterized the radical and 'pauper' press in the early nineteenth century (Chapter 3).
- *The public sphere* – as an idea – is an unsustainable notion; it needs to give way to the idea of 'public thought.' Public thought is produced and communicated in many different ways. It cannot be reduced to what a few self-selecting savants think, be they thinkers-on-behalf-of-the-public from academic (intellectual), political (community), or journalistic (commercial) situations. Even so, it is not a case of 'anything goes,' nor is every member of the public equal in the game of public thought. It is an organized and competitive market, best exemplified, I suggest, in the form of airport bestsellers (Chapter 4).
- *Television*, as it has been buffeted by technological and social change, has changed the most profoundly in the significance attached to it. It no longer counts as the metonymic stand-in for society-as-a-whole. Even if it is still the most popular pastime in the world in terms of raw numbers, it is no longer the case that those numbers are seen as one aggregated audience (coterminous with 'the nation') whose television habit is endlessly inspected for pathological symptoms to demonstrate to the public just how fearful it should be of its own agency. Instead, television is dispersed across different platforms, diffused among different audiences, and distributed by its fans and viewers. It is no longer 'popular' in the sense that it has power to unite whole populations in observation of one ritual act of drama (factual like 9/11 or fictional like 'who shot J. R.?'); but it

is more 'democratic' in the sense that people have more say in producing as well as consuming their own viewing and sharing practices
(Chapter 5).

- *Citizenship* has changed by being practiced in conditions of semiotic
plenty, play, and commercial consumer culture, all of which are ampli-
fied, networked, and coordinated anew in online media. While the idea
of citizenship is clearly historical, governmental, top-down, and policy-
led, its uptake and practice by those who are about to become citizens
– children and young people – appears not to be modeled so much on
social theory as on the 'dance-off' (Chapter 6).

- *The archive* is immense, but uncertain. Ideas are rather easier to come
by now that they can be Googled. Among the internet's many other uses,
it is also an archive, because whatever is uploaded is also stored, down
to the minutiae of phatic chatter or entire (unwanted, unlooked-at)
camera rolls of an event, as opposed to one redacted image. In conditions of unthinkable plenty (who can imagine a zettabyte?),[3] the status
of any object in this archive is unlike that of artifacts in conventional
galleries, libraries, archives, and museums. I shall argue that the only
way to explain what is going on is to take seriously the uncertainties
and indeterminacy of the archive, as well as the immensity of digital
information, by using probability theory (Chapter 7).

- *Human identity* does not escape these developments, or, at the very
least, the way we think about it needs to change. Instead of seeing it
as an intrinsic property of individuals who *then* enter society, we can
now claim that identity, like rational thought and purposive action,
emerges – it *results* – out of social networks and relationships connected via language, culture, social institutions, and various organized
forms of collective agency that use 'social technologies' (from firms,
markets, and the law to media and digital technology) to *produce* our
individual capacity for signaling (sense-making practices), copying
(cultural behavior), and networking (intersubjectivity). How we
produce and communicate our identity within a competitive social
network and an economy of attention is well-exemplified in the fashion
system. Individuality proceeds not from inner essence but from species

---

[3]   See Blake (2010). Blake tries to imagine a zettabyte: 'The current size of the world's digital
content is equivalent to all the information that could be stored on 75bn Apple iPads, or the
amount that would be generated by everyone in the world posting messages on the micro-
blogging site Twitter constantly for a century.'

identity; humanity is the *messaging* species or *Homo sapiens nuntius* (Chapter 8).

Chapters 2 and 9 do slightly different work, being focused on the problem of *renewal* rather than on specific ideas or media platforms. Chapter 2 locates that problem in the traditions of study that media and cultural studies have inherited, arguing that a *disciplinary* renewal is required in order to resolve the intellectual problems that the fields set out to tackle in the first place. Chapter 9 opens up the question of the renewal of cultural and economic *systems* more generally. Here, the argument is that the clash of difference and the wiles of deceit are both mechanisms for the emergence of the new. 'Creative destruction' is as much a feature of the deepest traditions of mythology (the humanities) as it is of evolutionary economics (the sciences). The agent of renewal – the trickster in one tradition, entrepreneur in the other – is the 'go-between,' who exploits the very differences between systems to make possible new meanings, even as they disrupt and challenge existing meanings. They provide one answer to the semiotician Yuri Lotman's challenging question: 'How can a system develop and yet remain true to itself?' (Lotman 2009: 1). That is the question for cultural and media studies. The agency of disruptive renewal, which I call 'cultural science,' is itself a 'go-between' that brings the humanities and the sciences into mutual dialogue. This is sometimes noisy with mixed ambitions, disagreement, and mutual incomprehension, but it may enable new approaches to emerge and thus the field of media and cultural studies to be renewed for a digital future.

Distributed and Dialogic Productivity

Each chapter in this book contributes towards two overarching claims about contemporary media and culture. First, the current era of digital transformation is one where 'command and control' centralization is giving way (often unwillingly) to 'self-organized' networked complexity, in which new ideas, public thought, entertainment platforms, information archives, and human identity itself are produced by innumerable 'agents' in a dynamic process that demands our analytic attention – and requires new analytic tools compared to those elaborated when 'analogue' media/cultural studies was started.

Second, it is no longer adequate to posit a powerful corporate or state agency as *producer* and a powerless individual or private *consumer* in any model of communication, even where the relationship is asymmetrical. Equally, however, consumption or reception is never done by a collective, whether understood as an audience or as a social group (such as a class, gender, ethnicity, etc.), but only by individuals whose choices are also patterned by association with such collective identities, among others. On both 'sides,' producer and consumer, there is both individual agency and collective productivity. It is a dialogic relationship. At a higher level of integration, it is possible to conceptualize the *overall* productivity of communication, culture, and media through what E. O. Wilson dares to call 'the communal mind':

> In his 1941 classic *Man on his Nature*, the British neurobiologist Charles Sherrington spoke of the brain as an enchanted loom, perpetually weaving a picture of the external world, tearing down and reweaving, inventing other worlds, creating a miniature universe. The communal mind of literate societies – world culture – is an immensely larger loom. Through science it has gained the power to map external reality far beyond the reach of a single mind, and through the arts the means to construct narratives, images, and rhythms immeasurably more diverse than the products of any solitary genius. The loom is the same for both enterprises, and there is a general explanation of its origin and nature and thence of the human condition, proceeding from the deep history of genetic evolution to modern culture. Consilience of causal explanation is the means by which the single mind can travel most swiftly and surely from one part of the communal mind to the other. (Wilson 1998: 12)

Everyone in *Homo sapiens nuntius* is part of the 'communal mind,' adding, whether purposively or unwittingly, to the process of 'weaving [...] tearing down [...] inventing [...] creating' the cumulative and dynamic archive of 'literate societies.' Everyone is a producer, publisher, journalist, scientist, artist . . . and everyone can *use* the archived 'communal mind' as a resource for identity, citizenship, and public thought – even more readily than when Wilson wrote this passage in the 1990s, given the continuing exponential (or power law) expansion of digital media. Thus, disciplinary media and cultural studies need to think again about the basic model of communication. The academic and scholarly tools that have been elaborated over the past few decades to *explain* the media are also in need of transformation; they cannot simply be 'applied' to 'new' media platforms (Gray 2010). Each chapter is therefore an attempt to reposition and repurpose media and cultural *studies* for a digital future.

Part II: A Short History of Representation – From Print to User

How well he's read, to reason against reading! (*Love's Labour's Lost* I.i.94)

Abstraction of Knowledge

The tradition of modern scholarship – now some centuries old – has tended to favor the abstraction of knowledge from action in order to develop explicit rather than tacit knowledge. From the Renaissance onwards, and at a gathering pace after the scientific revolution of the seventeenth century (associated with the foundation of the Royal Society), knowledge (in books, libraries, journals; also 'objective' knowledge in Karl Popper's sense) was radically separated from knowing subjects. This unleashed the growth of knowledge that we call modernity. During that lengthy period there were many instances of such abstraction across the whole field of the economy, society, and culture. In the industrial revolution, for instance, 'workers by brain' were abstracted from 'workers by hand,' white collar from blue, art from artisans, design from fabrication, knowing from doing. Without abstraction and specialization there could have been no exponential economic growth; no modernity.

The *medium* through which abstracted knowledge was collected and communicated was of course print. Printing by moveable type was invented around 1450 to serve the interests of religious and business activists in a still-feudal middle-Europe. Its ability not only to abstract knowledge from the knowing subject (Ong 2004 [1958]) but also to 'broadcast' it around the globe made it the first mass medium, and emancipated it from the control of its inventors. It was at this point that it became an 'enabling social technology' for the growth of knowledge in general. The unintended consequences of socially ubiquitous print literacy could emerge and grow. These consequences proved to be spectacular and included the development of all three of the most important realist textual systems of modernity – science, journalism, and the novel.

In the Middle Ages the university library evolved from the monastic scriptorium, but with print it too could be 'abstracted' – emancipated – from its institutional origins in the church. As a result, even though this process took time and was never uncontested, science was freed from both religiosity and the authority of ecclesiastical hierarchies. Similarly, spare capacity on printing presses and the growth of a secular reading public allowed for the development of prose fiction and later the newspaper. 'Dispatches,' 'Intelligences,' and 'Mercuries' about current affairs were 'abstracted' from the secret dealings of courtiers and merchants and broadcast to the reading public at large. Meanwhile, the development of vernacular printed prose and of middle-class leisure enabled the rise of the novel – the form in which psychological individualism (pioneered in Shakespearean theatres) was generically elaborated and socially propagated, recruiting writers as well as readers (especially women) from previously unrecorded origins. In all of these contexts, print was an agent of generative change, not a neutral tool; it carried the modernizing force of realism – science, journalism, imaginative individualism – to that most 'abstracted' entity of modernity, the reading public.

Print was vital to the emergence of secular industrial society; it was the very agent of knowledge. Small wonder, then, that those trained into modern scholarship are children of print and remain wedded to a model of intellectual emancipation based on print. Print was the means by which knowledge could be *extracted* (abstracted) from its context, from the knowing subject, and from the temporality of its first production. It was then available for archiving and dispersal among a general population that was at least in principle indifferent to birth, rank, or wealth. This in turn allowed experimentation, correction, and expansion of ideas on a scale hitherto impossible to imagine. Print was so suited to the 'emancipation' of knowledge from its context of production that many came to see it as an agent of rationality; the means by which the ideas of the Enlightenment were disseminated. The technology itself came to be associated with freedom – political, philosophical, religious, and personal. The famous emancipationist slogan of the nineteenth century, 'knowledge is power,' was routinely shown as the caption to a picture of the printing press.

However, the democratic and scientific supremacy of print was challenged by 'new media' during the twentieth century, especially film and broadcasting (radio and then television). These audio-visual media were not welcomed by many print-based thinkers, including scientists, journalists, and authors, because they seemed to rely not on reason and ideas but emotion, desire, and corporeal attraction for their communicative impact. They may have made millions of people laugh, cry, fear, or even wonder, but they did not seem suited to 'public thought' as it had been institutionalized since the American, French, and Industrial Revolutions. A division between print-based (abstract) knowledge and audio-visual (embodied) knowledge has persisted to this day, and forms part of the institutional setting into which the latest surge of 'new media' has erupted. Nevertheless, the audio-visual media carried all before them in terms of popularity and reach, so a long-term process of mutual accommodation occurred, at an increasing pace from the 1960s, whereby news, and thence politics, as well as imaginative fiction 'went over to the other side' – from print to broadcasting and film. Science held out longer, maintaining what was increasingly a fiction: that it is based on 'papers,' 'publications,' and 'print,' even when none of these is used to disseminate its rationalist ideas.

Thus, in order to understand the impact and politics of 'new media,' the field of media and cultural studies needs a better grasp of the history of sense-making practices in large-scale modernizing countries of the post-Enlightenment era (from the seventeenth or eighteenth centuries to today). At the most general level, just as communication has been modeled in a particular, limiting way, so the history of sense-making has been narrated as if it is self-evidently *representative*. Indeed, the stories we tell each other in mainstream media involve both a *semiotic* theory of 'representation' and a *political* theory of 'representativeness,' each infecting and amplifying the other:

- Semiotically, the default setting for signification-in-general is that of representation, where one thing (word, image, sound, phoneme, or 'sign') stands for another (meaning, referent, signified), often in a *realist* relationship with one another, where a real object leaves a trace of itself in the sign, as in photography.
- This realist representation is then caught up in political *representativeness*, where something stands for something else *proportionately*, as when an elected politician 'represents' in one person many thousands of constituents or voters.

'Our heroes,' on screen and on the page, 'represent' the supposed readership or audience as a whole, condensing in one celebrity body characteristics, desires, and actions that seem naturally to be representative of those of everyone. Combining semiotic and political representation makes for a powerful sense of realism or naturalism in the spectacle of celebrity culture: our screen gods and goddesses don't just *stand for* 'everyone'; if successful they *sum up* who 'we' are *on our behalf*.

This apparently natural or self-evident model of signification is, however, strictly historical. It belongs to a specific time – modernity – and a specific place – the West. This can be demonstrated both synchronically, by comparing the system of Western modernity with other co-present systems, and diachronically, by showing that the system itself is, historically, internally dynamic and changing, such that even as we speak (or write, read, etc.) it is in process of transformation. In both cases it is possible to find systems of representation that don't involve either realist foundations or conflation with representativeness. Just look at any culture's traditions of classical dance or drama; or at Australian Aboriginal painting; or at verbal dueling and ritual insult in many oral traditions. Here, courtly ritual, place-based cosmology, and competitive signaling are abstracted and elaborated, often with secrecy or interpersonal relations playing a more important role than open communication in the reproduction of knowledge within such systems. Nowhere here can you instantly scale up from comic-book character to superpower nation (Superman), from flawed hero to foreign policy (James Bond), from individual personality to universal gender role ('Brangelina'). Modern-Western 'representative representation,' apparently naturalistic, is contextual, contingent, and contestable. Its realism is conventional. It is not simply that a restless age tires of its representatives quickly or that competitive commercialism requires constant A-list turnover and renewal. It is the *system* that is localized to a particular time, place, and sense-making regime – no matter how global and permanent it seems to the gaze of the immersed onlooker – even as it changes under pressure of its own internal dynamics.

Representative Realism → Productivity of the Sign → Productivity of the User

Thus, my own reconceptualization of the realist 'representative representation' model of signification replaces the model with a periodization in which the modern Western model is reconfigured, slowly at first but at an increasing rate, into what I call a 'productive' model.

- Representative representation (realism): modernism;
- Productivity of the sign (abstraction and emancipation of signification): postmodernism;
- Productivity of the user (socially networked self-representation): digital futures.

In my analysis, this shift occurred via an interim stage when signification became abstracted from 'the real.' That stage was widely known as 'postmodernism.' There, *the sign* ceased to stand for anything much beyond itself, and thereby became massively more productive – but, catastrophically (for realism), less 'authentic.' This interim phase marked the *productivity of the sign*. It was soon replaced by the stage of the *productivity of the user* – the current era of interactivity, social networks, and the internet. Here, we are not 'represented' by others but can self-represent, making choices, taking decisions, or pursuing actions *directly*, not via 'mediated' heroes and celebrities. We are not represented by delegates or surrogates, but self-mediate. We are directly *productive* of both meanings and actions.

A couple of notes of caution may be in order here. First, periodizing does not tell a settled truth about a period. It gives a language with which to rethink periods and it may in the end overplay the differences between them, neglecting the fact that much change is imperceptible, especially to its own agents. Thus, it is only once a transformation has occurred that we can interrogate the former period (modernism) using the terms we have elaborated to account for a later one (postmodernism), only to discover that under the then 'obvious' modernist veneer there were already all sorts of ideas, actions, practices, and textual systems that could easily be described as 'postmodern.' It is just that the modernist lens could not see them and the modernist lexicon could not explain them. During the modern, representative era, people were *also* able to self-represent, achieve productivity, and the like, but *media and cultural studies* found this hard to see.

Second, the sequence I am proposing, from modernist realism, via the postmodern productivity of the sign, to the current productivity of the user, is not meant to suggest that 'naturalism' has disappeared. This concept still plays a crucial role in the sciences, where it is axiomatic that the study of something implies that it can be observed and that observing something requires attention to the nature of the thing rather than to the ideas of the observer. All this I accept; indeed, I am very much in favor of 'consilience,' where the sciences and humanities are seen as unified in principle and the hope is that both may be 'explained by a small number of natural laws' (Wilson 1998), such that what holds for one holds for the other. I am making no claims for cultural exceptionalism. But, equally, cultural specificity and media history need to be investigated in their own terms, both at the 'micro' level of specialized topics and at the 'macro' level of large-scale systems.

One such system is language, which while real enough and naturalistically evolved does not work the same way as do other natural phenomena, because its capacity to signify and thus to tell the truth is equally its capacity to deceive and thus to lie. They are the same capability, where the same sign may signify both truth and falsehood; a peculiar semiotic productivity whose ramifications will be taken up in more detail in Chapter 9. The discovery by the structuralists and continental philosophy of the 'productivity of the sign' was not itself a sign of the humanities going off the rails of the real, but a rational attempt to understand how humans make sense of anything, the real included, using something that lies and is purposed to deceive. Then, the 'postmodern' delight in the emancipation of the sign from mere realist referentiality was an *advance* in consilience, not its negation. The shift was observable in the accelerated mediation of contemporary global culture; it was not a mere fantasy of the theoretical imagination.

Further, interactive user productivity is now the mainstay of the internet (Gantz and Reinsel 2010). It could not have occurred without a prior process of the *abstraction* of the sign, from localized particularity of reference to global potential for meaningfulness, and its emancipation from the regime of producer-only causation (one-way communication). With the internet and digital communication, mediated communication has been restored to a two-way dialogic model in which everyone is understood as productive. Postmodernism, it transpires, was a halfway house to consilience. Scientific scoffing was premature. But a final general lesson follows. What's sauce for the goose is sauce for the gander. Media and cultural studies as a field needs to attend more to the causes and mechanisms of change, focusing the analytical lens on the dynamics of systems, not just on structural oppositions within them.

The Era of Representation, Semiotic and Political

The broadcast era was the heyday or culmination of *representation*, which is itself the semiotic and political form taken by abstraction. In the movies, and then in celebrity culture more generally, human traits and forms of identity were *represented* on screen, through look, dialogue, action, costume, and the company kept by characters (not to mention the stars who played them). The indeterminacy of the socially mobile self was also represented, through plot, narrative, and character development. Semiotic representation consisted in taking both identity and the mutability of modern experience and universalizing them on screen: the star stood for everyone; the story for reality.

Semiotic representation, however, requires a highly asymmetric relationship between the human attributes represented on screen and the myriad selves sitting in the dark. In this unequal exchange, the experts who produced media realism prospered while their customers were left with what the psychoanalysts liked to call a 'lack' in self-realization. Luckily for capitalism, the mass audience obsessively returned to the screen to fulfil that lack vicariously, for instance by gazing intently at Lauren Bacall, fifty-feet high and cool as a cucumber, while she taught their (alter) ego how to whistle. A standard critical response to this asymmetric relation is to dismiss it as a fraud: the audience were somehow deceived or duped, over-powered by the representation itself, which in any case did not stand for their reality.

Meanwhile, the same audience, now reconfigured as private citizens, faced the same Faustian bargain in politics, where they ceded to their elected representatives the power of political action, governmental decision-making, and administrative process, in exchange for . . . what? Again, a standard critical account looked for a lack, this time in power. Critical theory in the Marxist and Frankfurt School traditions, often recast in more recent work as 'political economy' critique, saw representative democracy not as winning the vote but as losing freedom of collective or class action. Nothing was 'gained' but powerlessness. The return on citizens' investment in political representation, according to this logic, was a straight loss. This was the logic that Monty Python sent up in *Life of Brian*: 'What have the Romans ever done for us?' – to which rhetorical question the answer is obviously *nothing* . . . except for what turns into a hilariously long list of concessions:

> REG [JOHN CLEESE]: All right, but apart from the sanitation, the medicine, education, wine, public order, irrigation, roads, a fresh water system, and public health, what have the Romans ever done for us?

Alright, point taken, but clearly the system of representation was flawed, its extreme asymmetry seeming to separate both political and semiotic representatives from the mass audience of citizen consumers, who were left hanging around on the amphitheatre steps with little to do but moan sedition.

Representation also looked suspect to those who were active in the *pro-duction* of print-literate knowledge, for among the capabilities ceded to professionals was the ability to *write*. Audiences could only 'read' images and stories. They couldn't produce and publish them in the broadcast media (another 'lack' filled in by representation). Therefore the 'reading public' for broadcast media appeared not as co-equal subjects of knowledge who might write as well as read but as passive consumers, the end point of a chain of causation that had those fifty-foot stars and *their* producers as 'cause' and the punters as 'effect.' This notion of a value chain (rather than a dialogue) transformed audiences from 'subjects' of knowledge and sov-ereignty to 'objects' of manipulation and mystification. Not surprisingly, therefore, scientists and intellectuals – adepts of print media – remained skeptical of 'read-only' popular media. Knowledge forged in *that* crucible was hardly to be trusted, and was routinely dismissed as demagogic or delinquent.

But, while it is easy to see how literate specialists, habituated to publish-ing their own thought as well as reading the thought of others, might feel short changed by the asymmetric deal offered in representative cinema and democracy, the same cannot be said for the popular audience. For them the contemporary media have offered a technological route to semiotic and intellectual emancipation that traditional arts denied to them. There was even some mobility between popular classes and popular media: the meri-tocratic principle recruited talented workers to creative and professional occupations, and any Betty Joan Perske could aspire to become a star (Lauren Bacall). Modern representation (both semiotic and political) offered something real to those who had no stake in traditional forms of artistic and intellectual expression or public participation. Movies and media seemed more transparent, less subject to artistic or ideological shaping, and therefore closer to ordinary life (despite the asymmetry between fans and their representatives on screen).

The 'mechanical arts' held the promise of greater objectivity and truth-fulness than sermonizing professionals. Mass media could not exist without scientific invention, industrialized production, and modern marketing. Science was recruited to the cause of art. The popular audience was primed for the idea that truth might be revealed by technological means. No matter how far-fetched the story line, from Chaplin onwards the diegetic screen world was real: human-scale but technologically enabled; populated by 'ordinary' characters who were engaged in self-realizing narratives and participating in imaginative responses to the rapid changes of the times.

Science itself became a staple of both realism and fantasy (e.g. *Metropolis*, *2001: A Space Odyssey*, wildlife documentaries, the dinosaur industry, and all those mad-scientist horror movies). For good or ill the representation of the human condition migrated decisively from art to science.

Like printing, the internet was invented for instrumental purposes (security, scholarship), but it has rapidly escaped such intentions and is evolving new 'affordances' unlooked for a mere decade ago. The most important change is that the structural asymmetry between producers and consumers, experts and amateurs, writers and readers has begun to rebalance. In principle (if not yet in practice), *everyone* can publish as well as 'read' mass media. Users play an important role in making the networks, providing the services, improving the products, forming the communities, and producing the knowledge that characterize digital media. We are entering an era of user *productivity*, not expert *representation*. It is now possible to think of consumers as agents, sometimes enterprises, and to see in consumer-created content and user-led innovation not further exploitation by the expert representatives but rather 'consumer entrepreneurship' (once a contradiction in terms).

Once again, as was the case for print in early modern Europe, a means of communication has become an agent as well as a carrier of change, extending the capabilities of the publisher across social and geographical boundaries and producing unintended consequences that have hardly begun to be exploited. The attention-grabbing aspects of digital media have been those related to private self-expression (albeit conducted in public), social network markets, entertainment media, and celebrity culture. Already it is evident that all three of print's unplanned progeny – science, journalism, and realist imagination – have also begun to colonize the web, using it for the 'higher' functions of objective description, argumentation, and research. Now, however, instead of abstracted individual authorship using spatialized monologue, users can exploit the social-network functionality of iterative and interactive digital media to create new knowledge using such innovations as the wisdom of crowds and computational power.

There is of course plenty of resistance to such changes. One thing that stands in the way, ironically, is print, or rather a print mentality that, because of the suspicion of media by modernists, persists in characterizing 'new' media as somehow demotic and unworthy – even untruthful. This is especially prevalent in schools, many of which still ban students' access to Google (especially Google Images), Wikipedia, social networking sites, YouTube, and so on, preferring to insist on the control culture of the expert paradigm rather than facilitating the open innovation networks of digital media. Given that the latter is indeed what students need to know (and to be able to do) in order to navigate the evolving digital mediasphere, the world of print-based scholarly modernism falls further out of step with the times, and scholarship threatens to become just as irrelevant as professional practitioners like to say it is.

There is therefore a clear choice to be made if those who wish to pursue the serious study of communications media wish to avoid the stand-off that persists between print and its latter-day competitors. We must follow science, journalism, and realism across from the arts to the sciences, and from print to digital media. We are entering a period in which the tensions between print-based scholarship ('papers' about *knowing*) and practice-based training (hands-on *doing*) can and should be superseded. Such a move would also challenge the current disciplinary distinctions between humanities (cinema studies has drifted towards literary and philosophical traditions of scholarship) and social sciences (media studies was captured early by social psychologists and political economists) on the one hand, and the math-based sciences (particularly evolutionary theory, game theory, and complexity/network studies) on the other. Indeed, so far has change proceeded, in both digital media and in the history of science, that film, media, and journalism scholars must face the question of how and what they know, and consider afresh whether their scholarly and pedagogic armamentarium needs a makeover. Instead of retreating (further) into hyper-literate philosophical speculation (cinema) or post-literate voca-tional guidance (media), it may be time to consider a digitally literate and unifying alternative, which I am calling 'cultural science.' This investigates the population-wide propagation of ideas and the future possibilities of knowledge in the context of cultural and economic dynamic systems – the 'active audience' as socially networked and actively learning *agent* of the media's unintended consequences.

2

Cultural Studies, Creative Industries, and Cultural Science

Questions of right and wrong in the arts and sciences should be settled through free discussion in artistic and scientific circles and through practical work in these fields. (Mao Zedong 1957: 49–50)

Why is Cultural Studies not an Evolutionary Science?

In 1898, long before we heard about Kuhnian paradigms and 'normal science,' the American economist and social theorist Thorstein Veblen made this comment on what can happen to a field when it stagnates:

> The well worn paths are easy to follow and lead into good company. Advance along them visibly furthers the accredited work which the science has in hand. Divergence from the paths means tentative work, which is necessarily slow and fragmentary and of uncertain value. (1898)

What's more, he says, 'departures from the accredited method have lain under the odium of being meretricious innovations.' Veblen was referring to economics, about which more later. At this point I simply want to suggest that his characterization of a non-dynamic field applies equally to cultural studies. The reason for making such an invidious comparison is, first, to emphasize that cultural studies is not the first field to face such issues (indeed, it seems to be lagging a full century behind economics) and, second, to suggest that the question posed by Veblen in 1898 – 'Why

---

Digital Futures for Cultural and Media Studies, First Edition. John Hartley.
© 2012 John Wiley & Sons, Ltd. Published 2012 by John Wiley & Sons, Ltd.

is economics not an evolutionary science?' – needs to be applied to cultural studies. More about that later, too. First, though, we must face the question of intellectual stagnation. Cultural studies was once an intellectual powerhouse. Is it now merely doing 'accredited work,' or even simply seeking 'good company'? Are attempts at new departures dismissed as 'meretricious'?[1]

As it has become institutionalized, some of the intellectual adventurousness of early cultural studies may have been lost, especially among senior figures with turf to defend. An exception is Tony Bennett, who has proclaimed the demise of cultural studies at least once before, when he was preaching cultural policy studies in the late 1980s (see Bennett 1992). He has recently struck out again, in a new direction, precisely on the premise that cultural studies is a spent force. He recently launched a new journal, the *Journal of Cultural Economy*, saying that the 'various schools of cultural constructivism […] have now pretty well run out of steam' (Bennett, McFall, and Pryke 2008: 2).

Meanwhile, the field is marked by infinitely extensible micro-level analysis. It has not even gone so far as to establish a system for taxonomic classification of these micro-descriptions. According to Veblen, such a taxonomic phase is a necessary *pre*-evolutionary stage for any discipline, just as descriptive 'natural history' became taxonomic 'botany' and 'zoology' before both could be synthesized into evolutionary 'biology' and, later, geneticist 'bioscience.' Economics was already at a taxonomic stage in Veblen's day; he sought to push it towards an evolutionary synthesis, a process he foreshadowed in 1898 that is still not complete. But there seems to be little appetite for any systematization of the field in cultural studies, not even taxonomy. Nor does the field pay enough attention to the macro level; rather, it is still using theoretical approaches, terms, and concepts that were elaborated in the 1970s. Thus, in the style of Marley's Ghost, it is proper to ask 'what are the past, present, and future of cultural studies?'

---

[1] A good example of the use of this very word to dismiss an attempted innovation in the field is in Jim McGuigan's (2006) review of *Creative Industries*. Given the quality of that volume's 30 authors, it seems inescapable that McGuigan's odium is directed, in just the way that Veblen had predicted, at my attempt, as editor of the book as a whole, to move the field in a new direction.

Part I: Past – Cultural Studies

The formation of different languages and of distinct species, and the proofs that both have been developed through a gradual process, are curiously parallel [...] The survival or preservation of certain favoured words in the struggle for existence is natural selection. (Charles Darwin 1871: III)

Although he did not cite Veblen directly, it was Veblenesque impatience with 'well worn paths' and 'accredited work' in his own field – the field of literary criticism, or 'English' – that drove Raymond Williams towards cultural studies during those same 1970s, when the field seemed 'emergent' rather than 'residual,' to use Williams' own terms for cultural dynamics. He gave a speech to the UK Council for National Academic Awards, the statutory accreditation agency for degrees awarded at polytechnics and institutes of technology (as opposed to universities, which had their own degree-awarding powers), and this speech was subsequently published in the US *Journal of Communication* (Williams 1974a). From this context, it is clear that Williams saw the alternative to English as coming from the outside in three ways:

- Disciplinarily (from continental social theory and US-based communication studies);
- Institutionally (from the non-university sector of adult education); and
- Geographically (from Europe and the US).

In other words, he saw cultural studies as an 'exogenous shock' (as economists may have put it) to his own subject specialism, *English* (see Lee 2003 for a comparative analysis).

Williams particularly despaired of English departments in England, which were then much more influential than they are now. Despite the loss of empire and the rise of an affluent consumer society, English retained the Arnoldian ambition of providing a literary education (Arnold 1869), which was justifiable only on the grounds of 'civilization,' that graduates destined for government need to learn to appreciate the points of view of others; to recognize ambiguity and complexity in human affairs; thence to recognize both long-haul impersonal cultural values and immediate moral dilemmas; and thus, finally, to be able to form judgments independently. Graduates could then safely be despatched to administer a global commercial empire.[2] Small wonder, then, that English was known by some, including Terry Eagleton, for instance, as the 'Queen of the Humanities' (this was before Freddy Mercury).[3]

Despite the lofty ambition of its inherited imperial purpose, by the 1960s English had shriveled to what Williams described as a 'small world of small cultivators, heads down to their own fields,' where

> You can go on doing, in effect without challenge, virtually anything that has ever been done, but if you propose anything new you are lucky if your integrity escapes whipping; your intelligence and sensibility will have been long given up as dead. (Williams 1974a: 18)

Such an anti-innovation climate was sustained by 'the defences of vested interests, the general drizzle of discouragement,' and 'inertia' (25). In this bleak characterization of the departmental climate, Williams may in fact have been erring on the generous side. Fred Inglis has described Cambridge's English department, where Williams worked, as a 'little boiling vat of spite' that 'seethed with detestation' (1995: 181). It was this to which Williams wanted to propose a radical alternative, which he called 'cultural science.'

Cultural Science 1.0

A professor of *English*, Richard Hoggart was founding director of the Birmingham Centre for Contemporary Cultural Studies (CCCS). One of

---

[2]   Matthew Arnold's 'theory' of English was implemented in the Edwardian era, when English departments were established at Oxbridge. The sense of *noblesse oblige* for English graduates was well conveyed by the first King Edward VII Professor of English Literature at Cambridge, Sir Arthur Quiller-Couch, who wrote:

> Since of high breeding is begotten (as most of us believe) a disposition to high thoughts, high deeds [...] I shall endeavour [...] to scour that spur of ancestry and present it to you as so bright and sharp an incentive that you, who read English Literature and practice writing here in Cambridge, shall not pass out from her insensible of the dignity of your studies, or without pride or remorse according as you have interpreted in practice the motto, *Noblesse oblige*. (Quiller-Couch 1946 [1916]: 102)

[3]   Terry Eagleton is upbraided (Wilson 1995) for his use of the term 'Queen of the Humanities' to criticize the work of gay historical materialist critic Alan Sinfield. On Sinfield and me, see Hartley (2009): 7–10.

his first acts was to invite the *sociologist* Alan Shuttleworth to introduce the work of the continental 'cultural sciences' to the Centre. One of the earliest of the CCCS's famous 'Stencilled Occasional Papers' – the second, in fact – contained Shuttleworth's *Max Weber and the 'Cultural Sciences'* (1966). Following this lead in his 1974 speech, Williams called his model of intellectual innovation 'cultural science' too, citing in particular the work of Max Weber and Wilhelm Dilthey. Williams traced the study of culture from early modern attempts to understand it as general human development driven by 'spirit' or 'consciousness' to the Marxist notion of culture as material production. He wanted to move on further, to identify the 'central problem' of cultural science for the latter part of the twentieth century as 'the relations between different practices' – and thence to see *communication* as a practice amenable to analysis by cultural science.

'Cultural science' is still used in this way by Tony Bennett, where the formula is 'the social, cultural and human sciences' (Bennett, McFall, and Pryke 2008), and also by the Australian Minister for Innovation, Industry, Science and Research, Senator Kim Carr, who let it be known that for certain funding purposes the word science 'is now to be interpreted in the broadest, Latinate sense' – that is, to include 'humanities and arts scholarship.'[4] Such 'Latinate' usage has never really caught on in the Anglosphere, even though it represents a strong current in European philosophy and epistemology, where *kulturwissenschaft* (cultural science) was established in the late nineteenth and early twentieth century by German-speaking sociologists, historians, and philosophers, notably Weber, Dilthey, and Heinrich Rickert, who sought to unite the study of objective reality and cultural values under that title. Thus, 'cultural science' is a common and uncontentious term in continental disciplinary traditions and departmental structures. I am calling this 'cultural science 1.0' to distinguish it from the later, evolutionary-complexity approach ('cultural science 2.0'), which I go on to describe below.

Raymond Williams introduced 'cultural science' thus: 'The approach I want to describe is that of cultural studies, which is English for "cultural science"' (Williams 1974a: 19). In other words, 'cultural studies' was defined

---

[4] See http://www.humanities.org.au/ISL.html; see also http://minister.innovation.gov.au/Carr/MediaReleases/Pages/$1MFORINTERNATIONALHUMANITIESANDSOCIAL SCIENCECOLLABORATION.aspx.

by one of its founders as a translation of continental cultural science. Williams was attracted to it because of its *openness*, praising its 'spirit' as 'profoundly open, alert, and general,' and he sought to emulate its 'vigorous and general humanity' (22). He used it to proclaim what he called 'an open conspiracy' that would work 'in new ways, by trial and error but always openly and publicly' (25) . . . which is a good description of scientific method. Cultural studies was imagined at the outset as a humanistic science, studying 'real expressive and communicative process' (20) not just 'isolable objects' such as texts.

Using such means to study the *relations between different practices* remains the purpose of cultural studies in the current revival of the 'cultural science' venture that I urge here – 'cultural science 2.0,' as it were. The most important difference now is that cultural science can move beyond its 'Latinate,' pre-evolutionary phase (Veblen 1898). In the light of developments since the 1960s and 1970s, the project needs to be updated to study *evolutionary change* in practices, and therefore to study *causal* rather than just *structural* relations.

What is 'evolutionary change'? According to Veblen, it is 'causal relations' in the 'cumulative sequence' of 'economic actions.' In cultural studies, it refers in the most general terms to the *growth of knowledge*. It is important here to distinguish recent neo-Darwinian evolutionary science from the social Darwinism that many in the cultural studies tradition 'hear' whenever evolution is mentioned. The approach recommended here does not seek to justify current power relations by reference to imagined origins; on the contrary, it seeks to account for change, using naturalistic methods. In this it is no different in purpose – although it may have access to better tools – from the most exemplary works of early cultural studies, for instance *Policing the Crisis* (Hall et al. 1978).

The neo-Darwinian formula for causal sequence is 'VSR' – variation, selection, and retention (Herrmann-Pillath 2010). Can such a formula be applied to culture? Veblen predicted in 1898 that an evolutionary approach to the 'process of cultural growth' was inevitable in the 'social and political sciences' as well as in economics:

> An evolutionary economics must be the theory of a process of cultural growth as determined by the economic interest, a theory of a cumulative sequence of economic institutions stated in terms of the process itself. [...] Under the stress of modern technological exigencies [...] the social and political sciences must follow the drift, for they are already caught in it.

In the same paper, Veblen made an important distinction between 'animistic' and 'materialistic' thought:

- *Animistic thought* is based on *individual experience*, which is elaborately projected on to the external world of nature, finding gods, 'natural' laws, and anthropomorphism.
- *Materialistic thought* is based on *impersonal scale*, where phenomena and causation cannot be understood by reference to individual people's perceptions, ends, or values.

Veblen argued that the kind of thought that proceeded from defined norms and supposedly 'natural laws' had not escaped from 'archaic' animism:

> When facts and events have been reduced to these terms of fundamental truth and have been made to square with the requirements of definitive normality, the investigator rests his case. [...] In effect, this preconception imputes to things a tendency to work out what the instructed common sense of the time accepts as the adequate or worthy end of human effort. It is a projection of the accepted ideal of conduct.

This critique applies just as trenchantly to social Darwinism as it does to pre-evolutionary thought. Such knowledge is not science – even in the Latinate sense – but ideology.

Unfortunately, Veblen's century-old critique (of economics) seems to apply with uncanny accuracy to some current tendencies within cultural studies itself, where both cultural practices and the work of other writers in the field are judged against moral, political, or artistic standards external to the process under investigation, ranging all the way from individualistic accounts of artistic and cultural genius to paranoiac visions of the malevolent agency of abstract entities, currently 'neo-liberalism.' Anyone caught practicing cultural studies without displaying the 'instructed common sense of the time' (what kinds of practices should be approved and what kinds of politics should be denounced) is likely to attract the 'odium' mentioned by Veblen, or, in Williams' words: 'you are lucky if your integrity escapes whipping; your intelligence and sensibility will have been long given up as dead.' In other words, we have turned our own world upside down, pursuing the very reverse of what 'cultural science 1.0' was meant to do. It was important *then* for cultural studies – as part of the 'cultural turn' more generally – to open up the field of culture, not to close down the terms of debate. Thus, it sought to include a wider array of practices than had hitherto been canonized in the literary tradition, by introducing popular culture and everyday life into an analytical system that had been designed to form aesthetic and moral judgments about elite arts. And, it drew new attention to the political and economic dimensions of culture, asking of any 'relational practice' the question 'cui bono?' – who benefits; for the good of which purpose? – as Williams himself put it (see Brunsdon 1997). Thus did cultural studies – 'cultural science 1.0' – seek an appropriate practical method for analyzing the constructed nature of the supposedly natural. Following Roland Barthes in particular, it refuted the 'instructed common sense of the time' as a form of bourgeois ideology. It increasingly sought an overarching 'macro' theoretical model for understanding the systems and structures within which such 'micro' constructions could be made.

Cultural studies proceeded in these tasks via a series of encounters with other disciplinary domains. First was sociology, via Shuttleworth and others including Weber. Subsequently, especially after Stuart Hall's ascendancy, the CCCS entered into dialogue with Marxism; with semiotics and textual formalism via a dialogue with 'screen theory'; and also, in a more troubled way, with feminism and thence other types of identity politics including those of race. Its most sustained dialogue was with Marxism. This was not the *political* or activist Marxism of communist parties in this or that country, but *theoretical* or 'scientific' Marxism, especially the work of Louis Althusser and Antonio Gramsci and the Marx of the *Grundrisse* and *German Ideology*, rather than *Capital* or even the *Communist Manifesto*. The CCCS were not alone in this move towards 'continental' Marxism. Cultural studies derived its own most sustained version of 'macro' structural relations from the Marxist 'base and superstructure' model that Williams himself borrowed (1973) on the way to publishing his own *Marxism and Literature* (1977).

These preoccupations with social structure (class inequality), textuality (constructions of meaning), identity (the politics of the personal), and structural Marxism (base and superstructure) have driven cultural studies ever since. Cultural studies retains a structuralist interest in systems (in which *oppositions* can be identified) rather than an evolutionary interest in 'cumulative sequence' and change. And it has modeled 'macro' change as *exogenous* not *endogenous* – it would come from revolution (external shock) not evolution (cumulative sequence). It was captivated by the notion of *power* (where various structural oppositions clashed) as the agency of causation, and it tended to universalize power, knowing in advance of any given analysis that this would be the explanation for whatever particular inequality, textuality, identity, or structure was being investigated (Gibson 2007).

Although cultural studies has gone on to have productive encounters with many other fields, including anthropology, postcolonialism, and more recently geography, it has not enjoyed a sustained dialogue with economics, except in the truncated form of 'political economy,' neo-Marxist versions of which have dominated the field despite their marginality in economics as such (e.g. Chomsky, Garnham, T. Miller, H. Schiller). Cultural studies has therefore remained aloof from the turbulent changes *within* economics, as neo-classical economics has faced multiple challenges featuring such tendencies as the 'post-Autistic' network,[5] heterodox economics – especially, from the point of view of this cultural science 2.0, *evolutionary economics.*

Meanwhile, lacking an 'evolutionary turn,' cultural studies was prone to backsliding and stagnation: it too became normative, moralistic, looking for 'natural laws' (e.g. Marxist explanations for power), and tended to pre-judge 'causal sequence' by knowing in advance the moral value of agents, whether they were artists, intellectuals, or larger-scale agencies, for example:

	Hooray!	*Boo!*
Artists	Avant-garde/youth	MoR entertainment
Intellectuals	Hall, Williams	Hayek, Schumpeter
Organizations	Public institutions (state)	Commercial firms (market)
Analytical positions	'Critical'	'Neo-liberal'

It is all too easy to know in advance where to find fault, where sympathies should lie. Cultural studies today has departed radically from its original project, which I am calling 'cultural science 1.0,' even as its latter-day adherents laud and lionize pioneers such as Hoggart, Williams, and Hall (without necessarily reading them in any detail). Cultural studies was established to use empirical facts (e.g. texts), to employ empirical analysis (of closely-observed practices), and to develop theoretical synthesis with due attention to Williams' 'relations between structures.' Cultural studies

---

[5] See http://www.paecon.net.

needed that 'open, alert, and general' spirit to *analyze* ideology. But, over the years it has fallen foul of its own purposes. It has imported ideology, in the form of pre-judged (prejudiced) political affiliations and allegiances, organized not around current problems of knowledge but under the shade of inherited prophets. It is important *now* for cultural studies – 'cultural science 2.0' – not to remain stuck in that Birmingham 'moment.' It is time to move on, and perhaps also for a little Schumpeterian 'creative destruction' to clear the way. That is what 'cultural science 2.0' is for.

Disciplinary Migrations

Before moving on from the past, it does need to be understood that cultural studies does not have the field of culture to itself, and it seems likely that 'cultural science' is going to be invented whether we in the 'Latinate' sector wish it or not.

In the first place, the distinction between the humanities and sciences is itself dynamic. A centuries-long trend can be observed where knowledge domains that started out as part of the humanities have evolved (or drifted) ever more firmly into the sciences, sometimes completely, sometimes causing a rift within a discipline, sometimes stopping halfway (marooned in the 'social sciences'). Thus, for instance, 'natural history' has evolved through botany, zoology, and biology to (evolutionary) bioscience. Other migrants from the humanities to science include geography (once descriptive, it is now computational), psychology (now neuroscience), linguistics (now highly computational and evolutionary; and let it not be forgotten that Saussure proposed semiotics as the 'science of signs'), and economics, to name a few. Some disciplines (among some practitioners), in anthropology in particular, show signs of moving in the opposite direction; from 'description of the real' to discursive ambivalence.

There have been many attempts to shift the study of human associated life (society and culture) over to the sciences. When Raymond Williams published his article on 'cultural science' in the *Journal of Communication* (1974a), positivist behaviourism was in its heyday in US communications science. His European-style 'open conspiracy' must have looked pretty alien to the alumni of that industrialized grad-school system, trained in quantitative methods that were the route to tenure in 'mass comm' at the time – and for some decades thereafter, since 'mass comm' is still the biggest of the divisions of the International Communication Association (the principal US professional association for communications scholars). Ever since the eruption of cultural studies into the field in the 1970s, US communication science has been riven between 'quantitative' and 'qualitative' methods, and this fault line tends to reproduce the distinction between 'scientific' and 'humanistic' approaches rather than overcoming that deep divide. However, it has also reified an impoverished notion of science, based on a rigidly enforced research methodology that serves more adequately as a modern-day 'puberty rite' for graduate students than it does as a description, never mind an imaginative reconceptualization, of the real.

Many in cultural studies, including myself, have thought that a shift towards such a version of 'science' – the enforcement of behaviorist positivism – is premature and misconceived. This version of psychologistic empiricism more or less defined culture out of account, seeking generalizability on the basis of methodological individualism and abstracted (universalized) individual 'subjects,' in a context where it is clear that there is a great deal more going on than individual rational choice. Meanwhile, communication science in its quantitative mode is not always closely in touch with recent developments in the sciences more generally, especially recent work in genetics and evolutionary science, and in complexity and network mathematics. Instead, 'science' has come to signify a certain style of academic conservatism, while a preference for 'qualitative' methods is equally often code for 'liberal' (i.e. left-leaning, not 'neo-liberal') scholarship.

In other words – but words that are not available to cultural studies if it refuses to engage with the disciplinary history of economics – US-style positivist communication science was a 'neoclassical' initiative that proved limited in its applicability to 'lived' culture or experience even as it produced quantitative data. In cultural studies, as also in economics in reaction to the neo-classical model, various 'heterodox' tendencies emerged, of which 'Birmingham' cultural studies was but one, that sought to provide explanations for culture based not on rational individualism and equilibrium models but on situated and contextual determinants, such as institutions, history, and social structure.

Given the model of 'science' that was dominant in US-style communication departments, where, like wind-blown invasive weeds, media and cultural studies took precarious root in the 1980s, the whole idea of 'science' was troublesome: a source of politicized antagonism rather than disciplinary hope. In reaction to behaviorism, and to science more generally as part of the Vietnam-era 'military-industrial complex,' an allergic reaction to the very term 'science' became common in cultural studies. A stand-off was staged between science *as such* and cultural – or 'critical' – inquiry based on values, judgment, and political affiliation.

Cultural studies offered a cogent critique of 'neoclassical' or positivist communication science. But it was a mistake to withdraw from exposure to scientific endeavor altogether. Cultural studies would have done better, as heterodox economics has done, to maintain a scientific ambition while critiquing science. Of course, some influential figures such as Poulantzas and Althusser claimed Marxism *as* a science (as the Communist Party of China still does), a form of knowledge that stood outside of the ideology it analyzed. However, 'scientific Marxism' was not in dialogue with scientific method in other domains; instead of unifying the field of knowledge it further sectarianized it.

Even so, because 'communication science' was itself ideological, pre-evolutionary, and tended to universalize humanity from the experimental sample-base of mid-western college students, it was appropriate for scholars of culture to resist *premature scientism* in the study of meaning systems. There was much to be learned from humanities-based, in-close analysis of contextualized constructions of meanings where power is reproduced. In a sense, this was like the taxonomic phase of Linnaean botany – identifying and classifying the systemic connections between types of cultural action (lived experience) or artifact (text). Without such careful description, culture presented as a wild profusion with no pattern other than what the observer could make out of the experiential immediacy of observation itself – which is a 'method' proper to art (J. M. W. Turner) rather than science (Joseph Wright 'of Derby').[6]

Cultural studies was surely right to try to describe and trace the organizing principles that 'determined' such profusion. The problem, though, is that unlike botany it has failed to 'self-correct' or to draw its theorizing and practical elements together in order to develop a model of such determinations that can be tested and built upon. Indeed, many in cultural studies rejected the 'grand narrative' of science altogether, and with it any commitment to incremental improvement in knowledge among a common-purposed group of investigators. This was held to betray a vestigial loyalty to the idea of rational progress, which was in turn associated

---

[6] Contrast the 'visions' of science in J. M. W. Turner's *Rain, Steam, and Speed: The Great Western Railway* (1844; accessible at http://www.j-m-w-turner.co.uk/turner-rain-steam.htm) and Joseph Wright ('of Derby')'s *An Experiment on a Bird in the Air Pump* (1768; accessible at http://www.nationalgallery.org.uk/server.php?show=conObject.1453).

not with knowledge but with imperialism and patriarchy. Instead, cultural studies turned back to evaluation, based now on political affiliation not aesthetics. It was not so much a case of 'anything goes' (the common scientific accusation against postmodernism) as a case of 'each for themselves,' in the sense that what any given analyst 'discovered' in their research could be ignored quite safely by all the others. The test for 'advancing' the field (though such a term was suspect) was not 'discovery' but 'like-mindedness,' resulting in various overlapping webs of mutual citation (and mutual criticism) among self-selecting groups whose affinities were based on identity politics. Cultural studies became stuck in an adolescent phase of argumentativeness, where each practitioner was free to argue whatever they liked. No-one was bound by anyone else's findings, and the field as a whole moved on by following trends and social movements (class, colonialism, gender, race, sexuality) rather than by reference to previous work in the field.

As a result, cultural studies has ignored developments in other scientific fields, which have changed radically since the time when Williams and Hall were writing, especially in the biosciences, which have completed their 'evolutionary turn' after a long period of taxonomic description, and in mathematics, which has benefitted from the incredible expansion of computing power, such that complex networks can be tracked and modeled where once they were what Benedict Anderson famously called 'imagined communities.' They need be imagined no longer; they are data.

Not surprisingly, then, the computational and evolutionary sciences are becoming ever more confident about explaining culture. The Santa Fe Institute, for one, was ambitious enough to ask: 'Is there a physics of society?' (this being the name of a workshop held there on January 10–12, 2008) – and is confident that it can explain culture, if only as what Jenna Bednar and Scott Page call 'suboptimal behaviour' in complex models, preventing rational choice.[7] Similarly, Baroness Susan Greenfield (see e.g. 2002, 2008) is one of many neuroscientists who think – in her case without experimental evidence for a link between her scientific observations and social fears – that they can explain culture (watching television and computer screens) as well as brains (the action of neurons):

---

[7] Scott Page (n.d.) wrote: 'In this project, Jenna Bednar and I construct models of culture that build from standard game theoretic models of institutions. In our conception, culture consists of mental models that are consistent both within and between people in a community that [...] may sometimes result in suboptimal behavior.'

> My fear is that these technologies are infantilising the brain into the state of small children who are attracted by buzzing noises and bright lights, who have a small attention span and who live for the moment. (quoted in Derbyshire 2009)[8]

'Cultural science 2.0' ought to be mindful of these attempts from within science to explain culture, as well as to seek to adopt for itself, following Veblen, a more systematic and less 'animistic' method of inquiry. 'We' may think we can do a better job of explaining culture than the physicists and neuroscientists have done so far, and certainly a better one than the positivist quantoids managed in what passed for communication 'science,' but we also need to engage with what (and how) the sciences know, and we need to convince them that what we have to say should be added to the knowledge base rather than continuing to be discounted as non-scientific.

Does it follow that humanities-based disciplines are of declining utility? What can they offer to the study of culture *as a science*? The physicist Alan Sokal opened his famous parody of cultural studies with the standard answer:

> There are many natural scientists, and especially physicists, who continue to reject the notion that the disciplines concerned with social and cultural criticism can have anything to contribute, except perhaps peripherally, to their research. (Sokal 1996: 217)

However, times may change. Where once this question was an excuse for insults across the divide of the 'two cultures,' now it opens a much more productive possibility. What is bringing science and the humanities together is evolution – the adaptation of complex systems to change. The present moment offers a chance to *fulfil the promise* offered by cultural science 1.0, not to bury it.

Cultural studies has included the study of:

- *Popular* culture and the emancipatory potential of popular media;
- *Language* as a sense-making system or network as well as an evolving historical artifact;
- *Media* such as printing, broadcasting – entertainment and information;

---

[8] See also Mitchell (2008) and http://www.abc.net.au/tv/bigideas/stories/2009/10/09/2709586.htm for Australian airings of the same fears.

- *Distinction* (class, popular/high culture, etc.) – raising questions regarding structure, power, and change as well as values, quality, and teaching.

That combination involved experiential aspects (reflexivity, agency, identity, and context) as well as 'objective' ones (the 'thinginess' or materiality of culture, including the empirical form taken by texts). Indeed, cultural studies was a powerful tool for showing how subjectivity had thoroughly invaded and compromised the supposed objectivity of knowledge and of structures based on differential evaluations. This was one of the main attractions of cultural studies. Self-reflexive and 'committed to a radical contextualism' (Grossberg 1993), it sought to show how the evaluations and hierarchies of society as well as literary and intellectual merit actually worked, rather than trying to assign evaluative places within them. Experience, identity, and reflexivity – the politics of the personal – were part of an important challenge to positivism and scientism, not least by feminism. This challenge was part of the so-called 'cultural turn' in the sciences, and cultural studies raised interesting questions for the domain of knowledge more generally:

- How can someone *inside* modern urban popular culture analyze it, combining reflexivity and agency with naturalism and objectivity?
- How can sign systems (such as language) in mediated forms (such as television) be propagated among whole populations? Shakespeare was the model (not the exception) for analyzing any elaborated textual system that combined human values with aesthetic and communicative elements for large, heterogeneous, and anonymous audiences/publics.
- How can popular, commercial forms carry serious content (again, with Shakespeare as the model), from comedy television to fashion photography? Clearly, these days, serious reflexive thought on the human condition is carried by film, television, and online media. These same media are just as available for popularization of scientific, historical-political, and imaginative work as they are for entertainment – indeed, as in Shakespeare, there is no distinction between the two.
- How can systems and media *be used*? This question becomes more interesting the more that such users exceed and transform the expectations of corporate or state 'providers.' How can active *audiences* and *social* networks be seen as creative agents of innovation, renewal, and productivity of large-scale media systems?

- How is the future open? Another attraction of cultural studies was that it was clearly committed to *producing* as well as *reporting* change, using scholarship *for* change, for what I once called 'intervention analysis' (Hartley 1992a), allowing for open-ended communication systems where media can be put to uses not imagined by their producers and owners.

Veblen (1898) calls this kind of purposefulness 'teleological, in the sense that men [people] always and everywhere seek to do something.' There is a vital distinction to be made here. It is as important to pursue 'teleological' *action* as it is to avoid teleological *theory* – one must act with purpose but not explain the world as if it shares that purpose. It is thus important for the (political or social) 'end' not to leak across into the (scientific) 'means' of investigation. Thus, cultural studies (cultural science 1.0) was an approach to culture that was purposeful, not seeking to describe natural laws, least of all aesthetic ones where the taste of one generation, class, or culture has power to command others. Instead, it broke the previously tight bond between three different types of teleological tendency:

- Teleological *actions* – the purpose of actions as seen by the agents involved: what were *their* ends? This question applies not only to individuals but also to governments, where it is called 'policy.'
- Teleological *explanations* – fitting facts to the model (this is or is not 'great' art).
- Teleological *world* – events are driven by spirits, or natural laws, or moral force, towards a preconceived end (e.g. profit, salvation, progress, racial domination).

The first kind of teleology is inevitable, a spur to action by individuals, and capable of being studied. The second two types are impossible, leading to bad science. What is it that can study and understand change (including purposeful agency) without falling for the wrong sort of teleology? Evolution, of course.

Part II: Present – Creative Industries

Creativity and culture – perhaps more than any other area of our lives – is in a state of constant reinvention. When we act as though culture is the product of fixed organisations and structures to be preserved and defended, we miss the point. Culture isn't just about preserving the legacies of the past. It's also about us. It's about realising the unique possibilities of now. Sometimes creativity needs a little creative destruction. (Westbury 2009)

A Present Moment

In *Policing the Crisis* (1978), Stuart Hall and his colleagues took a particular 'moment' – UK news reports about the sentencing of West Indian youths to lengthy jail terms for the 'new' crime of mugging – and asked how it could be explained. They used this trivial but telling moment to trace the cumulative causal sequence of hegemony in post-World War II Britain, and to theorize that there was a crisis of hegemony; a theory that not only explained the micro-events unfolding in a British courtroom but also sought to explain macro-level change in the Western political-cultural system. Michel Foucault opened *Discipline and Punish* (1977) with a more gruesome 'moment' – an instance of pre-modern spectacular capital punishment. He used it to contextualize his study of the change from medieval pain-of-death to modern administrative methods of government, and to theorize that these amounted to what he called 'panopticism.' 'Moments' are thus part of the cultural studies kitbag: an ordinary event – minor, local, and sometimes confronting – becomes the means by which a much larger and more complex set of historical determinations can be unraveled. This is Veblen's 'causal sequence.' Long-term and large-scale evolutionary processes operate in the here and now to produce what Hall called a 'conjuncture.'

Following this practice, the initiative that I want to describe now constitutes such a 'moment': the *creative industries*. Its birth was marked by the 1998 publication of the British government's 'mapping document' (Department for Culture Media and Sport (DCMS) 1998, revised 2001; see also Hartley 2005). Such an event may invite a feeling of bathos when compared to Hall's imprisonment or Foucault's execution, but bathos should not blind us to the fact that all three of these 'moments' are governmental actions reported in documents that allow the analyst to glimpse, in Williams' words, 'relations between practices.' It may then be appropriate to use the 'method' of the 'conjunctural moment' to explain the creative industries.

Needless to say, although it attracted attention around the world among state agencies for regional and industrial development policy, this bathetic birth was not accepted as conjunctural by many observers close to the scene at the time. In the UK in particular, it attracted a chorus of social-theory critique (see Hesmondhalgh 2007; Pratt 2008; O'Connor 2009), being dismissed as opportunism (a government department currying favor with the Treasury), local boosterism, and a garish combination of New Labour and neo-liberalism – 'third way' style without economic or cultural substance . . . or so said the critics. But such instant judgments – like those of competitor playwrights who derided Shakespeare as 'an upstart crow' in the 1590s – may not stand the test of time. They may even say more about the position of the social-theory critic, sidelined by policy-wonks and techno-business consultants, than about the creative industries.

Even so, the critics had a point. The DCMS initiative could certainly be explained as a bit of political opportunism by Chris Smith, incoming minister for Culture, Media and Sport in the UK government, taking over a renamed 'National Heritage' department. He sought to boost the culture budget by associating the arts with economic growth, not just with 'heritage' values. This was doubtless another example of New-Labour spin of the kind that so infuriated the academic left as well as the media throughout the Blair decade. There was also much to criticize about the DCMS definition of the creative industries, including the inclusion of certain sectors or the exclusion of others for purely local reasons – for example that London has an antiques market (included) or that tourism (excluded) came under a different departmental policy portfolio. In other words, the 'definition' was self-serving, insular, and partial. So, it was hardly surprising that it was regarded as unworthy, compromised by short-term self-interest, parochialism, political spin, and bad reviews.

Nevertheless, the moment of the creative industries may still yield important insights into longer-term changes in and among culture, the economy, and politics, and not just in the UK. Internationally, the idea was quickly adopted and customized to local requirements in different countries across Europe, Asia, and Australasia. Therefore, it is worth trying to explain this 'moment.' In essence, that is the task that the ARC Centre of Excellence for Creative Industries and Innovation (CCI) in Australia has undertaken over a sustained period (since 2005). Indeed, just as the Birmingham CCCS had sufficient scale and ambition to attempt large-scale or 'macro' explanations of culture, so the Queensland University of Technology-based CCI has taken on an ambitious, team-based program of work that seeks to explain 'creative innovation' from first principles, by moving as systematically as possible from the here and now of the 'present moment' to an analysis of the conceptual underpinnings of creative identity, and thence to an understanding of real creative productivity and 'actually existing innovation' from the perspective of dynamic change, as the generative edge in the growth of knowledge.

Thus, the CCI team approaches the DCMS moment as symptomatic of a much more important set of changes. The much-cited 'mapping document' (DCMS 1998; revised 2001) raised in a new and urgent way the question of the relation between economic and cultural systems. But that was not all – it was also *purposeful*, seeking to *do* something about culture, not simply to produce a finished definition. The DCMS document sought to identify the *source* of economic value in creative production. Thus, precisely because it hypothesized a strong economic role for culture, it demanded that we investigate 'causal sequence' in the role of creativity, innovation, and culture. Further, the DCMS approach sought to *change* cultural and creative productivity; naturally, to grow 'ours,' preferably at the competitive expense of 'theirs,' but always to understand and intervene in the process of positively aspirational socio-economic change, and if necessary political change too, in order to enhance the prospects of creative culture and innovation more generally. Put that way, and without any of the agents involved necessarily seeing it this way themselves, here was a version of the 'project' of cultural studies going back to the 1950s and 1960s: in Veblen's terms, 'teleological *action*' of an entirely defensible kind.

From Creative Industries to Cultural Science

That is what we have been trying to do at the CCI. We wanted to understand creativity in terms of 'cumulative causal sequence' and purposeful change. What tools were available for the job? Here we have benefitted from an intensive encounter with economics. It transpires that the discipline of economics is every bit as turbulent as that of cultural studies, some of the most familiar issues of which are mirrored in economics. In our attempt to explain creative innovation from first principles, neo-classical economics was not challenging enough, for it accepted a 'market failure' explanation of culture and provided descriptive accounts of the 'cultural economy,' in which a very traditional notion of the arts (i.e. 'high' culture) was interrogated for signs of economic activity (Caves 2000; Throsby 2001). At the other extreme, the kind of 'political economy' familiar from media and communication studies (Garnham 1986; T. Miller – see http://www.tobymiller.org) was *too* challenging, knowing what was wrong in advance. New information is hard to extract from such 'critique.'

The most productive interdisciplinary interlocutor turned out to be neither neo-classical economics nor political economy, but *evolutionary economics*. Like cultural studies in its early days, evolutionary economics occupied a marginal, agent-provocateur position in relation to mainstream economics. Both were the disruptive irritant that, along with complexity science, sought to reconfigure the nineteenth-century disciplinary knowledge system (Lee 2003). We have found this dialogue both provocative and productive, just as did the pioneers of cultural studies in their encounters with their interdisciplinary neighbors. We have now begun to publish the main conceptual advances of our approach so far, in economics journals such as the *Journal of Cultural Economics* and *Industry and Innovation* (Potts et al. 2008a, 2008b) as well as in more familiar humanities journals, and in our own experimental journal, *Cultural Science*.[9] The convergence of cultural studies and evolutionary economics is based on the recognition of problems common in 'culture' and 'economy' that centre on the attempt to understand the drivers of creativity, innovation, and change in contemporary cultural processes, economic actions, and the growth of knowledge. We have been calling this enterprise 'cultural science' – cultural science 2.0, in fact.[10]

We locate the cutting edge of research on creativity at the point of triangulation between three domains: evolution, complexity, and creative media communication. This interdisciplinary interface is counterintuitive, but highly productive:

- *Creativity* can be understood as reflexive adaptation to unpredictable change within complex systems.
- *Complexity studies* explain how 'social network markets' are a vital enabling technology for the distribution of choice.
- *Evolutionary theory* focuses on the dynamics of change in the growth of knowledge.[11]

---

[9]   See http://cultural-science.org.

[10]   See http://cultural-science.org. See also http://www.cci.edu.au and http://www.apo.org.au/creative-economy for information about the CCI's research programs.

[11]   We are not alone in seeking to introduce evolutionary thinking into the humanities, of course. A notable comparable venture was The Darwinian Renaissance in the Humanities and Social Sciences, a research symposium held at Queen Mary University of London in November 2009.

These developments, added to those coming from anthropology, cultural studies, and creative arts, enable us to rethink creativity as a property of agency in dynamic systems, not as an expression of the essence of uniquely talented individuals. The emergent form of 'cultural science 2.0' that we are exploring seeks to identify patterns of action in complex social networks, their past evolution, and possible future scenarios, including paying attention to unintended consequences of choices at any given 'moment.'

Social Network Markets and other Novelties

The future-oriented view of the loose network of the 'cultural science' group is that creativity, both expert and amateur, is driving change in the nature of markets as well as dynamic growth in creative sectors such as digital content. More fundamentally, reflexive creativity is what enables human culture to adapt and change. Despite some 'mass extinctions' throughout the millennia, this process has resulted in the long-term growth of knowledge and in the creation of new values, both economic and cultural. In such company, culture can no longer be seen as the preserve of artists, nor can innovation remain the preserve of corporate engineers. Both require the activities and productivity of the millions who interact in the social networks that are now dispersed among whole populations. With the growing ubiquity of digital media these are becoming a more dynamic source of productivity than industrial-era innovation based on expert invention and the closed pipeline of the corporately controlled value-chain. The social network 'swarm' outperforms the IP-protected 'lab,' and at twice the speed.

Already, this work is gaining traction. Among other outcomes, we are reconceptualizing how markets themselves work, including the idea that creativity is an 'enabling social technology' – just as markets themselves are. Like markets, science, the law, and other such social technologies, creativity is required in order to enable individual choice, agency, and enterprise to be conducted in a rule-governed but open-ended environment. We have defined the 'creative industries' *as* 'social network markets,' where choices are made not on the basis of rational choice in perfect equilibrium but on the basis of competitive status among networked agents. Individual choices are determined by the choices of others (Potts et al. 2008a), and thus markets are systems made up of those who are *paying attention* to certain types of choice. An example of this is fashion, in which competitive attention creates the market (Hartley and Montgomery 2009).

Social network markets have two main peculiarities. The first is that people's choices are *determined by the choices of others* in the network. The second is that *choices are status-based*. Why are these characteristics peculiar?

- Markets are supposed to be based on self-interested choice, which is assumed to be individualist and rationalist, not determined by the choices of others. In social network markets choice is externalist or system-based, produced by relationships, not reason – reason is the *outcome* of collective choices in a system of relations, not an *input.*
- Choice is meant to satisfy wants or needs. But in social network markets it expresses status relations. Thus, the creative industries don't look very much like a neo-classical market. The choices of high-status celebrities will often be preferred, and those of low-status people avoided, creating a market in celebrity endorsement. Celebrity itself is not a product of but an input into such a market. Emma Watson made Burberry cool again, but she had to be Emma Watson first.

'Entrepreneurial consumers' (Hartley and Montgomery 2009) can signal and gain status by making admired choices, not just in high fashion but also in street fashion, like Harajuku in Japan.[12] And, because status is both relative and transient, the continuing process of making choices in social networks has an impact on status and thus on values (and further choices), both cultural and economic. This is what Jason Potts (2010) calls 'choice under novelty' as opposed to choice under uncertainty or choice under risk, both of which have been studied in behavioral economics. When faced with new knowledge, new connections, or new ideas, people cannot reduce uncertainty by getting more information, precisely because what they're facing is new. Thus, suggests Potts, 'rational economic agents' – that's everyone – observe and learn from how others are making choices, and thus learn how to respond to the new. This is how they get into social network markets in the first place. Once there, by observing and connecting with others, not least by random copying (Bentley 2009), new possibilities open up for them, including other opportunities for 'consumer productivity' and co-creation – hence the opportunity for consumers to act entrepreneurially,

---

[12] See http://www.japaneselifestyle.com.au/tokyo/harajuku_fashion.htm.

taking a risk on the new, in a role that classical economics and mass consumption theory alike would see as a contradiction in terms, because entrepreneurial productivity and consumption are at opposing ends of the value chain.

Further, much of what constitutes social networks, and therefore the creative industries, is not market-based at all, at least not in the usual sense. This is because social networks exist prior to and outside of markets, among families, friends, neighbors, enemies, and so on, and because they belong to the *economics of attention* (Lanham 2006) as much as to the monetary economy.

People place value on the *attention* they give and receive. This is an economy of *signals* as much as one of monetary values, which is why it needs a 'convergence' of cultural studies (semiotics, anthropology, media analysis) with economics to make sense of what's going on (Herrmann-Pillath 2010). People may invest time, creativity, and material resources in creating the right signals to attract more attention. They also value *paying* attention to favored others. Fans, for instance, invest in the attention they offer to their idols. Attention may be 'payed' in many ways, not all of them monetized. Choice may just as easily end in a marriage or friendship as a sale.

Evolving Creative Industries

Creative innovation is dynamic. It is therefore important to keep up conceptually as well as commercially, moving beyond 'creative industries' as a specialized industry sector to investigate creativity as an input into the economy generally, thence to broaden the term to include the whole population by incorporating 'creative culture.' Users and consumers as well as producers need to be incorporated into the model of creative industries as social network markets. There have already been at least three phases of the creative industries, each generating a different model rather than conforming to one definition. Each model has supplemented – not supplanted – the one before.

CI-1: Creative clusters

- *Industry* definition.
- Closed expert system.
- 'Creative clusters' of different 'industry sectors' – advertising, architecture, publishing, software, performing arts, media production, art,

design, fashion, etc. – that together produce creative works or outputs (the DCMS list).
- 'Provider-led' or supply-based definition.

The first phase is the *industry* definition (DCMS), which I call 'creative clusters.' It is made of clusters of different 'industries' – those listed above – that together produce creative works or *outputs*. This is a 'provider-led' or supply-based definition. The sector is reckoned to be anywhere between three and eight percent of advanced economies (Australia, the UK, the US), of growing importance to emergent economies (e.g. Brazil, China, Indonesia), high-growth, and with an economic multiplier effect. Looked at this way, the creative industries are nothing other than *firms* whose livelihood depends on creating intellectual property and protecting it with copyright, enforced against both commercial copying and consumer 'piracy.' The sector is thus modeled on the industrial-era closed expert pipeline (invent → patent/copyright → manufacture → distribute → sell), preferably with all of these functions controlled by one firm (e.g. News Corp, Viacom).

CI-2: Creative services

- Economic *services* definition.
- Closed innovation system.
- 'Creative services' – creative inputs by creative occupations and companies (professional designers, producers, performers, and writers).
- 'b2b' (business to business) or hybrid producer/consumer definition.

The second phase is the *services* definition, which I call 'creative services.' It is characterized by the provision of creative *inputs* by creative occupations and companies, most obviously where professional designers, producers, performers, and writers add value to firms or agencies engaged in other activities, from mining or manufacturing to health, government, and other public services (Howkins 2001). Creative services expand the creative industries by at least a third, according to research at my centre (Higgs, Cunningham, and Bakhshi 2008), using the concept of the 'creative trident.' Creative input is high value-added, stimulating the economy as a whole and boosting innovation in otherwise static sectors (e.g. manufacturing). This kind of creativity can transform old-style services such as transport into creative services such as 'experience'-based tourism. Because this version of the creative industries is economy-wide and involves *occupations and agencies* other than firms, it may be regarded as a hybrid system, in which social networks play a role, but it remains focused on market-driven activity; it is only 'demand-led' in a b2b environment. Nevertheless, here is where innovation policy can gain traction, encouraging firms of all kinds to collaborate with creative entrepreneurs and to innovate using creative inputs.

CI-3: Creative citizens

- *Cultural* definition.
- Open innovation network.
- 'Creative citizens' – population, workforce, consumers, users, entrepreneurs, artists.
- 'User-led' or demand-based definition, bearing in mind that, in the creative industries, supply *precedes* demand (people don't know what they like or dislike in advance).

The third model is the *cultural* definition, which I call 'creative citizens.' Here is where creativity spills both out of the economy and into it, being an attribute of the population at large – the workforce, consumers, users, and entrepreneurs, who become hard to distinguish from artists in how they go about pursuing an idea and a market for it and creative reputation. This is a *user-led* or demand-side definition, where in principle everyone's energies can be harnessed. It adds the value of entire social networks and the individual agency of whole populations to the *growth of knowledge*. It is the domain of experimentation and adaptation, where *individual* agency may have *network-wide* effects: thus it is the dynamic 'edge' of systemic *emergence*. Such a vastly expanded definition of creative agency is only 'thinkable' with complexity/network theory and the notion of open complex systems. It is most easily evident in computer-based social networks, but is not confined to the digital domain. Creative citizens are 'navigators' rather than 'consumers'; they may also act in concert as 'aggregators' to produce crowd-sourced solutions to creative problems.

Following this line of thought it is easy to see that there is more to creativity than what is taught in art schools – or business schools. Creativity is generalized as a population-wide attribute, it requires social networks, and its 'product' is the growth of knowledge, sometimes within a market environment, sometimes not. This is a radically democratic move, although it is far from universally adopted and its implications have barely begun to be worked through. However, it is possible to identify the new value propositions associated with an evolved and expanded notion of population-wide creative industriousness in this formula:

Agents (both professional and amateur)
  + *Network* (both social and digital)
    + *Enterprise* (market-based and other forms of purposeful association)
     = *Creative value* (in a complex open system)
     = *Growth of knowledge*

The first two models – CI-1 and CI-2 – are based on the economy. CI-3 is based on *technologically equipped culture.* In Clay Shirky's (2006) phrase: 'Here comes everybody!' In this model, everyone's creative potential can be harnessed for innovation, which can come from anywhere in the system. In fact, CI-3 is radically different from CI-1 and CI-2, because:

- It focuses on culture, not economy; consumer or user, not producer; and whole populations (social networks), not firms.
- It is the beneficiary of the digital revolution, posing a direct and fundamental challenge to 'industry' business models.
- Potentially it is a more productive model of creativity than the ones that are tied to expert systems alone.

It includes myriad acts of what I call 'microproductivity,' among large-scale but connected populations, where previous unproductive end-user consumption (say, taking a photo) is but one move in a creative and potentially innovative process. This can happen at both the 'micro' scale (e.g. an amateur cell-phone photo of a newsworthy scene) or at the 'macro' scale of complex systems (e.g. Flickr, Panoramio). CI-3 is therefore another example of how the clash of opposites is proving to be the driver of change in creative productivity. Rather than being seen as the output of an industry, creativity becomes a property of complex systems, socially networked relations, and the interaction of cultural and economic activities. Further, social networks themselves are sources of innovation; they are not simply distribution media.

Systems such as social network markets can be analyzed using evolutionary economics, but they cannot be understood without an interdisciplinary approach that includes both in-close contextual techniques derived from the humanities (textual and ethnographic) and computational power from the science and technology side. Examples might include *modeling* social networks using complexity mathematics; *mapping* networks of choice and influence in digital media such as the blogosphere; or *monitoring* large-scale changes in the way that people perform their cultural identity and relationships. Here again, we bump up against work that is already under way in neighboring disciplines such as network theory, web science, and internet studies. Theory-building is also vital, to model how such actions may be patterned in complex adaptive systems and how agents and enterprises navigate those systems. Again, such work is already well under way, for instance in ANT (actor network theory; Latour 2005) and its successor techniques (see Hawkins 2009 for a good example).

Investigation of these questions has already led a book called *The Economics of Identity and Creativity: A Cultural Science Approach*, by Carsten Herrmann-Pillath (2010). This is a thoroughgoing evolutionary approach to creativity and culture. It is:

- Naturalistic (not mentalist) – the world of ideas and that of 'matter-energy' are one and the same;
- Externalist (not individualist) – which means that identity is produced within networked interaction among brains mediated by language: the 'extended mind';
- Anti-Cartesian (mind and matter are the same) – so 'rational individualism' cannot be founded on a theory of mind; and
- Premised on the idea that knowledge is material not mental.

Herrmann-Pillath writes:

> I submit that the externalist approach to human knowledge boils down to the *cultural science paradigm*. Cultural science explains human knowledge in terms of naturalism and externalism, and therefore uses an evolutionary paradigm to investigate the generation, diffusion, and maintenance of human knowledge

In this context,

> markets can be seen as external knowledge systems, i.e. a special aspect of the 'extended mind' phenomenon. Markets as an outcome of cultural evolution are part and parcel of the knowledge structures that underlie individual action in markets.

Thus we seek to account not only for creativity but for the evolving knowledge structures – including markets – within which it operates.

Part III: Future – Cultural Science

I believe the enterprises of culture will eventually fall out into science, by which I mean the natural sciences, and the humanities, particularly the creative arts. These domains will be the two great branches of learning in the twenty-first century. (E. O. Wilson 1998: 12)

Cultural Science 2.0

An important focus for future work must be *population-wide* analysis in an evolutionary approach. Cultural studies has made significant progress in reconceptualizing culture, and creativity with it, as part of 'ordinary life' rather than as the emanation of individual genius (art) or corporate power (media). But it has not followed through on the implication of this move. It is no good looking at creativity, culture, or knowledge *as professional or expert systems*, whether individualist or corporate, any more than it would be to see them as expressions of spiritual inspiration or natural laws (in Veblen's sense). We need to understand cultural, creative, and knowledge systems *across whole populations*. This is why we have taken a strong interest in social networking systems where consumer productivity and user co-creation are important features, including in the games industry, because it is clear that innovation occurs in the interaction between producers and consumers, professionals and players, and not within the confines of the production company. However, in this context, new problems arise, across the range of institutions, in distribution, and in relation to the role of the 'user.' Naturally, methodological problems also abound, as does the persistent difficulty of doing truly interdisciplinary research.

In relation to institutions, there are problems in coordinating and scaling creative innovation. How do large-scale systems self-organize when productive agency is adding to their scale and complexity every day? How are individual actions organized into clusters, rules, hierarchies; how are these related to each other; and what causal force does institutional agency exert on the system as a whole? What role do existing institutional agencies play in the emergence and elaboration of the new, especially when such novelties are technologically disruptive? What is the balance between expert elaboration and amateur emergence in the institutional production of the new? In relation to distribution, what is the role of *property* in the creation of wealth – intellectual property and intellectual capital are not worth much unless they are shared, but sharing them decreases their value. In relation to users, when considering the productivity of whole populations, it is a mistake to plump either for methodological individualism (as some versions of psychology, as well as neo-classical economics, have done) or for single-cause determinations of entire systems (as Marxist-derived political economy has done). Instead, an 'externalist' (extended brain) approach to creativity and identity requires intermediate levels of agency and organization. Social networks *self-organize* via institutional forms, a process of coordination that forms one of the main objects of cultural science inquiry.

Institutional organization is unavoidable – it is not an external force impinging on individual freedom of action like Charlie Chaplin's famous machine; it *enables* and coordinates individual action, intensifying and directing individual creativity and productivity. Thus, we cannot remain satisfied with an approach to institutions that condemns the most elaborated versions of them as somehow inhuman, as in 'capitalism,' 'globalization,' 'the market,' 'corporate power' – or 'Rupert Murdoch,' and at the same time endowed with human purposes, as in capitalism's 'wants' or 'desires.'

Nor are we any longer in a cultural universe where individual access to creative culture – that is, literacy – can be seen as emancipationist in itself, as seemed to be the case as print literacy was being universalized in industrial countries during the twentieth century. Now, the information universe is too large – or in economic terms transaction costs are too high – for mere access to ensure intellectual freedom; organizational forms and interactions also determine how individual agency operates in practice. New attention is needed to trace and understand the role of *selection*, *management*, *order*, and *redaction* (creative editing of existing material) in networks and archives even as they continue to expand faster than exponentially.

A further problem is that of distribution. Chris Anderson's 'long tail' (2006) has alerted everyone to 'power law' distribution (see Figure 2.1 and Figure 8.1), which seems to explain why some systems seem to favor a 'winner takes all' scenario, from blockbuster sales to bankers' bonuses. How widespread is this pattern of distribution in cultural and media forms? It is necessary to test the possibility that relationships previously regarded as in opposition (e.g. elites as opposed to masses) may in fact be power law gradients.

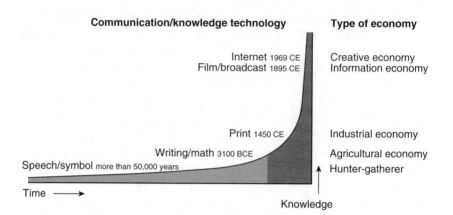

Figure 2.1   A short history of the future. This power-law curve (long tail) models the growth of knowledge via technologies of speech/symbol, writing/math, print, broadcast media (inc. film), and the internet. The list of 'types of economy' on the right suggests that the evolution of each new knowledge technology coincides with economic epochs: speech = hunter-gatherer; writing/math = agricultural; print = industrial; broadcast/electronic = information-based; and, most recently, digital = creative. (Not to scale.)

Social distinctions, up to and including class, may be better explained by network theory, with 'hubs' and 'nodes' (in Barabási's (2002) terms; see Figure 8.1) within a complex open network of relational identities, in which 'elites' have many connections within the network and 'masses' (the long tail) have few. In other words, is what separates celebrities like Paris Hilton or Stephen Fry from the rest of us simply the number of connections they have within a social network market? Certainly such things are avidly measured. The number of friends on Facebook or followers on Twitter someone has is publicly monitored, and if of sufficient scale is further cause for celebrity coverage.

Such models are interesting because they focus on what connects all of the agents in a system, not on what divides them, and they allow for dynamism (change) in the position, status, and action of any 'node' or agent, as well as in the network as a whole. Thus, 'distribution' can no longer be seen as shifting finished goods, meanings, or knowledge *from* a productive centre (or cause) *to* a passive recipient (or effect); instead it requires attention to *distributed productivity* throughout the system. Of course, one of the main attractions of a population-wide cultural science approach is that it focuses on creativity among 'users' as much as 'producers,' thereby continuing the cultural-studies tradition of focusing on ordinary culture, the active audience, and 'bottom-up' causation in meaning systems. Problems arising from this perspective include a major question about how to shift from small-scale, in-close 'micro' analysis of diverse local practices to large-scale, system-wide 'macro' understanding of the web of mutual causation.

Finally, cultural science presents problems of *method*, for we don't yet know how best to model change; how to measure 'cumulative sequence'; how to identify and describe population-wide processes of variation, selection, and retention in the cultural sphere; how or what to predict in the growth of knowledge. It does seem at the very least that we need to focus on probabilities in large-scale systems (e.g. 'what can I find on YouTube?') rather than on essences found in single texts (e.g. the signed work of art in a museum); this is the subject of Chapter 7.

'Thought Control'

Cultural science draws our attention to the extent to which the 'cultural' as a special sphere of peculiar value has converged with the 'economic' – which itself turns out to be inexplicable without attention to identity, creativity, and language.

Does this collapse of economic and cultural values into each other mean we are stalking horses for neo-liberalism? Many of our colleagues seem to think so (O'Connor 2009). But an alternative view comes from a surprising source. One of the most prominent contemporary organs of radical activism – the magazine *Adbusters* – devoted its September/October 2009 issue to heterodox and evolutionary economics. This is a counter-intuitive choice, because evolutionary economics is most often associated with the Austrian school of theorists, for example Friedrich von Hayek (1944) and Joseph Schumpeter (1942), whose economic radicalism is not normally recognized on the Left. But it seems that radical theory can come from somewhere unexpected on the old style political spectrum. It is now the chosen weapon with which to *oppose* the status quo. Addressing students of economics directly, editor Kalle Lasn (2009) says:

> Your university is a police state […] not a free marketplace of ideas in which innovation is acknowledged and rewarded. But outside your department, a vigorous heterodox economics thrives […] there are social economists, feminist economists, interdisciplinary economists, ecological economists and

hundreds of intellectuals and maverick professors who are openly critical of the neoclassical paradigm and fighting to overthrow it.

The editorial concludes by giving the student a choice:

> You can ignore all of the screaming inconsistencies and accept the status quo […] Or you can align yourself from the get-go with the mavericks […] You can bet your future on a paradigm shift. I hope this book inspires you to take the riskier, more exciting path.

It does seem strange to read the fiery rhetoric of the barricades in the context of the economics lecture theatre. *Adbusters* seems to be channeling the radical appeal of early cultural studies, which itself, however, seems less and less able to offer its devotees a 'riskier, more exciting path.' Strangely enough, that old radical rhetoric may itself be exerting a form of 'thought control' in cultural studies – making it hard to recognize that things are changing over in the economics department. As the *Adbusters* editorial puts it:

> economics is a highly contested field […] a profession whose axioms, principles and credibility are being questioned like never before. The prevailing neo-classical paradigm is crumbling and a new, more chaotic, more biologically based paradigm is struggling to emerge.

Certainly, cultural studies needs to distance itself from neo-classical economics, where, in the immortal words of Veblen (1898), the individual sits as 'a self-contained globule of desire.' But it must not reduce itself to that same status – self-contained, desiring, but unconnected to others. Such work may simply reproduce (unwittingly or not) the neo-classical model. To the extent that we still tend to treat both *identity* and *creativity* in terms of the desiring individual, that is just what cultural studies does.

We need to move on: '*Economic action* must be subject matter of the science if the science is to fall into line as an evolutionary science' (Veblen 1898, my emphasis). By that token, the subject matter of an evolutionary 'cultural science' is *creative action*, which in the case of our own work, especially if it is allied with similar movements in economics, can be just as radical as ever.

3

Journalism and Popular Culture

I think the trick is that you have to use words well enough so that these nickle-and-dimers who come around bitching about being objective or 'the advertisers don't like' it are rendered helpless by the fact that it's good. That's the way people have triumphed over conventional wisdom in journalism. [...] I can't think in terms of journalism without thinking in terms of political ends. Unless there's been a reaction, there's been no journalism. It's cause and effect. (Hunter S. Thompson in Hahn 1997)

In this chapter I turn from the creative industries in general to one in particular: journalism as the factual-realist textual system of modernity. I offer a historical account to show that popular culture was the *source* of the first mass circulation journalism, via the so-called pauper press of industrializing Britain (1790s to 1840s), but that journalism was later incorporated into the mechanisms of modern government for a very different purpose, first theorized by Walter Bagehot (1872 [1867]), whereby popular culture became the *object* of journalism. In the process journalism's own polarity was reversed – it turned from 'subjective' to 'objective.'

This history gives rise to more-general methodological and categorical considerations that demonstrate how media history itself – as the study of causation and change in dynamic human made systems – is necessary for the process of critiquing and developing conceptual frameworks, especially 'models of communication,' which may not be so self-evident as contemporary common sense seems to indicate, given that completely different

Digital Futures for Cultural and Media Studies, First Edition. John Hartley.
© 2012 John Wiley & Sons, Ltd. Published 2012 by John Wiley & Sons, Ltd.

models may have animated the system in previous times. I conclude with a discussion of YouTube and the resurgence of self-representation, using the resources of popular culture, in current election campaigns. Are we witnessing a further reversal of polarity, where popular culture and self-representation once again become the 'subject' (rather than the 'object') of journalism?

Part I: Popular Culture – Subject or Object?

In this way a reading public which was increasingly working class in character was forced to organize itself. (E.P. Thompson 1963: 799)

Popular culture, understood as modern, industrialized, urban 'associated life' (Veblen 1899) and media, is both 'object' and 'subject' of representation in journalism. As object, popular culture is the familiar consumer market, over which the press barons and their international corporate successors preside. Here, professionals and proprietors take it upon themselves not only to sell representations of the world in commodity form to 'the people' but also to set themselves up as representatives of their readership (using that term to cover all forms of semiotic engagement), whose abilities to choose and act – for example to buy, vote, or riot – they arrogate to themselves as part of their power to influence economic and political decisions. But as subject, popular culture is the source and means of self-representation by various self-constituted versions of 'the people.' It is the place where individually and collectively, as persons or as classes, ordinary people get to speak for themselves. Clearly journalism takes different forms depending on whether popular culture is understood as object ('they') or subject ('we') in the process of production (Sonwalkar 2005).

Journalism studies is interested in journalism; cultural studies is interested in culture, as you would expect. Each field has properly concentrated on its own object of study, investigating with its own evolving set of methods and problems, to such an extent that the two specialisms now present to the observer as two different species. If they ever were varieties of the same discipline, it seems that at last they have speciated; intermarriage among their populations is impossible. In this divergent evolution, journalism studies has tended to take the view that popular culture is an object (of manipulation; behavior), while cultural studies has tended to view popular culture as a subject (of emancipation; action). Journalism research tends to prioritize the perspective of the producer (the professional, the industry, the firm); cultural studies that of the consumer (identity, meaning, use).

It seems that fear of miscegenation among journalism educators means that neither cultural studies nor popular culture are welcome in J-school environments; that is, in the context of the professional training of newsroom journalists. From that perspective, studying popular culture is seen either as siding with a depoliticized celebration of consumerism or as giving way to theory-driven relativism (Windschuttle 1998, 2000; *Media International Australia* 1999). But such a view of popular culture and of cultural studies is mistaken, both historically and conceptually. Journalism studies would benefit from recognizing more directly that the historical co-evolution of journalism and popular culture, the 'subjective' tradition of self-representation, and the methodological purposes of cultural studies, are all important to a proper understanding of journalism's place in contemporary culture.

The object of study has not speciated, so the means of study ought not to either. Journalism and popular culture are part of the same unified field. To adopt an 'objective' or a 'subjective' stance is not a matter of discipline but of politics (or interest at least). And, while it might seem obvious that an 'objective' stance is preferable for journalism, the history of how popular culture was turned into an object suggests that this is by no means a reliable conclusion. Rather, popular culture as subject is the source of popular self-representation, a practice that was decisive in the evolution of mass communication, and which is now resurgent. With the current emergence of digital online self-made media, the need for an integrated understanding of journalism and popular culture is once again urgent, and cultural studies can assist in reaching it. Journalism studies would therefore benefit from giving consideration to the 'subjective' as well as to the 'objective' traditions; for example to YouTube as well as to 'newspapers of record,' because they are part of the same system, and any research field that focuses on just one of them is the poorer for it.

Liberty and Libertinage

We are forced to ask ourselves how inflammatory language and mythologizing can offer a legitimate exegesis on the politics of the day. (Antoine de Baecque 1989: 168)

Popular culture is the true seed bed of modern popular journalism. Although newspapers for the gentry and merchant classes had been around since the seventeenth century, it was only when they became popular in the context of modern democratic and industrial revolutions that they took on contemporary shape, and only then that journalism achieved its potential of communicating with entire populations regardless of their local class or status. In turn, journalism played a strong role in developing popular culture as a modern, urban, mediated experience, as opposed to the prevailing notion of it at the time as craft-based folk art.

Popular journalism was born of the European Enlightenment, French Revolution, and British industrialization and urbanization during the period from the 1790s to the 1840s. In that half-century, motivated by a desire for political emancipation as well as an entrepreneurial bid for profit, radical journalists and publishers, from Tom Paine and William Cobbett to Richard Carlile and Henry Hetherington (see Simkin n.d.), perfected the means for secular, cross-demographic communication about public (and private) affairs to 'ordinary' readers numbering in the hundreds of thousands and – by the time the ultra-radical Sunday newspaper *The News of the World* came onto the scene in 1843 – in the millions. This was, as historian Robert K. Webb puts it, 'a pioneering effort to solve the problem of getting ideas across from one man, or one class, to another' (1955: 35; and see Hartley 1996: 94–9). The 'pauper press' succeeded in creating the popular 'reading public'; an achievement won by people without the vote, often poor, in the teeth of government suppressions, and with no established business infrastructure or market.

'Getting ideas across' was not a merely cerebral business, however. Modern political journalism was founded as much on scandal, gossip, and sensationalism as it was on reason and truth. As the *ancien régime* slid towards political modernization via the French Revolution, salacious novels and pornographic pamphlets were the 'real sources from which political journalism originated in France,' according to historian Robert Darnton (1982: 203). Sex and politics were coterminous, as the bedroom antics of *Thérèse philosophe* (1748, attributed to Marquis Boyer d'Argens) and her many successors demonstrated by the simple narrative device of equating the achievement of orgasm with that of freedom. Sexual gossip, scandal, and innuendo about the king, queen, courtiers, and clerics were used to undermine deference towards royalty and aristocracy, while stories of sexual awakening and libertinage were grand metaphors for political self-realization and philosophical freedom. The most celebrated writers of the Enlightenment – Diderot, Mirabeau, Montesquieu, Voltaire – wrote bawdy and pornographic works as well as political journalism and philosophy, without making a distinction between the personal (popular culture) and the political (journalism). Indeed, the genre of publishing that gave birth to popular journalism in France, the *'livres philosophiques,'* lumped porn together with philosophy (Darnton and Roche 1989: 27–49). The radical underground was not squeamish about where journalism stopped and other forms of writing and representation began; and not only in France (McCalman 1992, 1993). 'Liberty' and 'libertinage' shared the same philosophical history (Grayling 2005: 116–8).

Two Models for 'Two Nations'

It was not easy to escape from politics in nineteenth-century Britain. It filled the newspapers; it was a principal means of mass entertainment. (Robert K. Webb 1955: 83)

During the early nineteenth century, when industrialization took hold (first of all in Britain), only three men in a hundred and no women had the vote. There was a sharp divide between the working class and the political class: they were, in Disraeli's famous phrase, 'two nations' (1980 [1845]: 149). The propertied, educated, and enfranchised class, both conservative and liberal (as famously satirized in *Iolanthe*), followed public affairs in papers such as *The Times* and *The Economist*. These were dedicated to politics (confidence or otherwise in the government of the day), public administration (e.g. campaigns for army reform, or against slavery or capital punishment), and the economy (e.g. promotion of or opposition to free trade). Meanwhile, the other nation, the unenfranchised popular majority, developed their own press, both radical popular (e.g. the *Northern Star, Poor Man's Guardian,* the *Republican*) and, increasingly in and after the 1840s, commercial popular (e.g. *Lloyd's Weekly News, Reynold's News*). There was a telling mismatch between scale of readership and degree of political influence. With a circulation in the low thousands, *The Times* could topple governments; with sales in the hundreds of thousands, and multiple readers per copy (Webb 1955: 33–4), the pauper press was physically attacked *by* the government: their premises were raided, their property seized, and their proprietors imprisoned.

Because of these asymmetric purposes and powers, the respectable and the radical press were expressions of different models of communication. *The Times* and *The Economist* developed journalism as professional expertise, to serve a readership with a stake in both economic and political questions. These papers connected the minority of emancipated citizens to each other, and for them a three-link supply chain of sender/text/receiver was appropriate, because the producer and consumer were co-subjects, equal in status if not in information. The pauper press, meanwhile, saw itself as part of the struggle against the current economic and political arrangements and, as the current phrase has it, sought to 'speak truth to power' (Kennedy-Cuomo 2000). Its mode was as much to accuse opponents as to address its own readers, because it spoke on behalf of – as the voice of – a class that had not attained citizenship (and therefore the idea of the informed citizen did not apply). The poorest sections of that class were not even counted in the census (Mayhew 1849: preface). For activists, who agreed that 'the ideas of the ruling class are in every epoch the ruling ideas,' a two-term base/superstructure model was appropriate (Marx 1845). The productive or laboring classes and the poor were on one side, confined by penury and policing to a rather direct relationship with the economic base; the titled, landed, and educated (middle) classes were on the other side, occupying the superstructural heights of politics and culture (while benefiting from basic economic power). Here already there appeared to be a chalk and cheese distinction between professional journalism (*The Times*) and popular culture (*Poor Man's Guardian*), even though journalistic skills were to be found on both sides of the fence.

This was the basis for a divergence between journalism that saw popular culture as object (to be feared and controlled) and journalism that saw popular culture as subject; 'we the people.' The early mass-circulation newspapers were produced by radicals among whom were also entrepreneurs, who had the 'ability to harness commercialism for the purposes of political dissent and cultural populism' and who were proud to use the latest high-tech industrial inventions such as the steam-powered rotary press (Haywood 2004: 164) in order to reach a mass reading public. They pioneered the 'mass' media. However, as time unfolded, the commitment to oppositional self-representation in these newspapers declined as their scale and profits increased. As the nineteenth century progressed, wages, leisure, literacy, and the franchise were progressively increased and extended. The 'radical popular' (we) press began to give way to the 'commercial popular' (they) press. A good example is the *News of the World*, launched as an unstamped 'ultra-radical' Sunday newspaper in 1843 (Maccoby 2001: 420). Eventually it became the newspaper with the largest circulation in the world, when it was widely known as the 'News of the Screws' because of its penchant for exposing sex scandals, in the honourable tradition of the *livres philosophiques*. It was Rupert Murdoch's first Fleet Street acquisition in 1969. It remained Britain's biggest-selling newspaper until 2011, when it was unceremoniously closed by News Corp after a phone-hacking scandal, in a bid to protect Murdoch's attempt to gain full control of the more valuable subscription-TV company BSkyB. *The Sun*'s own career followed the same route in the twentieth century. It began in 1911 as the *Daily Herald*, a strike-sheet published by printing unions as part of an industrial dispute. It was taken over by the Trades Union Congress with the help of the publisher Odhams and became the official mouthpiece of the union movement and the Labour Party. For a while in the 1930s it too was the biggest-selling newspaper in the world, but suffered in brutal circulation wars with the *Daily Express*. When the Mirror Group took over Odhams in the 1960s they revamped the *Herald*, changed its name to the *Sun*, and then sold it to Rupert Murdoch in 1969 (see National Museum of Photography, Film and Television 2000). Both papers were transformed from radical popular agents of workers' self-representation to commercial popular mechanisms for turning them into a market; from 'subject' to 'object.'

Constitutional Journalism: A 'Certain Charmed Spectacle'

It is nice to trace how the actions of a retired widow and an unemployed youth become of such importance. (Walter Bagehot 1872 [1867]: III)

By the turn of the twentieth century, the popular press had largely fallen to conservative press barons, who launched commercial picture-tabloids such as the *Daily Mail* and *Daily Mirror*. Their proprietors addressed the laboring classes and their families not as radical activists but domestic consumers (and biddable voters). They boosted their circulation with stunts and prizes and pretty girls rather than firebrand politics (although the *Mirror* did a bit of both). During World War I they were fully incorporated into the purposes of the state, their proprietors becoming cabinet ministers. They ushered in the *Citizen Kane* era of press lords whose political clout was based on popular reach. They were exemplified by Lords Beaverbrook, Camrose, Kemsley, Northcliffe, Rothermere, and Thomson on one side of the Atlantic and on the other by William Randolph Hearst ('you furnish the pictures, I'll furnish the war!' *Time* 1942).

In the process, the self-representative communication model of the radical press was recast into the sender–receiver model that still characterizes journalism research. The latter model connects journalism to popular culture only indirectly. Journalism is seen as a production system that conveys news to the public, while popular culture is a consumption system of commercially purveyed entertainment. But, despite the asymmetry, each side needs the other: no readers, no news; no entertainment, no readers. However, compared with the earlier radical popular press upon which commercial popular journalism is built, in this model representation has shifted from the demand to the supply side.

What kind of representation did commercial popular journalism proceed to supply? In 1867 Walter Bagehot, journalist, influential editor of *The Economist* for 17 years, and author of the standard work on the English constitution, made a famous distinction between those component parts of the constitution that excite 'the reverence of the population' and those 'by which it, in fact, works and rules' (1872 [1867]: II). He called them the 'dignified' and 'efficient' parts respectively. The monarchy and aristocracy (House of Lords) were the dignified part; the Cabinet and the House of Commons were the efficient part.

Following the extension of the vote to unskilled male laborers in the 1867 Reform Act, Bagehot feared what he called 'the supremacy of ignorance over instruction and of numbers over knowledge.' Indeed, he wrote, 'I am exceedingly afraid of the ignorant multitude of the new constituencies,' in the industrialized metropolises (1872 [1867]: II). To counter their numerical supremacy Bagehot made a less-well-remembered distinction between 'deference' and 'democracy.' He preferred deference, where electors defer to wealth and rank and thence to 'the higher qualities of which these are the rough symbols and the common accompaniments,' over democracy, which exalts the 'vacant many' over the 'inquiring few' (III).

Bagehot felt, however, that the parliamentary system itself could be used 'to prevent or to mitigate the rule of uneducated numbers,' so long as deference was maintained. By deference he did not mean – or mean alone – the forelock-tugging deference of what Marx called 'rural idiocy' towards the country squirearchy. Bagehot had something much more modern in mind:

> In fact, the mass of the English people yield a deference rather to something
> else than to their rulers. They defer to what we may call the theatrical show
> of society. A certain state passes before them; a certain pomp of great men;

a certain spectacle of beautiful women; a wonderful scene of wealth and enjoyment is displayed, and they are coerced by it. Their imagination is bowed down; they feel they are not equal to the life which is revealed to them. Courts and aristocracies have the great quality which rules the multitude, though philosophers can see nothing in it – visibility. (VIII)

mechanism of hegemony?

Bagehot is describing nothing less than the genesis of what is now more easily named as celebrity culture (Plunkett 2003; see also Rojek 2004; Turner 2004). Rather than siding with those 'philosophers' who would 'deride this superstition,' he makes celebrity journalism central to the constitutional arrangements of what was at the time the most powerful empire on earth. He argued that the 'charmed spectacle' and human values of the royal and aristocratic families could succeed in preserving popular deference, under the cloak of which the mundane business of government could continue in few but expert hands:

> What impresses men is not mind, but the result of mind. And the greatest of these results is this wonderful spectacle of society, which is ever new, and yet ever the same; in which accidents pass and essence remains; in which one generation dies and another succeeds. [...] The apparent rulers of the English nation are like the most imposing personages of a splendid procession: it is by them the mob are influenced; it is they whom the spectators cheer. The real rulers are secreted in second-rate carriages; no one cares for them or asks about them, but they are obeyed implicitly and unconsciously by reason of the splendour of those who eclipsed and preceded them. (VIII)

This distinction between the dignified (deferential) and efficient (ruling) parts of the constitution is crucial to any consideration of the relationship between journalism and popular culture. It makes of the 'charmed spectacle,' and thus of the popular/media culture that is the stage for it, what may be called a ruse to rule. Journalism on both sides of this divide is part of the 'constitutional' mechanism for social order: there is journalism for efficiency (*The Times, The Economist*) and journalism for deference (celebrity spectacle). The overall system requires both parts for the ordered continuation of good government in a polity governed by fear of a democratic majority that has no direct role to play in rule. Bagehot's schema makes clear what subsequent familiarity may well have blurred: that the spectacle of 'wealth and enjoyment,' the celebrity of 'great men' and 'beautiful women' and the 'theatrical show of society,' are all *an essential part of government.*

'A Universal Fact [...] Rivets Mankind'

A family *on the throne is an interesting idea also. It brings down the pride of sovereignty to the level of petty life.* (Walter Bagehot 1872 [1867]; emphasis in original)

Popular culture is the domain of spectacle and celebrity. These are communicated to the 'mob' of 'spectators' via popular journalism. Therefore, in line with Bagehot's insight about the need for both rule and the spectacle of rule – and that these are distinct but equally necessary as the efficient and dignified parts of the constitution – journalism also has two essential 'constitutional' components: one that follows the 'real rulers secreted in second-rate carriages' and another that follows the 'charmed spectacle' of high society:

> No feeling could seem more childish than the enthusiasm of the English at the marriage of the Prince of Wales [...] But no feeling could be more like common human nature as it is, and as it is likely to be [...] A princely marriage is the brilliant edition of a universal fact, and, as such, it rivets mankind. (1872 [1867]: III)

The 1867 Reform Act enfranchised over a million working men. Modern journalism (as part of Bagehot's constitution) is founded on the fear of this newly sovereign demos. How to 'rivet' the popular mind to a constitution in which 'real rule' might remain with those 'secreted in second-rate carriages,' so as to avoid succumbing to 'the supremacy of ignorance over instruction and of numbers over knowledge'? The cultivation of deference via popular culture, using 'universal facts' and 'common human nature' to 'rivet mankind,' was, however, not straightforward but a hazardous venture, not least because a 'princely marriage' may swiftly be followed by royal adultery and marital scandal – as has duly unfolded for not one but three princes of Wales since then (Edward VII, Edward VIII, and Charles). Further, the people who really enjoyed that 'great quality' of visibility seemed to be the respectable classes themselves, not to mention the courtiers whose job it was to attract the attention of the press. As Lord McGregor (then chair of Reuters Trust) noted:

> At the time of the wedding of the Prince of Wales [1863], sales of *The Times* increased to 108,000 copies compared with its average of around 60–65,000

during the 1860s. In 1864, the Prince and Princess visited Denmark accompanied by Lord Spencer who [...] went on to complain that court officials with their '*adulation of reporters* show great want of dignity.' (McGregor 1995, my emphasis)

Thus, it was not by any means a case of the posh papers providing rational information for rulers while popular culture laid on celebrity, spectacle, spin, and bread and circuses for the masses. It was if anything the other way around. Circulation of *The Times* nearly doubled on Royal Wedding day. For the have-nots, on the other hand, the spectacle was not always so welcome – it served to inflame 'the knockabout anti-monarchism of the popular press [...] and [...] the republican political rumblings in the 1860s and 1870s, some of which found a parliamentary voice opposing grants to the Queen's children on occasions such as royal marriages' (Thompson 2001: 75).

Similarly, it should not be assumed that the respectable press was always pro-*government* (it was always pro-*rule*). Thomas Barnes in *The Times* joined with Richard Carlile in the *Republican* in denouncing the Peterloo Massacre of 1819. *The Times* thundered: 'nearly a hundred of the King's unarmed subjects have been sabred by a body of cavalry in the streets of a town of which most of them were inhabitants, and in the presence of those Magistrates whose sworn duty it is to protect and preserve the life of the meanest Englishmen' (August 19, 1819). *The Times* was in favor of the 1832 Reform Bill to extend the franchise, while the *Morning Chronicle* commissioned both Charles Dickens' *Sketches by 'Boz'* and Henry Mayhew's reports on the condition of the laboring poor in England and Wales (Mayhew 1849). In other words, the top people's press was averse neither to spectacle and sensation nor to social reform. What really differentiated the two types of journalism discussed here was their *readership*: understood at the time as 'two nations' and still now not fully integrated into one public – politically, journalistically, or culturally.

Walter Bagehot was candid about the rationale for a constitution with a dignified part that was literally useless but vital in terms of 'visibility,' spectacle, and narrative. It was straightforward fear of 'numbers over knowledge.' He was 'exceedingly afraid' that popular sovereignty would overwhelm established arrangements. To counter the influence of the 'ignorant multitude,' however, Bagehot proposed not to educate the masses as to their 'real rulers' (much less to educate them to rule themselves) but to put on a good show – 'not mind, but the result of mind.' In this endeavor he was aided and abetted by the 'efficient' papers, the conservative press barons, and the sender–text–receiver model of communication, all of which were dedicated to riveting mankind; that is, trying to hold on to real rule, albeit from a second-rate carriage, and seeking to unite the two nations under one constitution. It is this model of communication that underlies commercial popular journalism to this day, and this is also the model most widely taught to journalists.

Popular Culture and Journalism Studies

Popular culture is thus the true origin of modern journalism, taking 'origin' to refer both to empirical historical beginnings, in revolutionary France and industrializing Britain, and also to theoretical first principles, where popular culture is the subject (source) of journalism, not its object (destination). Therefore, I argue, the relations between journalism and popular culture, and between journalism studies and cultural studies, are best studied historically, but within such histories can be discerned the working through of contrasting underlying models of communication and determination. In one the consumers of news are an effect of media; in the other they are a source of meaning. One model leads to a representative, expert journalism; the other to emancipationist self-representation (see Table 3.1). Both are present throughout the history of modern media, although during the long reigns of the press barons and broadcast monopolies the top-down version has predominated. This predominance is currently in crisis; my argument is that scholarly attention to the historical relations between journalism and popular culture can help to explain what is at stake in that crisis.

There are two methodological lessons that may be drawn from this history. First, journalism as such is not the fundamental point of difference.

Table 3.1   Two paradigms for the study of journalism

Journalism studies	*Cultural studies*
Object(-ive)	Subject(-ive)
Supply side	Demand side
Popular culture as effect	Popular culture as cause
Producer-provider perspective	Consumer-citizen perspective
Representative	Self-representation
Professional expertise	Popular emancipation

The practice of journalism has evolved through both the expert and the emancipationist traditions. Second, the 'popular culture' model, based as it is on the underlying notion of an 'active audience,' has received an immense boost in recent times owing to the growth of user-led innovation, consumer-generated content, self-made media, DIY culture, citizen-journalism, the blogosphere, and peer-to-peer social networks.

The Popular Extension of the Reading Public

Modern journalism and the mass reading public were unplanned outcomes of efforts directed to other ends. It was only after their scale and adaptability had been demonstrated that their general importance to such a complex open system as modernity could be discerned. But to establish a reading public that could be taken to be coterminous with 'the nation,' or with 'society' in all its populous unenfranchised multifariousness, was not a straightforward process. Nor did it go uncontested. Inventing, extending, and stabilizing the 'mass' reading public took longer than a generation. Nor was it achieved by the press alone. The pulpit took printed form too, and so did fictional entertainment. But *journalism* could not have developed without the pauper press, and the 'reading public' – *the* public of modernity – could not have developed without journalism.

From the point of view of production and distribution, establishing 'the public' required technology, capital, industrious enterprise both collaborative and competitive, a network of agents for newsgathering and vending, a creative imagination, 'popular address' (discursive and rhetorical populism), fast distribution (railways), and a willingness to persevere in the face of official suppression and frequent incarceration. From the point of view of the readership, it required non-instrumental literacy, sufficient disposable income, and a desire to keep up with events as they unfolded, resulting in the habit of reconsumption. This could only occur when 'consumers' liked what they read and wanted to be part of the movement or community 'hailed' by their paper, believed they had a personal stake in the outcomes for which it campaigned, and were willing to be represented by their own 'organ of enlightenment' in the competitive contestations of opinion in 'the public sphere.' In this sense the pecuniary nexus that laid the foundation for the commercialization of the press – that is, myriad individual artisans and their families, exchanging a penny for an unstamped paper – was also a 'vote' by each of them for the political program espoused within its pages. They had no other vote.

Here, then, over a 50-year period (the 1790s to the 1840s) was the beginning of that peculiarity of modernity: the marketization of democratic representation. The market came into play only after a two-way connection had been firmly established. In other words, the representation came first. Representation was also two-way. The paper *represented to* the readership their co-subjectivity with a 'class-action' cause or movement, and the paper was *representative of* its readership (the larger the better) in the political arena. Purchasers received not only a regular dose of information and entertainment but also access to a 'global' textual system and resources for autodidactic political and social education. The vendors received not only an income but also ongoing confirmation that they were leading a campaign, not simply exploiting a market.

And thus, out of this combination of economic enterprise, political emancipation, and personal hazard, and via a laborious process of contested construction, journalism won a place as an essential mechanism of modern societies. Its importance remains not so much as an industry or economic sector as a general enabling 'social technology' that is just as important as (say) the law and the financial system. It is the *textual system* of modernity (Hartley 1996). It has only achieved this condition because it actually does, or at least it is taken to, reach the whole population of a given ethno-territorial polity, creating for the first time on a mass scale what is now called the 'collective intelligence' of social networks. Modern journalism is embedded within, representative of, and speaking both for and to *popular culture*. It was in place by the 'year of revolutions,' 1848.

This was a new invention on an unprecedented scale, an 'imagined community' of nevertheless real co-subjects, attending together in the here and now to the same events or issues and occasionally capable of concerted action too. It reached across demographic boundaries of class, gender, age-group, region, and ethnicity to forge a national public for modern industrialized countries. Popular culture provided a new, secular means of public communication for changing societies. Instead of binding 'the people' to authority and tradition, as had the only hitherto 'mass medium,' namely the pulpit, it focused public attention on contemporary life and future possibilities. It took the quotidian measure of competitive political, economic, and personal development ('scandal'). It brought to everyone's attention the specialist knowledge distributed across a highly differentiated complex social system ('muckraking'). Equally it was a vehicle for various interests, associations, and ideologies to contend for popular support, taking the oratorical traditions of the pulpit into the service of politics ('rabble-rousing').

Truth and Textuality: A Short History of 'Truthiness'

Popular culture is often taken to be a domain of leisure entertainment and fictional narrative, while journalism is often taken to be a part of the democratic process. The lesson of history is that these are not conflicting attributes but part of the same generative process, the same *realist* textual system. Popular journalism predated popular democracy by decades. The agitation for popular emancipation required masses of potentially activist readers, and in order to attract and retain them the pauper press had to learn the tricks of textuality, or what Stephen Colbert – reminding us of the central role of the comic satirist in the politics of truth (and the truth of politics) – has called 'truthiness' (see 'Truthiness' n.d.).

The radical papers pioneered the union of entertainment and emancipation, narrative and nationhood, realism and representation. They sought to propagate commanding truths in the form of compelling stories. They spoke directly to the experience and in the language of those whom they wanted to represent, drawing together and encapsulating the identities and aspirations of myriad individuals in an imagined commonality of which the paper itself was the voice. They did not baulk at using fiction, in addition to fact, as a means to this end and indeed the line between the two was not clear. For instance a personalized account of the privations of a family, a worker, or a region, often in the form of a letter, might stand in for a sociological truth, whether the featured family or correspondent actually existed or not. Conversely, imagined human frailties were clothed in the garb of truth, with petty criminals, pretty girls, and attractive victims in an incessant parade across the page as personifications of imaginary fears and desires. The *most* popular journalism remained that which tapped into human conflict (i.e. *drama*): 'true crimes' and scandalous disclosure (news); ferocity, exploit, and arrested development (sport); and marriageability and its vicissitudes (human interest).

What was new was that these longstanding elements of popular narrative were combined with the great fantasies of the modern imagination – narratives of progress and equality, of both competitive individualism and class consciousness, of the power of knowledge, and of the emergence of the ordinary as a positive social value. And let it not be forgotten that straightforward fiction – thrillers, romances, and crime stories – was a staple of journalism and remained prominent even in the daily press at least until the arrival of television. Popular culture was the nutrient of democratic action; it succeeded in (and by) combining the rationalist, secular progressivism of the Enlightenment with the emotionalist, narrative 'sensationalism' borrowed from the popular dramatic and musical traditions. It gave both individual agency and systematic shape to 'the public.' Democracy was precipitated out of popular journalism rather than being a precondition for it, and the admixture was saturated with potent concentrations of fiction, fun, and faith, as well as realism, righteousness, and reason. Catalyzed by simple, well-told stories, this incendiary mixture of journalism and popular culture generated much more political energy than either 'rational' journalism or 'emotional' popular culture taken alone, and it was capable occasionally of causing a truly explosive reaction.

'The Popular': Radical Versus Commercial

Both the *study* of the relationship between journalism and popular culture and the *conduct* of that relationship in everyday life and enterprise have pivoted about the question of what is at stake in the word 'popular' (Dahlgren 1992: 5–6). Early cultural studies theorists including Raymond Williams (1976), Richard Hoggart, and E. P. Thompson, in different ways, were interested in the relationship between popular culture and class. The main problem here was a conflict between 'popular culture' construed as a 'whole way of life,' a life literally *made by* the working class for and by itself, the classic statement of which is Thompson (1963), and 'popular culture' construed as pleasures and entertainments laid on for the enjoyment of working-class people by commercial enterprises, the classic critique of which is Hoggart (1957). Out of the former came the Labour movement, trade-unionism, and other collective mechanisms for self-representation. Out of the latter came commercial media including the press, television, cinema, magazines, and the like.

Journalism occurred on both sides of this conflict: it could be 'radical popular' or 'commercial popular' (Hartley 1992b: 177–81), and the two types could co-exist, although the commercial popular press did not take off until the second half of the nineteenth century, after a popular reading public had been established by the pauper press. Indeed, it may be argued that commercial popularity systematically supplanted the radical popular (Conboy 2002: 80–6). Increasingly, the commercialization of the entire media sector tended to exclude all but a few radical popular voices in favor of commercial properties owned by 'press barons' whose own political views were more likely to be reactionary than revolutionary. The 'radical popular' retracted to a committed readership that was eventually far from 'popular' in number, while the 'commercial popular' remained dominant numerically but treated the populace as a mass market, the object of campaigns both political and commercial.

Not surprisingly, observers from the radical side of politics continuously criticized these developments, berating the commercial popular media for 'dumbing down' as well as 'demagoguery.' They objected to the fact that 'popular' journalism had stopped speaking *for* or even *as* 'the people' and instead spoke *to* them, seeking to manipulate their behavior rather than to represent their voice. Thus, by the time the serious academic study of *popular culture* began in Britain in the 1960s and 1970s, there was felt to be a need to understand how 'radical' communicative action by oppositional classes, which themselves were proliferating beyond the industrial proletariat to include identity groups based on gender, ethnicity, nationality, sexual orientation, and the like, might survive and even prosper in an era of commercial media.

The answer to this problem took two forms, one practical and the other theoretical. In practice, radical communicative action abandoned the field of formal journalism almost entirely, emerging instead within the 'whole way of life' associated with counter-cultural alternatives, especially those associated with music and subcultures, from flower power to the hippies; the blues to punk. In the era of identity politics and the 'politics of the personal,' self-representation was carried on largely through the entertainment aspect of popular culture, by musicians and artists who combined commercial success, entrepreneurial acumen, and an image of freedom. Successive singers – Pete Seeger, Bob Dylan, Jimmy Hendrix (Gilroy 2006), John Lennon, Bob Geldof, Bono – seemed to speak on behalf of a global, anti-war, pro-ecology generation that saw mainstream journalism as part of the problem not as their representative voice. Lennon in particular was willing to use his mass mediated fame to put items on the political agenda that were entirely consonant with the 'radical popular' media of a previous century – opposition to state control, advocacy of peace, and pursuit of an alternative lifestyle, all conducted through popular media, in which journalism was simultaneously an adversary, a foil, and an ally.[1]

---

[1]   See http://www.theusversusjohnlennon.com.

Accompanying such efforts, entirely new forms of journalism arose in the spaces between music, counterculture, politics, and identity, including what was called the New Journalism, and exemplified in the 'underground' press and 'alternative' magazines such as *Ink, Oz, Rolling Stone*, and *Spare Rib* among many others, continuing though the punk period via fanzines such as *Sniffin' Glue* and into the era of DIY culture and digital media. These models of self-representation and in-group distribution left the mainstream media looking distinctly flat-footed, representing as they did a rich vein of journalism that is simply invisible in journalism studies, in J-school curricula, or in discussions of the 'democratic process' and 'professional journalism.'

Meanwhile, the theoretical attempt at a 'solution' to the conflict between radical communicative action and commercial media was the Marxist concept of the 'national popular' (Gramsci 1971; Laclau and Mouffe 2001 [1985]), which substituted 'nation' for 'class' and 'popular' for 'proletariat' in an attempt to identify the 'alliance' needed to win power by constitutional rather than revolutionary means (Forgacs 1984). Many countries in Europe and Latin America for example built 'national popular front' parties or alliances to pursue that goal. Such political efforts influenced the study of journalism. Researchers sought to identify what the prospects were for building a 'radical popular' media in the context of 'commercial popular' media dominance (Hall et al. 1978). Since the diffusion of cultural studies into the academic mainstream following its internationalization in the 1980s, this specifically political agenda for popular journalism studies has also dissipated somewhat, although vestiges of the 'class war in language' approach survive in many studies of the 'capitalist' press and media (for an interesting reworking of this trope see Lewis 2005). At the same time, interest in the radical possibilities offered though music and other forms of countercultural consciousness has remained a central concern of cultural studies.

However, the basic proposition, that *popular journalism is a creation of popular culture*, just as the labor movement is, has been almost entirely forgotten in journalism studies. J-schools have tended to focus on journalism as an occupation, one moreover linked to the formal political process and the specialist needs of business, not to the myriad-voiced expression of popular aspiration. Indeed, the most recent commentators judge that 'bottom-up' journalism is literally unthinkable. Martin Conboy, for instance, introducing a special issue of *Journalism Studies* on 'Popular Journalism,' admits defeat:

> In our contemporary capitalist consumer culture, it is hard to envisage much in the way of journalism which is produced entirely by ordinary people and consumed by sufficient numbers of them to maintain regular production as journalism given the institutional and financial demands of the genre. (2007: 2)

Such a view clearly requires the restriction of what is meant by 'journalism' to its highly capitalized 'industrial' form (i.e. 'the press' or 'the media'). It does not admit *as journalism* the self-representations characteristic of Web 2.0 applications, including e-zines, the blogosphere, citizen journalism, and 'collaborative' online news production. Here it is at odds with those analysts who see journalism not as an industry but in terms of its ability to 'help enable, extend, and enhance public discovery, discussion and deliberation of the news' (Bruns 2005: 317) – a function that can be performed by anyone and indeed everyone (Hartley 2009), despite professional misgivings about the 'cult of the amateur' (Keen 2007).

Tabloidization and Celebrity

Within the converse 'cult of the expert,' as it were, the excision of 'bottom-up' popular and countercultural journalism from the equation leaves only 'commercial popular' forms. Here the chief problem associated with popularity is what has come to be called *tabloidization* (Langer 1998; Lumby 1999; Bird 2003; Hargreaves 2003; Turner 2005) and *celebrity culture* (Ponce de Leon 2002; Rojek 2004; Turner 2004). The nature of the 'problem of the popular' changes from a debate about *representation* ('by' or 'for' the people?) to a debate about *reason*. Popular culture has come to be associated with emotion, irrationalism, affect, sensation, and embodied experience. As mentioned above in relation to the nineteenth-century pauper press, journalism was first popularized with the aid of these dangerous allies, which were harnessed in the cause of popular emancipation. But as time wore on, and as popular sovereignty became routine and the popular press commercial, the use of sensation in the service of truth began to jar the modern sensibility.

As a child of the Enlightenment with strong investment in the liberal values of reason, truth, science, progress, and realism, journalism has had a tough time coming to terms with the corporeal basis of knowledge. Despite the empirical fact that no journalistic enterprise has ever succeeded in separating reason and emotion, information and entertainment, the real and the imagined, the facts and the story, the idea persists that journalism *shouldn't* deal with the 'naughty bits.' Reason fends off its opposite number with revealing squeamishness (Lumby 1999); a combination of lust and loathing (not excluding self-loathing), which divides the profession of journalism itself.

But the problem remains as it was in the beginning, when the pauper press attracted readers with rapes, murders, and pugilism in order to hold them for radical reform. How do you get uncommitted ordinary people (voters, citizens, consumers, audiences) to take an interest in things they don't know or care about? How can you impart information to the public if they don't pay attention to you? How can you confine journalism to the doings of one elite (the politico-business decision-makers) while scorning those of another (celebrity-entertainment role models). Why fetishize facts when journalism deals in stories? Why is it OK to write about Monica Lewinsky's encounter with cigars or Camilla Parker-Bowles' with tampons on the grounds that these raise constitutional issues, but to declare 'a vacancy at the Paris Hilton' (Sconce 2007) in relation to popular celebrities on the grounds that citizens *ought not* to be interested in, or told about, the sex life (or the *Simple Life*, or the prison life) of the rich and famous (Lumby 1999: 65)? Why lament a generation that doesn't vote while lambasting the same group for its devotion to peer-to-peer social networking and self-expression through entertainment? Trying to hold a middle line in this environment is more difficult than it may seem, despite the very obvious fact that any form of communication must appeal to those addressed in order for them to attend to it, and despite the less obvious one that even the most 'low-brow' entertainment may carry important information, teach some truth, or engage with real experience. For instance, Liz Nice, former editor of *Bliss* magazine, writes:

> Teenage magazines are not big on social and political debate so may not encourage their readers [...] to do something about social problems and start campaigns. But editors insist that they do empower them to deal with peer pressure, teenage pregnancy, bullying and drugs. And through continuing interactivity, via text messaging, letters pages, e-mail and the magazine's website, they offer readers a forum which helps editors to understand them better and give them a voice. (2007: 132)

Such sentiments are not confined to editors of consumer magazines. Ian Hargreaves, former deputy editor of the *Financial Times*, editor of the *Independent* and the *New Statesman*, and director of news and current affairs at the BBC, put the same case in his book *Journalism: Truth or Dare*:

> It is a difficult line to tread between appealing to the audience's natural point of interest and emotional pressure points, without trivializing events. It cannot be denied that there is plenty of bad tabloid journalism [...] But there is also brilliant tabloid journalism, in newspapers, magazines, television and radio, that brings issues alive and broadens popular engagement. (2003: 134–5)

Indeed, Rupert Murdoch himself has claimed that his most famous tabloid title is in fact a *radical* newspaper: 'The *Sun* stands for opportunities for working people and for change in this society. It's a real catalyst for change, it's a very radical paper' (Murdoch cited in Snoddy 1992). The problem of the popular returns unchanged, except that now the 'radical popular' is *conflated* with the 'commercial popular' (Allan 1999).

Citizenship and Self-Representation

The current research environment is one of furious convergence among many different and previously contending positions on the problem of the popular. Despite their disciplinary, ideological, professional, and geographical diversity, a common focus has emerged, centered on the idea of cultural citizenship. The question that was once posed at the level of class is now posed at the level of the individual consumer-citizen: what are the prospects for informed, embodied self-representation (Bird 2003; Hermes 2005; Rennie 2006)?

The very idea would have horrified the pioneers of 'commercial popular' journalism, for whom the salient fact about individual bodies was that there were multitudinously too many of them, and that if left to their own devices they would destroy knowledge rather than share and expand it (Bagehot 1872 [1867]). This tension between democratization and dumbing down still infuses the study of journalism (Rusbridger 2000). A question for future research, then, is how do divergent but overlapping energies – for instance globalization, economic growth and competition, internet affordances, the commercialization of culture, and the agency of myriad individuals located in diverse contexts – enable or inhibit popular self-representation?

Part II: Methodological Considerations

The field of cultural studies is both educationally corrupting and profes-
sionally embarrassing for journalism education. (Keith Windschuttle
2000: 145)

Popular culture has featured in journalism studies largely as an 'other,'
associated not with freedom, truth, power, and organized news-making but
with entertainment, consumerism, persuasion, and personal identity. As a
result, especially in English-speaking countries, the research field of journalism studies is frequently at loggerheads with cultural studies (Windschuttle 1998; Zelizer 2004). This methodological stand-off is debilitating
to a proper understanding of the relationship between the two fields. The
gap that is now evident between journalism (studies) and popular culture
(studies) is real, but it is also a link. They are linked because they are at
opposite ends of the same information supply chain; at one end the 'writer'
(producer) and at the other the 'reader' (consumer). Journalism studies in
the US, UK, and other countries such as Australia have tended to focus on
the occupation of the news reporter, often with scant regard for the readership (beyond an interest in its scale). Cultural studies, conversely, has had
more to say about the cultural form of journalism, investigated from the
point of view of the reader or audience, giving no special status to journalists themselves. The often strained relations between those who study them
may be 'referred pain' – an expression of a real but indirectly experienced
conflict of interest between producers and consumers of news in modern
societies.

Model 1: The Value Chain (Objective, Supply-Side Journalism)

This 'value chain' model, through which journalism is both practiced and
studied, seems also to show causal sequence: A causes B; B affects C, therefore C is an effect of A (where → = direction of causation).

$$A \rightarrow B \rightarrow C$$

I argue that this chain of causation is but an artifact of the model – causation does not in fact flow one way through such a linear process.
The apparent logic of interconnected linear models makes it seem almost
unarguable, however. Journalism (the modern occupation) is at one end

of the supply chain while popular culture (the modern experience) is at the other:

Journalist → News → Public

That linear chain is superimposed on another one; the commonsensical model of communication:

Sender/addresser → Message/text → Receiver/addressee

The apparent homology of these two models (as in Table 3.2) seems almost naturally to explain the relative position of journalists and their readers at opposite ends of a 'value chain of meaning' (Hartley 2008: 28; see also Porter 1985):

Producer/originator → Commodity → Consumer/user

Table 3.2 Model 1: The value-chain model of communication

	Supply side *Economy* ⇨	*'Medium'* *Politics* ⇨	*Demand side* *Culture*
Value chain	Producer/originator	Commodity/ distribution	Consumer
Communication	Sender (agent)	Message	Receiver (behavior)
Public affairs	Government ('makes')	Decisions ('affecting')	Citizens ('voters')
Journalism (form)	Writer/news-gatherer	Copy/script	Reader/audience
Journalism (occupation)	**Journalist**	**News**	Public
Commerce	Firm	**Entertainment**	**Popular culture** (experience)
Power	Cause	'Media'	Effect

Each horizontal line represents a different domain of action but, because of the strength of the 'chain' logic, values can slip between domains. Thus, the values of the journalist/news can become associated with those of entertainment/popular culture, and power seems to go with supply. An alternative model of the relationship between journalism, popular culture, and power is hard to imagine while value-chain logic presides over commonsensical thinking.

Firm → Entertainment → Popular culture

The doctrine of causation by agents further up the communication/value chain generates the familiar 'media effects' model. Despite criticism of it in cultural and media studies (e.g. Gauntlett 1998, 2005), 'media effects' thinking continues to exert force in both academic (e.g. political economy) and journalistic accounts of journalism. It implies that journalists are congregated at the powerful producer end of the value/causal chain while popular culture is massed down at the consumer end, a behavioral effect of corporate processes that have their explanation, and their pleasures and powers, elsewhere.

Government ('makes') → Decisions ('affecting') → Citizens ('voters')

Journalist → Copy/script → Reader/audience

Finally, all of these linked sequences express an underlying presumption (shared by Marxists and liberals alike) about the *chain of causation* in contemporary society:

Economy → Politics → Culture

The mainstream tradition of university-based journalism studies has been dedicated to the producer/publisher/provider, or supply side. Cultural studies is dedicated to the consumer/audience/user, or demand side. Both phenomena (journalism and popular culture) *can* be studied without reference to the other, because each is associated with a different version of the 'chain' metaphor. Nevertheless, the two chains are versions of a homologous relationship within the same overall system. Table 3.2 sums up what is at stake, which becomes clear when the terms introduced so far are read 'vertically' as well as horizontally.

This homology among different commonsensical models of communicative relationship demonstrates two things. First, the three-link structure of the model is extremely robust, embedded in common sense as a kind of retained resource of intellectual capital, a generally available means to make unreflecting sense of modern experience. In this respect the model itself is a component of popular culture. Second, it is a serviceable model in practice. It works. End of story? Not quite. The 'effects' model cannot help but cast consumers – and therefore by homology audiences, readers, and citizens – in a poor light; as behavioral 'effects' of media, dumbed-down dupes, and distracted dopes, manipulated or worse by firms or state agencies.

Small wonder that journalists, understood as those employed in news-rooms at the causal end of the information supply chain, literally 'in the know,' don't want to be associated with them, even 'in theory.' Instead of fraternizing with the punters, journalism research has focused on 'professional' practice, construing consumers of news as behavioral effects of journalistic causes. Tellingly, this is the journalistic culture that Prasun Sonwalkar (2005) dubs 'banal journalism,' predicated on a deeply assimilated 'us–them' binary.

Even as this way of modeling communication took hold in empirical social science, James Halloran (1981: 22) warned of the inherent danger of such a turn:

> It is now suggested that research [...] should be shifted away from such questions as 'the right to communicate' to 'more concrete problems.' But what are these 'concrete problems'? They are the same as, or similar to, the safe, 'value-free' micro-questions of the old-time positivists who served the system so well, whether or not they intended or understood this. All this represents a definite and not very well disguised attempt to put the clock back to the days when the function of research was to serve the system as it was – to make it more efficient rather than to question it or suggest alternatives.

While positivist accounts of 'the system as it was' continued to gain strength in journalism studies despite Halloran's worries (e.g. Donsbach 2004, 2007; Loeffelholz and Weaver 2008), the pioneers of cultural studies were also interested in 'concrete problems' but saw them in terms of political rights not supply-chain efficiencies, and analyzed them from a perspective grounded in the humanities not the social sciences. They approached both journalism and the study of popular culture from a true 'alternative': the point of view of the 'consumer.'

Model 2: Self-Representation (Subjective, Demand-Side Journalism)

From the perspective of Model 2, neither audiences nor popular culture are the end-point of a chain; they are the *source* of productive labor, of action (especially collective political action), and of language and culture (see Table 3.3).

Early cultural studies was an amalgam of Leavisite literary history and leftist or Marxist emancipationist politics, brought together in 1950s New Left activism in Britain through such figures as Richard Hoggart (1957,

Table 3.3 Model 2: The 'subjective' model of communication

Productive agent (labor, action, language)	⟨⟩	*Collective enterprise*
'Collective speaker' ('we, the people') (e.g. class, gender, ethnicity, sexuality, identity) Popular culture as subject, agent, cause		'Reading public' ('public opinion') (e.g. class, nation, species) Popular culture as network, dynamic change

1967), Raymond Williams (1968), and Stuart Hall (various works summarized in University of the West Indies n.d.). From this perspective, consumers were 'ordinary people,' and cross-demographic communication was not a three-link chain but an antagonism between opposed structural positions. Thus, the study of news media was part of a larger project in cultural politics (see Lee 2003; Hartley 2003; Gibson 2007). In this schema, ordinary people were – among other things – a 'reading public' (Webb 1955); a social network constructed historically, held together by cultural affinities, and grown to popular scale during more than a century of industrialization, the growth of the press, mass literacy, and both democratic and class politics ('struggle'). A reading public is a deliberative agent of knowledge, not a behavioral effect of media. It is the locus of 'cultural citizenship'; the place where 'we' engage with textual systems to 'reflect on, and reform, identities that are embedded in communities' (Hermes 2005: 10).

Journalism in Cultural Studies: You Have Nothing to Lose But Your Value Chains

Where the cultural studies pioneers were interested in journalism, it was to understand its role in a 'system of representation' and to show that such a system was determined by economic forces and political power. Raymond Williams wrote in 1968 about the need for 'a recognition of the social reality of man in all his activities, and of the consequent struggle for the direction of this reality by and for ordinary men and women' (16). We can now recognize that 'recognition' as the project of cultural studies. Williams was ready at the time to name the 'struggle for the direction of this reality': he called it 'socialism.'

Thus cultural experience was seen as the ground upon which both class consciousness (socialism) and ideology (e.g. consumerism) were propagated. Later, Stuart Hall made very clear why he thought popular culture was worthy of study:

> [Popular culture] is one of the sites where this struggle for and against a culture of the powerful is engaged: it is also the stake to be won or lost in the struggle. It is the area of consent and resistance. It is partly where hegemony arises, and where it is secured [...] it is one of the places where socialism might be constituted. That is why 'popular culture' matters. Otherwise, to tell you the truth, I don't give a damn about it. (1981: 239)

Popular culture was an arena of struggle, and, to the extent that power was concentrated in the hands of the owners and managers of the means of production and their hired experts, including journalists, such a circumstance called for change, not passive consent, so that 'ordinary men and women' might gain power over the 'direction of this reality' by their own collective efforts, guided by analysis from intellectuals working in the tradition of the rational left.

Among the issues that had divided those working in that tradition was whether to focus organized popular action on the economic sphere (the worker) via the labor movement and revolutionary parties, or on the political sphere (the voter) via reformist social-democratic parties and representative government. Cultural studies posed a third alternative: if change was not secured by direct struggle in the economic and political spheres, then perhaps attention needed to turn to the cultural sphere (the singer, dancer?). Was there something about the experience of culture that impeded (or might encourage) popular (or 'national-popular') political and economic action? This was the founding question of cultural studies, which turned out to be as much a challenge to existing dispositions of knowledge as it was to extra-mural action (Lee 2000, 2003; Wallerstein 2001, 2004: 18–22). Quite a few analysts feared, and still do, that in this context journalists were part of the problem, not the solution. Table 3.4 shows why.

The entry for 'media + ideology' in Table 3.4 may appear to be an odd one out or conceptually different from the other terms in the field. Whereas the class-based organizations of the labor movement were seen as 'bottom-up' agencies of self-representation for working people (e.g. Thompson 1963), the media were seen as 'top-down' and invasive, speaking to and for

Table 3.4 Cultural studies as the continuation of class struggle by other means

Sphere *(determination)*	Economy	Politics	Culture + society (Williams)
Subjectivity	**Worker**	**Voter**	**Consumer**
Site *(of struggle)*	Factory	Parliament/ government	Home + neighbourhood (Hoggart)
Representation	Labour movement	Labour parties	Media + Ideology (Hall)
Leadership	Revolutionaries	Reformists	Intellectuals (New Left/ CCCS)

'ordinary people' while actually representing the interests of the 'power bloc.'

One of the important innovations of early cultural studies was its interest in how the media ought to be understood both as a system of representation and as a means of popular expression. This work was initiated by Richard Hoggart (1957, 1967) and taken up by Raymond Williams (1974b) but it was most fully elaborated by Stuart Hall (often working with colleagues), who had built up over 30 media-related publications by the time the capstone *Policing the Crisis* was published (Hall et al. 1978; see also University of the West Indies, n.d.). As cultural studies turned from the 'worker' (economics) and 'voter' (politics) to the 'consumer' (culture) in order to investigate how modern subjectivity was formed, attention was inevitably drawn to the media, both the 'radical popular' press of self-representation and the 'commercial popular' press of expansive capitalist culture. Was the latter responsible for helping or hindering the process of self-representation by modern subjects? To answer this question, cultural studies turned to a different model of determination, the Marxist concept of base and superstructure, within which both politics and culture appear as effects (in the last instance) of causal determinations generated in the economic sphere. In such a structure, the media are not simply a system of representation but more to the point an ideological system; they cannot help but express 'ruling ideas' no matter how popular they are. It was within this model of determination that Stuart Hall proposed the 'encoding/decoding' model (1973), to 'answer back' to the naturalistic three-part value-chain/communication model inherited from common sense (see Table 3.5).

What follows from Table 3.4 and Table 3.5 is a rationale for a certain form of political action, based on the cultural domain, led by intellectuals,

Table 3.5   Hallism: Journalism as an ideological system of representation

Economy base	⟹	*Politics + culture superstructure*
Determination		Ideology
Encoding		Decoding
Objective		Subjective

including the avant-garde and artists, which was devoted to ideology critique *as* action, or what the communist tradition called 'agit-prop.' It was necessary to counter the hegemonic naturalization of ideology in mainstream media by means of a counter-ideological struggle. This was indeed the politics of the Hallite CCCS and *New Left Review*, which they hoped would be propagated through educational uptake in the form of activist cultural studies (Lee 2003). Despite the variety of personal political positions among those who took up journalism studies on the one hand and cultural studies on the other, this notion of cultural studies as a counter-hegemonic discourse whose ultimate purpose was to produce a new speaking voice for subjected, oppressed, or marginalized identities, in the cause of social renewal, has remained as a fault line between cultural studies and journalism studies – on one side 'the people' are construed as addressee or 'they' (journalism as 'dominant ideology'); on the other 'the people' are addresser or 'we' ('speaking truth to power').

Plus ça Change?

The logic of the history I have been outlining [...] is for the industry to keep flogging the dead horse of its weary old formats until they lose their audience entirely. At that point, the networks can claim to have proved there is no market for current affairs programs any more, and replace them with a game show. (Turner 2005: 159)

Since its invention in the French and the Industrial Revolutions, the popular reading public has migrated from press to broadcasting and thence to online media, and the scale of the potential readership has expanded from a class or a nation to a globalized social network market (which can sometimes also be a public). But the pioneering effort of the radical press to solve the problem of 'getting ideas across' demographic boundaries in conditions of economic change, political contestation, and cultural division was the crucial R&D for what later became a thoroughly commercialized media environment. The current period is experiencing a return to self-representation or demand-led rather than supply-led journalism, via user-generated content, citizen journalism, and self-made or DIY media of various kinds, all of which can be used for journalism as well as for self-expression and entertainment, including plenty of bawdy stuff that retreads the fuzzy line between liberty and licentiousness. These activities too are proving to be an energetic and surprising locus of innovation, as ideas and social networks form in the sphere of self-representation (daydreaming and mischief as well as freedom and comfort), and some are subsequently adopted in that of economic enterprise and professionalized production, crossing from culture to economy – subjective to objective – in the process.

Perhaps the model of communication established in the early pauper press is due for a revival. Certainly there are straws in the wind: one that blew by as I was writing this was a newspaper story in *The Australian*, syndicated from *The Times* – both newspapers of record. It reported on the popularity of a YouTube video of a model (Amber Lee Ettinger), 'prancing around New York in various states of undress while lip-synching the words of a song declaring she had a crush on presidential candidate Barack Obama' (Baldwin 2007). Among the lyrics quoted were these:

> Baby I cannot wait
> Till 2008,
> Baby you're the best candidate. [...]
> You're into border security,
> Let's break this border between you and me.
> Universal healthcare reform,
> Mmmm – it makes me warm. (Obama Girl 2007)

Quite apart from the combination of humor, sexuality, and politics, what links this to self-representative journalism is its non-canonical provenance and its popular reach. It was published on the 'broadcast yourself' platform, where by June 2007, when the story was published in *The Australian*, the video had attracted over a million hits, thousands of comments, and the attention of 'over 200 TV stations around the world' (Obama Girl 2007). It has remained popular, with over 22 million views by May 2011. Although it appears to have been professionally made, the video personifies the perspective of the citizen (whose part is performed by 'Obama Girl') while using the resources of popular culture, including comedy, music, dance, and a pretty girl to say something that is serious, at least to the extent that it addresses a notoriously non-voting demographic in the name of anti-Bush politics.

Fusing sex and politics (and rock and roll) in the name of liberty has remained a well-trodden route to fame (and sometimes fortune) from the *livres philosophiques* onwards. It has been continued in the present era via such figures as Felix Dennis (from *Oz* to *Maxim*)[2] in the UK and Larry Flynt (*Hustler*) in the US. An endless succession of scandals, from royal mistresses to Monica Lewinski, continually remind us that sex remains one of the most potent elements of political journalism. The staples of popular culture – scandal, celebrity, bedroom antics – are the very propellant of modern journalism and therefore of modern ideas (Hartley 1996: 114–20).

In a similar vein, during the Australian federal election campaign of 2007, the first YouTube election in that country, a 23-year-old law student at Sydney University named Hugh Atkin trumped the political professionals by uploading a self-made spoof called 'Kevin Rudd – Chinese Propaganda Video' (Atkin 2007). As Australian voters knew, this referred to Labor leader Kevin Rudd's fluency in Mandarin (he had previously served as a diplomat). It soon scored over 80,000 views and hundreds of comments, favorites, honors, and responses, and has gone on to garner over a quarter of a million views. It was shown on *The 7.30 Report*, the Australian Broadcasting Corporation (ABC)'s flagship current affairs program, and received copious coverage in the news media, most of which concurred with this assessment: 'The two main political parties, with their multi-million advertising budgets, are proving no match for the power and creativity of the guerilla videomakers of the internet' (Coultan 2007). While its qualities as satire were admired, its politics were ambivalent, as noted by a comment on the site:

---

[2] Felix Dennis won fame as a countercultural folk hero as one of the editors of the magazine *Oz*, whose trial for obscenity in Britain in 1971 was a landmark case (see e.g. http://www.bl.uk/onlinegallery/takingliberties/staritems/430oztrial.html; also dramatized in *The Trials of Oz* 1991). He went on to become a media mogul in his own right, and one of Britain's wealthiest individuals. His libertarian instincts remained undimmed, however – he was one of those who stood surety for Julian Assange's bail during the Wikileaks imbroglio of 2010–11.

> *This is pure, absolute, unadulterated genius. But I can't figure out if it's pro-Liberal or pro-Labor. Can I get some help here??? WHAT SHOULD I THINK??!?*

This was posted by Mark Pesce ('mpesce'), a prominent new-media entrepreneur and writer.[3] In the conversational mode of social networks, his rhetorical question was answered by Atkin, among a long string of others debating the issues. Another comment recommended viewers to look at an 'even funnier' video by 'Cyrius01' (Stefan Sojka), called 'Bennelong Time' (Bennelong is the name of then Prime Minister John Howard's parliamentary constituency, which he lost in this election).[4] It revoiced a Led Zeppelin classic with apposite anti-Howard lyrics, ending with a call to vote for the Greens. This too went viral, attracted over 50,000 views during the campaign, and was featured on ABC television. Sojka was interviewed on ABC Radio and in *The Australian*, where he said:

> For years and years you sit there looking at the television and screaming at it, trying to put your arguments across during all the political current affairs shows, and then I thought, well, there is a place where I can actually do it and say something and maybe be heard. (quoted in Canning 2007)

The Australian commented: 'It's unofficial, unauthorised and may yet have an influence on the voting intentions of generations X and Y.' In terms of popular appeal, it seemed that these spoofs were upstaging not only the parties and advertising agencies but also straight political journalism, which proved all too willing to limp along behind the YouTubers in search of the authentic voice of the populace.

Is this what has become of the tradition of popular self-representation: popular culture as subject? Certainly popular culture is the ground on which new experiments in journalism are propagating. Developments in online media are a definite challenge to expert, top-down, producer-led, supply-side journalism, as is well recognized in the industry and in the commentariat. The industrial-era model of one-way, one-to-many, read-only, mass communication that sees the populace as an object (of policy and campaigns) is now supplemented if not supplanted by two-way, peer-to-peer, read-and-write, networked communication where popular culture

---

[3]   See http://markpesce.com.
[4]   See http://www.cyrius.com.au.

is once again the subject and agent of its own representation. The reading public is at last evolving into a writing public. Now, in principle, everyone can be a journalist; anyone can publish journalism (Hartley 2009). The tradition of self-representation has found a mechanism to cut out (or never cut in) the intermediary agency of the professional expert and the political activist alike. People can and do speak for themselves in an expectation of being heard, whether by a small group of peers or more widely. The supply-chain model of journalism is again in conflict with the self-representation model, as was the case at the beginning of modern journalism in the period 1790–1830.

Both journalism and popular culture currently face the challenge of citizen consumers who produce as well as consume creative content across all domains including information, entertainment, and deliberative debate. The popular extent of this challenge is contestable, but it does bring into focus serious questions about the future of the modern professional, expert, representative journalist, especially when so many of this group are employed on non-news journalism, while traditional political journalism is driven by ideological agendas (Fox) and formula-driven reporting (*Daily Mail*).

That challenge extends to the study of journalism too. The curriculum of J-schools and the range of topics in academic journals have tended to restrict what counts as journalism to the democratic process (politics – including war and other forms of social conflict), the career of policy (public administration and its maladministration), and the business cycle (economics and its downside). Much of what journalists actually do is missing from the record. You wouldn't guess that they do astrology, beauty, captions, celebrity, competitions, crime, desire, domestic life, emotional experience, fashion, fear, fiction, gossip, human interest, jokes, liberation, lifestyle, media, medical procedures, oratory, pin-ups, puns, real estate, reviews, scandal, sex, shopping, sport, television listings, travel, and a lot else besides, or that they are active agents in PR, marketing, spin, propaganda, impression management, and the 'economy of attention' (Lanham 2006) just as much as in the democratic process or in constitutional journalism, whether dignified or efficient. Such aspects of journalistic practice go back to the eighteenth century. They are deeply embedded in popular culture even if they don't all originate there. However, they have had remarkably little impact on the *study* of journalism.

The familiar and widespread allergic response towards cultural studies (or any other theory) by professional journalism educators has had a negative effect on the academic advancement of the field (Zelizer 2004), but at the same time journalism courses in universities are increasingly popular as skills-based information management and writing programs, whose graduates may have no ambition to work in professional newsroom practice. Future research in the field might want to investigate the extension of journalistic capabilities into popular culture (and vice versa) via such training schemes, along with the impact of anti-expert DIY formats from blogs to YouTube. Are journalism and popular culture finally dissolving into each other? Is it possible to imagine both numbers and knowledge, subject and object, radical and commercial, in the rule and representation of (what's left of) modernity?

Carts and Horses

The seemingly inexorable tendency in current 'professional' journalism studies towards a top-down functionalist account of journalism as public communication, where journalists provide communication *to* the public, is not simply a choice between otherwise neutral models or paradigms. Historically it errs by putting the cart before the horse, which ought to be recognized if only to honor those whose struggle *against* the social leadership of their day produced the means for today's practitioners to grasp professional autonomy and social leadership for themselves. But, more importantly, putting the cart before the horse is an error of theoretical principle. It reverses the true *flow of causation*. The flow of causation in journalism is not *from* a professional provider *to* popular culture, but the other way round. Popular culture is the cause, the subject, the agent, the origin of journalism, no matter how professionalized, industrialized, and bureaucratized the latter may become.

This is what journalism studies neglects to its cost. It has fetishized the producer-provider (individual journalist and proprietor or firm); it ignores the agency of the consumer, except as a 'micro' or individualized behavioral *effect* of causation by professional-industrial expertise. It has no concept of a 'macro' textual system that is shared among a large-scale social network of attention-paying co-subjects and that forms the condition of possibility (the 'demand') for journalism to be practiced at all.

The importance of this blind spot in journalism studies and among journalists is that as a result they have diminished means to explain what happens when shifts occur in the reading public and evolution occurs in the textual system. For example, *systemic* changes are under way at the present time, in the shift from 'read-only' participation in public affairs and popular representation to a 'read-and-write' mode of socially networked mass digital literacy in which information, news, and representation are self-made but simultaneously socially scaled. This is where popular culture is currently most energetically concentrated, around Facebook, Myspace, Wikipedia, and YouTube. Here also is where enterprise, capital investment, and marketization have followed, just as was the case with the initial invention of the mass reading public in the nineteenth century. A model of journalism that focuses unduly on the professional provider, and sees self-propagating social networks as somehow irrelevant to that calling, will have little understanding of (and less sympathy with) this emergent social technology. As a result, journalism is being reformed from the outside, without the help of journalism studies, because in the end the social functionality of public communication belongs to the public, not to an autonomous caste of self-appointed representatives in the pay of corporate monopolies, no matter how 'popular' their work may seem for the time being. The relationship between journalism and popular culture is in flux, again, so it is important to understand the direction of causation. That is why it is necessary to analyze journalism from the perspective of popular culture, which may be taken as its subject, not its object.

4

The Distribution of Public Thought

Provided that the opinions which were quacked out were orthodox ones,
'duckspead' [the Newspeak word meaning 'to quack like a duck'] implied
nothing but praise, and when The Times *referred to one of the orators*
of the Party as a doubleplusgood duckspeaker it was paying a warm and
valued compliment. (George Orwell 1949: 249)

'Public Thought' and Shirky's Shock

This chapter is about the public sphere, an overworked concept burdened
with several decades' worth of Habermasian social theory. To work through
that in order to attempt a conceptualization better suited to 'digital futures'
may invoke the law of diminishing returns: much mental effort expended
for little result. Instead, I have recast the concept as 'public thought.' Far
from finding the latter in a state of collapse, as some fear, I argue that you
may find it operating online. For a working *model* of organized public
thought, I argue we should be looking at something much more contemporary than Habermas' ideal of the eighteenth-century coffee house. Public
thought is alive and well in a hitherto unlooked-for (and unloved) institution: the airport bookshop and the market of 'airport bestsellers' it
supports.

How I came to this conclusion has been a journey in itself, of which this
chapter is the record. What set me thinking was Clay Shirky's post called

Digital Futures for Cultural and Media Studies, First Edition. John Hartley.
© 2012 John Wiley & Sons, Ltd. Published 2012 by John Wiley & Sons, Ltd.

'The shock of inclusion' (2010) on *The Edge* site.[1] His was one of numerous contributions by various notables to *The Edge*'s 'question for 2010': 'How has the internet changed the way you think?' I really liked this short piece when I first read it, but there is also a niggling problem with it, which I'm going to try to write through. Along the way I'll include other materials that came my way while I was thinking about this, which makes the chapter as a whole a record of the actual process of 'public thought' (someone thinking in public).

First, let me quote from what Shirky said. The paragraphs that made me think are these (my italics):

> This *shock of inclusion*, where professional media gives way to participation by two billion amateurs (a threshold we will cross this year) means that *average quality of public thought has collapsed*; when anyone can say anything any time, how could it not? If all that happens from this influx of amateurs is the destruction of existing models for producing high-quality material, we would be at the beginning of another Dark Ages.

> The *beneficiaries of the system where making things public was a privileged activity*, whether academics or politicians, reporters or doctors, will complain about the way the new abundance of public thought upends the old order, but those complaints are like keening at a wake; *the change they fear is already in the past*. The real action is elsewhere.

> Given what we have today, the internet could easily become Invisible High School, with a modicum of educational material in an ocean of narcissism and social obsessions. We could, however, also use it as an Invisible College, the communicative backbone of real intellectual and civic change, but to do this will require more than technology. It will require that we adopt norms of open sharing and participation, fit to a world where *publishing has become the new literacy*.

The idea that most struck a chord was this one; that the 'average quality of public thought has collapsed.' Shirky probably meant this in a banal, arithmetic sense: given the same task (say, writing opinion columns in the press), two billion amateurs will score a lower individual average on any quality measure than a few experienced professional specialists. It seems therefore that he is conceding the *more means worse* argument (a classic

---

[1] See also http://www.edge.org/q2010/q10_index.html.

maneuver of the educated Left) (see e.g. Ryan 2001), for he talks about 'the shock of inclusion' as (potentially) 'another Dark Ages' where 'pancake people' (i.e. widely spread and thin; see Carr 2008) connect through 'an ocean of narcissism and social obsessions.'

Average Collapse

I am not ready to concede that argument. It has no basis in either mathematics or in history. In terms of the math, let's say that among internet users only a miniscule one in a thousand (0.1 percent) qualify as 'high' (as opposed to 'average') 'quality.' Out of two billion users, that still amounts to two million quality creators – more than any previous mass medium could muster. Of course the real proportion will be much higher. When I first went to university, only four percent of the UK population were graduates; now it is more like 40 percent. Not all graduates are high quality, so let's stick to the lower figure. Four percent of two billion is 80 million – the population of Germany. Could you call participation by such numbers in 'public thought' a 'collapse'?

In terms of history, *more* of anything worthwhile has never meant *worse* – more education, healthcare, affluence, freedom, comfort, intellectual or entrepreneurial activity, or whatever, has consistently resulted in, well, *more*. Growing up as a poor kid without a breadwinner in the family, I still had better dental care than Ramesses the Great (Pain 2005), better education than Queen Elizabeth II of England (who never went to school),[2] more intellectual freedom than the pope (Maurizi 2008) . . . and so on. Extending once-priestly or royal privileges to everyone benefits . . . everyone. Duh![3] Why would this not be true also of 'public thought'? So let's hear no more of the collapse of the 'average quality of public thought' *in general*.

Journalistic Collapse

None of this crossed my mind when I first read Shirky's piece, however. I took him to mean something else, because my imagination was caught by that word 'collapse.' I took the piece to refer to the collapse of the existing

---

[2]   See http://www.royal.gov.uk/HMTheQueen/Education/Overview.aspx.
[3]   See http://www.urbandictionary.com/define.php?term=duh.

system of 'public thought' and its *replacement* by the 'influx of the amateurs'; that is, that 'the average quality of public thought has collapsed' *among the professional commentator class*. This made sense, not least because I had been away from Australia for a few months and had only just started to pick up again on the op-ed columns in the *Courier Mail* and the *Australian*, the news and current affairs shows on television, and so on.

Just for a taste, on the day I first drafted this chapter, columnist Jane Fynes-Clinton (2010) offered this 'public thought' in my city newspaper the *Courier Mail*:

> WHERE have our little girls gone? In the past five years or so, a strange phenomenon swept them away, leaving swearing, smoking, fighting, drinking creatures in their place. These girls are as angry, fat and sexually active as they are too young for all those things. It is enough to make a caring society weep.

This was part of a concerted campaign by the *Courier Mail* against 'bad girls' – that being the front-page headline two days earlier:

> A MASSIVE spike in violent attacks by young Queensland girls has been blamed on internet 'fight sites' where videos of the attacks are posted. Authorities say a 44 per cent jump in assaults is being driven by the growing popularity of 'girl fight sites.' [...] Professor Kerry Carrington, from Queensland University of Technology's School of Justice, yesterday warned of a new generation of 'very nasty' and physically violent girls. 'There is no doubt girls are becoming more violent,' she said. 'The internet actually encourages this behaviour because kids from all over the world go on and rate the fights, so even when conflict doesn't exist this particular medium may be encouraging violence.' Prof Carrington said a simple internet search revealed 73 million hits for girls' fighting compared with 31 million for boys, and 24 million girl fight videos on YouTube – eight times more than those featuring boys. (Ironside 2010)

On the day between the 'bad girls' lead and the opinion column by Fynes-Clinton, another news story featured a 'teen girl' who was said to have 'got off lightly' with a 'rap on the knuckles.' She was pictured in a prominent color photograph as an attractive young woman in a summer dress, shown seated in the back of a car . . . wearing handcuffs.

Although no mention is made of the fact in this edition, that quarter-page photograph was nearly two years old. It was first published during the same teen's original trial for assault (April 24, 2008 – I found it because it was still attached to an online report of that case). You have to read quite a long way into the accompanying story to discover that this 'female ringleader' is in court on more recent charges, and that the assault in question had occurred two years previously. The story leads (paragraph 2) with 'But Tiani Slockee, now 19, has escaped actual jail time.' Only later (paragraph 5) does it transpire that she had already served 91 days in custody on remand. It is not until paragraph 7 that we learn that 'Yesterday' she was back in court for a breach of probation. And not until paragraph 10 (of 11) do we learn that in the meantime she has suffered the death of 'one of her premature twin children.' A bit of Googling reveals that, although it does not figure in this coverage, her side of the story had been reported – by the *Courier Mail* itself – in 2007:

> Defence lawyer Debbie Marinov said Slockee approached the couple – who were walking on East Dutton Street, Coolangatta, about 12.50am (AEST) Saturday – when she saw them arguing. Ms Marinov said Slockee had asked the off-duty police officer: 'Doesn't she love you any more?' The officer then made a derogatory remark and Slockee responded that she was 'only joking,' Ms Marinov said. The court was told the man then made another derogatory remark and tackled one of the youths in the group to the ground. '(Slockee) stood back in shock – she could not believe the level of violence and how it had escalated so quickly,' Ms Marinov said, adding that Slockee had said she did not touch anyone during the melee. As Slockee was led away from the court into custody, a tearful Slockee said to her mother in the public gallery: 'I love you, mum.' (AAP 2007)

Further hints of a different kind of life were also readily retrievable:

> The teenager was refused bail on Saturday because she was deemed at risk of reoffending, but yesterday [defence lawyer] Mr Winter revived an application for bail. He told the court Slockee [...] needed to return home to look after her sick, elderly grandmother, as she was her primary carer. Mr Winter said Slockee's grandmother suffered chronic lung disease and emphysema and her granddaughter was the only person available to shower and feed her. (Fineran 2009)

On Tiani's Myspace page we read: 'R.I.P. Nan. I'll never forget you,' and under 'ethnicity' she has entered 'Pacific Islander.'[4] Here I must interpolate some qualms about referring to a private citizen's Myspace page, not least

---

[4]   See http://www.myspace.com/tiani_69_gigaboo.

because this is a familiar ploy in journalism, especially where embarrassing photographs are concerned. However, I decided to go ahead, because (a) I want to show how easy it would have been for the news media to construct a humanizing picture of her and (b) because I'm quoting only her basic datasheet, not communicative content as such. Of course, I'm also (c) demonstrating that Myspace material, which may have been posted for a restricted circle, remains public and appropriable for purposes not imagined by the user.

By such means, public and instantly searchable, a potentially very different reality emerges. A person of Indigenous heritage is caught up in a 'who-started-it' dispute with a police officer that rapidly escalates out of her control. The upshot is a catalogue of catastrophic encounters with the law – for a recently bereaved young single mother. But all this is lost on the *Courier Mail*, for whom the cause of it all is . . . *the internet*:

> **Teen girls get off lightly for violent crimes**
> QUEENSLAND'S fastest-growing group of violent offenders are likely to be let off with a scolding as punishment for their crimes. *The Courier-Mail* revealed yesterday that girls aged 10 to 14 were responsible for a massive 44 per cent spike in assaults last year, a phenomenon child experts have linked to the explosion in the number of girl fight sites on the internet. (Stolz 2010; see also Ironside 2010)

Yes, I thought – even allowing for the silly season, the quality of public thought has indeed collapsed! And, given the Murdoch press' sustained campaign against internet sharing, while preparing their new subscription-based business plan, you may well say: well, duh! But this is quite a big admission for me, as I have spent an entire career *avoiding* making negative statements about the quality of popular media. I have argued instead in favor of the media's emancipationist potential.

Academic Collapse

One reason for my refusal to trash popular culture is that too many people are already lined up to take their turn at that sport. In the same week that Tiani's story 'broke,' if that's the right word, the *Times Literary Supplement* published a long letter from Gabriel Josipovici, an author and emeritus literary critic, under the heading 'What are universities for?' The letter was provoked by cut-backs announced at the local university in an email from the vice-chancellor that, for Josipovici, was 'couched throughout in the worst bureaucratese' and in 'execrable English.' The cuts sought financial savings across a number of schools, including English and an amalgamated department of History, Art History, and Philosophy (as well as Engineering, Informatics, and Life Sciences) and promised 'growth and development' for schools with 'future prospects,' including Business, Management, and Economics; Global Studies; and Media, Film, and Music. Here, then, in the contrasting fates of English and History on the one hand, and Media Studies on the other, was the rub:

> As one might imagine, this is not good news for those disciplines which have always been seen as at the heart of the Humanities side of English universities. [...] Clearly, this university at any rate is being treated strictly as a business, with the least profitable branches closed and the most profitable ones developed. [...] The question this raises is: Are universities really businesses? And if not, what are they? Are they to become forcing houses for the immediate economic development of the country and nothing else (i.e. are Business and Media studies to replace Engineering, English, History and Philosophy)? If that is what the country wants, so be it. But we should be clear that it means the end of universities as they have been known in the West since the Middle Ages. (Josipovici 2010)

Collapse is imminent! And the evidence is . . . that *media studies* will 'replace' . . . *English*. This, self-evidently, is the end of civilization as 'we' know it. Such harrumphing hatred of media studies as the proxy for 'the immediate economic development of the country' (understood as a calamity) is a longstanding genre in itself. Josipovici seems anxious to prove the point by invoking a recent contribution to the *Times Literary Supplement* by fellow-harrumpher Stefan Collini (a link is provided on the *Times Literary Supplement* website). Collini's expression of contempt for anything popular or media-related is dressed up as a witty critique of the UK's inclusion of 'impact' in research funding criteria. Following is a sample (it's a very long column):

> there is no reason to expect a literary scholar to be good at this kind of hustling and hawking. [...] If anything, meretricious and vulgarizing treatments [...] will stand a greater chance of success than do nuanced critical readings. [...] our sensibilities have been numbed by the proliferation of economistic officialese – 'user satisfaction,' 'market forces,' 'accountability,' and so on. Perhaps our ears no longer hear what a fatuous, weaselly phrase

'Research Excellence Framework' actually is [...] Instead of letting this drivel become the only vocabulary for public discussion of these matters, it is worth insisting that what we call 'the humanities' are a collection of ways of encountering the record of human activity in its greatest richness and diversity. To attempt to deepen our understanding [...] is [...] an end in itself. Unless these guidelines are modified, scholars in British universities will devote less time and energy to this attempt, and more to becoming door-to-door salesmen for vulgarized versions of their increasingly market-oriented 'products.' (Collini 2009)

The most-recommended comment on Collini's piece on the *TLS* site was this one, from a suitably patriotic correspondent:

John Bull [sic.] wrote: Why do not at least the older universities refuse to accept this anti-educationalism? If Oxford and Cambridge, and the respected London Colleges, refused to touch it, what could the government do? Will no one stand up for Western Civilization?

'We' all agree with Colllini, it seems, that defense of 'Western Civilization' will only be achieved if 'literary scholars' are protected from the 'hustling and hawking' required to explain their research to the public, which will inevitably result in 'vulgarising and meretricious treatment' in the media. Only the 'older' universities can save us now! So the forces of darkness and light are lined up in traditional opposition: the 'fatuous, weaselly phrases' and 'ludicrous' 'drivel' of 'economistic officialese' (boo!) versus 'what we call "the humanities,"' which is 'an end in itself' (hooray!). And what 'we' call the humanities, as Josipovici makes clear, extends only to 'those disciplines that have *always been seen as at the heart* of the Humanities side of English universities' – that is, anything but media studies, which is populated by Collini's evil 'door-to-door salesmen for vulgarized versions of [universities'] increasingly market-oriented "products."' *Are* there any such things as 'door-to-door salesmen' (or women) any longer? And what does 'vulgar' mean? It means 'of the common people' (you know, folk like Tian!). Re-enter ancient class prejudice, by the back door.

Keening at a Wake

All this flooded into my mind as I read Shirky's comments on the collapse of the 'quality of public thought.' Yes! Yes! It has collapsed! And I for one do not want to be pulled back into that slough of despond that we used to call an English Department – bogged down in stagnant purposelessness and willful disutility, tangled up with a deep-rooted but toxic sense of entitlement, and overhung by a superiority complex dripping with contempt for everyone else.

The siren wailings of professors Collini and Josipovici – who were singing the same song all those years ago when I started out – amounts to professional bad faith. If they weren't so stuck in the mud, sensibilities numbed by accidental exposure to economics, surely the purveyors of 'nuanced critical readings' would want to run away from these 'forcing houses' (publicly-funded universities) and set up their own 'vociferous opposition' somewhere far away from '"user satisfaction," "market forces," "accountability," and so on'? Of course they wouldn't. As Shirky astutely points out, they are the 'beneficiaries of the system where making things public was a privileged activity,' whose 'complaints are like keening at a wake; the change they fear is already in the past. The real action is elsewhere.' Yes, indeed – so let's hear no more about 'inclusion' signaling the return of the 'Dark Ages.'

Sequence of Collapse

The changes brought on by the 'abundance of public thought' hit the academy long ago; more recently politics itself and at last the public media too are feeling the winds of change. This is what really got me excited about Shirky's piece. It struck me that there might be a *sequence* in the collapse of the 'average quality of public thought.' If he is right – if it is true that the change feared by the 'beneficiaries of the system where making things public was a privileged activity' is 'already in the past' – then there must be a history or causal sequence of such change. If so, then 'keening' by 'beneficiaries' may in fact be used as an indirect measure of the location, presence, and intensity of change. Here is what I would hypothesize on that topic: The collapse was first experienced in the academy (a proxy for intellectual and literary life); then in politics (a proxy for community life); then in journalism (a proxy for corporate interests in the copyright industries).

(1) *Academic (intellectual/literary) collapse.* The social prestige and political influence of the professoriate – as a class – has been in genteel decline (especially in the humanities) since the mid-1900s or earlier. To some extent the collapse was internal, as imperial/modernist cer-

tainties were challenged by successive waves of critical theory (structuralism, feminism, identity politics, relativism, deconstruction, constructivism, postmodernism), critiquing the knowledge–power nexus and disputing the truth-claims of science. In recent decades this precipitated open hostility towards the academic left in the so-called culture wars. The 'quality of public thought' within and about the academy degenerated into mutual contempt or derisive spoof – witness the Sokal affair.[5] I don't know whether it was a consequence of this, but at the same time academic specialization ensured that debate retreated into ever-tinier enclaves, where more has been written about less than ever before. People responsible for 'public thought' were once proud to carry the moral, political, and aesthetic conscience of empires on their shoulders – remember, Kipling (Nobel laureate for literature) called it the 'white man's burden' (1899) and Sir Arthur Quiller-Couch (King Edward VII Professor of English at Cambridge) called it '*noblesse oblige*' (1946 [1916]). Now they are reduced to an ambition for satisfactory *impact metrics* – among which *forming the taste and judgment of future leaders* does not appear. Hence the harrumphing humanities.[6] Meanwhile, the trained expertise upon which our vestigial claims to a public platform might have been based was steadily eroded by the increasingly obvious fact that such expertise was neither scarce nor valuable – *everyone* is an 'expert' on popular culture, and few want to pay for knowledge about 'ordinary' life. Now, we may be able to produce high-quality 'public thought' on our specialist topic, but it is so micro, arcane, and impenetrable that there is no public paying attention, so who cares?

(2) *Political (community) collapse.* 'Public thought' on the question of 'Are we all going to die?' ceased with the end of the Cold War internationally and capitalist/socialist struggles internally. As the danger of 'mutually assured destruction' (by weapons or workers) faded, politics became *purer*; that is, more abstract, not *about* anything except adversarial opposition itself. Robert Hughes (1993) called the result the 'culture of complaint.' In a *Time* article on the 'fraying of America,' he wrote that the US had become 'obsessed with therapies and filled with distrust of formal politics; skeptical of authority and

---

[5] See http://www.physics.nyu.edu/sokal.
[6] Harrumphing for the humanities seems to be internationally contagious; for an Australian example see Turner (2010b).

prey to superstition; its political language corroded by fake pity and euphemism' (Hughes 1992: 44). Excessive politicization corrupts: 'Polarization is addictive. It is the crack of politics – a short, intense rush that the system craves again and again, until it begins to collapse' (Hughes 1993: 11). The 'quality' of *political* 'public thought' nose-dives. Instead of looking for reds under the beds, we are looking for child molesters – someone to blame for our continuing sense of risk in conditions of unprecedented security. Or perhaps it's those 'teen girls,' heads turned by the internet, roaming the Gold Coast, spoiling for a fight . . . or a party.

(3)   *Journalism (commercial) collapse.* It's the economy, stupid. Here's where Shirky gets interested – not when professions or publics suffer systemic collapse, but when business plans are threatened. The principal large-scale 'beneficiaries of the system where making things public was a privileged activity' were of course *publishers* – of songs, sights, and stories. That is, the music business, broadcasting and the movies, the press, and publishing – the existing copyright industries. The one bit of this sector of the economy where 'public thought' was linked directly to 'private enterprise' was journalism (loosely defined, i.e. including opinion, commentary, features, and PR). It's not just individual firms; whole industries are crumbling, business *models* don't work . . . hey, it's the *end of civilization as we know it!* So now journalism has something to campaign about in which its own fate is implicated. It's back to the good old days of 'are we all going to die?' . . . but now the 'we' is a plc. The campaign is not confined to editorials, the op-ed pages, and features, but permeates so-called hard news too. Journalism as a whole is geared up to turn 'public thought' into a culture of complaint . . . about *piracy.* Along the way, editors are quite happy to stage front-page news reports that undermine their online rivals in 'making things public,' by whatever pretext that comes to hand: 'A massive spike in violent attacks by young Queensland girls has been blamed on [the] internet.'

Every Time You Torrent

Here is where we are now: the latest outbreak of 'keening' is by commercial creators, manufacturers, and disseminators (up to and including Rupert Murdoch) and their freelance-consultant allies, such as Andrew Keen

(2007). Here he is, writing in the house magazine of the Directors' Guild of America, going about the business of foe-creation, the essential first move for any 'battleground' (Keen 2009).[7] Following a list of the 'digital literati' he opposes:

- 'The digital rebels use many names to describe themselves. They are "hackers," "bloggers," "longtailers," "diginauts," "socialista," and "digerati." Above all, however, they identify themselves as "pirates." They even now have their own international political movement, the Pirate Party';
- Andrew Robinson, 'the head of the United Kingdom's new Pirate Party';
- Stewart Brand, 'countercultural creator' of the *Whole Earth Catalog*;
- Matt Mason (author of *The Pirate's Dilemma: How Youth Culture is Reinventing Capitalism*);
- Lawrence Lessig (*Remix: Making Art and Commerce Thrive in the Hybrid Economy*), 'misty-eyed academic dream';
- Jeff Jarvis, 'pirate intellectual';
- Jay Rosen, 'digital liberation theologian';
- Cory Doctorow ('Media-morphosis: How the internet will devour, transform, or destroy your favorite medium'), 'pirate rebel';
- Karl Marx, as in 'Just as Karl Marx welcomed the industrial revolution . . . so Lessig welcomes the digital revolution as our savior';
- Siva Vaidhyanathan, 'left-leaning communitarianism gone amuck'; and
- David Weinberger (*The Cluetrain Manifesto: The End of Business as Usual*), 'academic cluelessness.'

Adopting the familiar dripping-with-contempt tone of Josipovici or Collini, Keen summarizes the manifesto of the 'pirate rebels,' among whom Clay Shirky must surely number:

> To critics of 'authoritarian' mainstream media like Lessig, today's Internet technology is the great emancipator, the enabler of the digital rebellion. We've supposedly arrived at another Gutenberg moment in history, one of those once-every-500-years historical events that forever alters the course of the human story. But instead of the old exclusive printing press, all we need now is a personal computer to become a Johannes von Gutenberg, a William Randolph Hearst and a contemporary Hollywood movie director all rolled into one noble citizen-creator.

---

[7] Subsequent quotations of Keen's words are from this source.

He sums up the case for the copyright industry:

> What these leveling 'democratizers' miss, however, is the reality of any crea-
> tive economy – talent. Utopians like Mason seem to believe that everyone
> – irrespective of their intellectual training, personal rigor, and innate ability
> – should have their work represented in the creative commons. This naively
> fails to acknowledge the inconvenient truth that not everyone is an artist, or
> has interesting things to say.

He seeks to undermine his opponents' credentials by association with
(discredited) academia:

> Perhaps it's not surprising that so many of the rebel pirate intellectual
> leaders are academics at leading American universities. [...] Despite trum-
> peting the rights of the individual creator over their corporate exploiters,
> none of these tenured ivory tower theorists appears to particularly respect
> the sensitivity of freelance artists dependent on the security of their creative
> content.

He concludes with the 'great cultural achievement' of the internet: it
is . . . bathos:

> So this is the great cultural achievement of the Internet? For all the promise
> of a glittering new cultural age, of radical democratization, of a renaissance
> in creativity, what the digital revolution is actually promising to deliver are
> 'cheap' and 'crummy' online videos with infinitesimal audiences and no way
> of realizing any meaningful revenue.

Just in case you stupidly think this is about art, or talent, rather than the
economy, Keen's article features a literal bottom line – a comment interpo-
lated from the President of the Director's Guild of America (DGA), one
Taylor Hackford:

> Your DGA leadership believes that Internet piracy poses a great danger [...]
> and a great challenge to this Guild. [...] This is a complex and multifaceted
> issue which is too often reduced to simplistic sound bites that hide the real
> threats we face from those who want our work 'for free.' It is only by educat-
> ing ourselves that we will be able to put forward our strongest and most
> effective offense to protect the creative and economic freedom of Guild
> members.

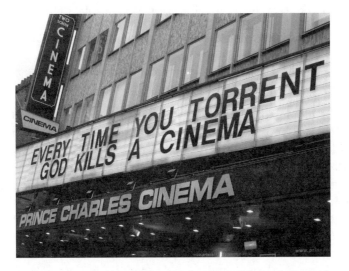

Figure 4.1   Leicester Square, London, October 2009 (Photo: J. Hartley).

An Invisible College – At the Airport

But, if Shirky is right, the complaints of beneficiaries are simply evidence that it is already too late for Keen's 'keening.' The real action is elsewhere. I think Shirky is indeed right. And I know where the real action is. It's *at the airport*. I'm thinking of the airport in relation to long-haul flights in particular (from recent experience), where time zones, jetlag, transit lounges, and complete subjection to the will of others relativizes everything, from your circadian rhythms to your experience of time, place, self, and society. That grey hub of artificially induced docility fails to mask the realities of uncertainty and risk, where no-one is at home (in equilibrium) but billions visit some time, myriad agents bent on different but mutually accommodating ends, finding ways to suspend time and live in pure relativism.

Airports are perhaps the best physical manifestation we have of humanity's skill in developing social-network infrastructure; they are an analogue version of the 'packet switching' that enables the internet to function. Here we come to the last bit of the Shirky piece that I quoted at the beginning of this chapter:

> We could, however, also use it [the internet] as an Invisible College, the communicative backbone of real intellectual and civic change, but to do this will require more than technology. It will require that we adopt norms of open sharing and participation, fit to a world where *publishing has become the new literacy*. (my emphasis)

As well as the democratization of knowledge, Shirky favors an Invisible College (precursor of the Royal Society) modeled on the network of experimental inquiry and open argumentation that we now call science, which was established among early-modern chemists in Europe. I support his sentiment that a world where everyone is a publisher may drive progressive intellectual and civic change and, like him, I am interested in ways of organizing and sharing knowledge outside of formal institutions. In fact I wrote a book on these topics (Hartley 2009). However, I do not follow Shirky's idea of an Invisible College (see 'Invisible College' n.d.). All his talk of an 'influx of amateurs' and 'another Dark Ages' has made me suspicious. If the Invisible College is just a few self-selected savants – the 'we' who 'adopt norms' – then it smacks of *Brave New World*, not to mention the latter-day Illuminati (see 'Illuminati' n.d.). But if, at the other extreme, it is taken to be the internet as a whole ('here comes everybody'), then such a vast system-of-systems cannot hope to achieve purposeful change, even if it is called for from within the ranks of users themselves. What then might be a model for directed, educative change, including 'open sharing and participation' among *any* if not *all* netizens, in the iterative improvement of contested knowledge (i.e. science) as a self-organizing, grass-roots approach to knowledge transfer, so as to use the emergent productive capacity of the internet to best effect?

The answer is staring us in the face. What does everybody do at airports? They buy books to read on planes. The Invisible College is . . . *airport bestsellers*. Such books belong to a peculiar genre. They must fit in with the realities of air travel: long but not too long, absorbing and narratively compelling, not like work . . . and extremely well promoted, branded, and celebrity-endorsed, because travelers must be able to choose on the fly, as it were, without access to their habitual feedback loops. Most such books are novels, but significant subgenres exist in non-fiction, including business, popular science, history, and biography. The whole point of them is that they address non-specialist, ordinary readers with other priorities and purposes. They address the *general public*, which is thereby constituted in the form of a constantly changing but continuously replenished market.

Please note that almost all of the 'digital literati' lambasted by Andrew Keen, along with Andrew Keen and Clay Shirky themselves, are authors of non-fiction bestsellers, the ideal type of which is the business book you buy at the airport. Where once these clustered around the prating of alpha males (Jack Welch syndrome), there is now a sizeable segment devoted to digital topics, often by (or co-authored with) those who have made some money. Indeed, such books are part of the definition of the 'digerati':

> The 'digital elite.' People who are extremely knowledgeable about computers. It often refers to the movers and shakers in the industry. Digerati is the high-tech equivalent of 'literati,' which refers to scholars and intellectuals, or 'glitterati,' the rich and famous. Digerati, 'technorati' and 'geekerati' are synonymous. See Technorati and Illuminati. (PCMag. com n.d.)

The airport bestseller is the type of book most likely to be cited by high-profile controversialists (such as Andrew Keen or Clay Shirky) as they conduct their online arguments. It is the common currency of communication about the internet among the diverse and multivalent, not to say mobile and shifting, population of non-specialist readers. It is the medium of instruction for the 'influx of amateurs' – a readily available resource that they can turn to for inspiration. Needless to say, this being the age of the internet, anyone can write one, and there is no shortage of advice on how to go about it. The advice website eHow.com has some deceptively simple instructions for tackling the 'challenging' job of 'how to write a business bestseller':

> [Step 1] Find an original idea or creative approach to an existing topic. A business book is marketed to a very discerning audience of highly intelligent people, so for it to be successful it must be a new idea; you can't just talk about investing the same way everyone before you has, or you will not have a book that will sell.
> [Step 2] Succeed in business. Your book needs credibility in order to become a bestseller. This requires that the author has succeeded in business. The buying public wants to know that the advice or ideas in the book have been successfully applied to the real world. They want to know that they can use them to achieve success.
> [Step 3] Write the book; this entails more than just putting words down on a page. Business people as a rule don't like to spend an excessive amount

of time on any one task. This means that in a book they are looking for clearly defined answers delivered succinctly and without unnecessary fluff. [...] The book also has to be interesting enough to read so that it doesn't put the reader to sleep.

[Step 4] Promote your book, as one can't just be content to allow simple market forces to compel your book to bestseller status. You might want to do a simple book-signing tour, or you might want to arrange a series of seminars and speeches; but either way you need to tell people why they should buy your business book instead of all of the others. Once you have them convinced that the book will change the way they do business for the better, they will buy it in droves. (*eHow* n.d.)

It's so simple! Lol. Rofl. LMAO. *eHow* gives good advice, but notice that this guide does require more than mere domain knowledge and authorial wordcraft (e.g. Step 2: 'succeed in business'). Note also that Step 4 is *promotion* – 'simple market forces' (i.e. Adam Smith's 'invisible hand'; see Joyce 2001) need a helping hand from marketing, as Joseph Schumpeter was the first to theorize (McCraw 2007).

Signaling the Quality of Public Thought

The problem of the 'quality of public thought' is solved. In the first place, those who have followed the advice above – from Eric Beinhocker (*The Origin of Wealth* 2006) to the *Freakonomics* guys – tend to write really good books. 'Quality' is condensed into the simple and unarguable form of sales data: if it's a bestseller, it's a good idea (until it is overturned by a subsequent bestseller). This system feeds on itself: if I've heard the buzz I'll buy the book. Conversely, if you academic experts – drear drudges of dismal data – have done nothing more than master your subject, perfect your methodology, and discover something new, then *der*.[8] You won't compete until you've caught the eye of public *attention*, as Richard Lanham and Brian Boyd have both stressed . . . in their own airport bestsellers (*The Economics of Attention* 2006 and *On the Origin of Stories* 2009). Promotion, including celebrity status, attention-seeking antics, polemical attacks, and controversies, turns out to be of crucial importance to the propagation of knowledge. Mere *expertise* runs a distant second, although professional expertise in

---

[8]   See http://www.urbandictionary.com/define.php?term=der.

promotion is still at a premium. The airport bestseller is thus a *signaling mechanism.*

Digital Literacy: 'Look at Moi!'

This takes us beyond Shirky's 'shock of inclusion.' The initial phase of Schumpeterian creative destruction 'upends the old order' (as he puts it). The existing 'beneficiaries of the system where making things public was a privileged activity' (among whom I've specified academics, political parties, and commercial publishers) are discombobulated and dethroned. However, they don't disappear – perforce, they regroup, trying to adapt to the new circumstances. Even the harrumphers and keeners are busy adapting. But the real action is happening over at the airport. Here we can observe the emergence of a new order – a market in ideas for busy, mobile, half-attentive but motivated and self-directing consumer agents. This market also establishes a pecking order among opinion-formers, who are the true educators of the 'here comes everybody' era.

The catchphrase of the old tailoring sitcom was 'never mind the quality, feel the width,' as if the two were incommensurable.[9] But now we are among the *long-tailers* of the power law generation, where quality (peak bestsellers) and width (broad sales of diverse titles among a heterogeneous public) are in a *relationship* (a mathematical one at that), not in opposition to one another. Airport bestsellers do for tradable ideas what newspapers once did for nations, and what universities are still supposed to do – they *create a public* for new knowledge, and they sort the ideas according to their uptake among that public. This process, of differential uptake, is what we might once have called *education* and even intellectual *emancipation*, except that now it is self-directed, demand-led, and self-organizing.

Of course, it's not entirely online. The 'shock of inclusion' proceeds in multiplatform mode. There is plenty of online chatter about the latest offerings, and many of the best titles are (legally) available online in their entirety (e.g. Leadbeater 2008; Zittrain 2008). But these books have to take physical form too; else why do we have Amazon . . . or airports, come to that? Clay Shirky says that 'publishing' by users, online, 'has become the new literacy' – and I agree with him (Hartley 2009). I also agree that the internet marks the most important evolutionary step in the growth of

---

[9] See http://phill.co.uk/comedy/quality.

knowledge technologies since Gutenberg. But we don't yet know how to harness all the new 'public thought' that's already out there, even if much of it is what the linguists call 'phatic' communication, designed for keeping in contact – which means *attracting attention* – rather than communicating thought (Hébert 2011). We know even less about how to stimulate, improve, or propagate its 'quality.' In this context, the argy-bargy of complaint, controversy, and keening should not be taken at face value. It is not important to decide on a winner or loser among all the arguments, nor to agree with this or that commentator. Instead, note the importance of *signaling* in the propagation of public thought. If you want to get an idea across, get attention. If you want attention, keep the lines of communication open. Thus, the rhetoric of polemical argument itself performs a phatic function (like 80 percent of internet traffic). As they say on *Kath & Kim*, it's going . . . 'Look at Moi!'[10]

Trust Me, I'm a Doctor?

The lesson we should be learning is that a mechanism for *extending* and *improving* the quality of public thought exists: airport bestsellers as Invisible College. The readership is proving both able and willing to take advice. It may take a while, but the real impact of print didn't emerge for about 150 years. However, we can see here a model for propagation and improvement of popular public thought. What we don't have yet is a mechanism for extending the system beyond readerships. Here there is plenty of room for improvement. The internet is populated by a much larger public than the one captured by the readership of even the most popular bestseller. Lots of people out there don't read books at all, but they do count among Shirky's two billion. Take Tiani Slockee, once again. Her Myspace page, now somewhat neglected, lists her interests, which centre on 'my friends, beach, DANCING' (see Chapter 6). But when it comes to books, rejection is total, and proud of it: Against the box marked 'Books' is written 'fuck that!!!!'[11] So the question is how to reach out to *everybody* – including those who don't want to be improved but whose life chances are liable to real, catastrophic 'collapse' if they don't get good advice on how to avoid sticky

---

[10] See   http://www.austrade.gov.au/Exports-Beckon-Look-At-Moi-Look-At-Moi-/default. aspx.

[11] See http://www.myspace.com/tiani_69_gigaboo.

situations: how to survive not only chance encounters with off-duty police-men but also parenting, relationships, bereavement, legal jeopardy, media attention . . . and being (as here) *public property*. In Tiani we have one among the self-published internet billions who could evidently use some 'invisible high-schooling' in identity management, on the street, in the media, and online. Where will she get it? What signal will attract her atten-tion? What knowledge will sustain her interest? What can she learn to lift the quality of her own 'public thought'? Is the new literacy any more up to this job than the old one was?

If there has been a 'collapse of public thought,' among academics, public representatives, and commercial media alike, it is in their combined willing-ness to exclude such folk altogether, or to assume that empty chatter (phatic entertainment) is enough for the likes of them. But it would be a big – epochal – mistake to imagine the internet in the same terms, making an invidious distinction between what Shirky calls 'a modicum of educational material' (hooray!) and 'an ocean of narcissism and social obsessions' (boo!), not only because we are slow to recognize the same elements in our own 'public thought' but also because we know in advance which way many users will choose to jump. The existing organs of public enlightenment – the pro-fessional beneficiaries of 'making things public' – have lost the attention of people like Tiani. The internet still has it. Let's start from there. What might they need to know? How might their attention be attracted to useful knowl-edge? How can media and cultural studies provide practical assistance in the broad-based project of providing 'public thought' for social learning?

Outlearning

The fact is that, not only as a resource for social learning but also as a competitive provider of learning-oriented *teaching*, the internet is already giving the most prestigious of all learning institutions, universities, a run for their money; and, simultaneously, there is a growing disconnection between lay populations and elite knowledge institutions. The *productivity* of 'new technologies' that have been able to exploit the abstraction of sig-nification from the page, and to extend the growth of knowledge among networked populations, is a long-term evolutionary challenge to universi-ties, despite the 'unworthy' provenance of social networks in market-based entertainment media. Look to the commercial internet – not the public education system – for radical advances in digital literacy, distributed expertise, consumer productivity, and networked learning. This applies not only to the affluent economies of plenty but also increasingly to developing countries and emergent economies, for example in China, where over 330 million people used the internet during 2009[12] (more than the total US population); moreover, countries like China and Korea are not making the mistake of letting their prowess in 'pop culture' digital media get away from their efforts towards educational modernization (see Morgan 2010).

In established universities, surprisingly little attention is given to consumer demand for knowledge, as opposed to disciplinary supply. The 'market' for university *research* is largely b2b, restricted to companies and governments – and tenure committees – rather than being aimed at the general population, who are regarded as b2c (business to consumer) clients at best, apt to get what they are given – which is what we professionals call *teaching*. The b2b function is high-cost, high-prestige, and tenure-track, while the b2c function is massified, outsourced to casual staff, and under-resourced. Compared with the 'academic freedom' enjoyed by tenured researchers at R1 universities, teaching is declining towards something akin to knowledge of the helots, by the helots, for the helots (the term 'helot' is Hoggart's (1957: 191)).

Now, with every improvement in digital interactive technology, change should be seen in a more positive light. The possibilities for lay people to engage directly but informally in social *learning*, knowledge *production*, and creative *innovation* continue to grow, at the speed of Moore's Law.[13] Learning and research organizations such as universities must venture much further into that intermediate space between expert elites and the citizen consumer, because this intermediate space of *popular realism* is the 'medium' for growing user-led, consumer co-created innovation. It is time, therefore, to turn from a 'provider' perspective on knowledge to a 'user' one.

For Karl Popper (1945: vol. 2, 275–8), the aim of education was modest (albeit rarely achieved): 'Do no harm' and 'give the young what they most urgently need in order to become independent of us, and to be able to choose for themselves.'[14] He preferred a learning mode motivated by personal modesty (not fame-seeking individualism), critical dissatisfaction,

---

[12]   See   http://www.web2asia.com/2009/07/17/q2-2009-china-internet-statistics-report-released; for annual statistics on internet development in China see http://www.cnnic.cn/en/index/0O/02/index.htm.

[13]   See Wikipedia's 'Moore's law' (n.d.) for a good account.

[14]   See also http://www.the-rathouse.com/RC_PopperEdu.html.

and eagerness for improvement. If that is what education is *for*, the question is how to combine the reproduction and renewal of disciplinary knowledge (understanding and teaching the object of study) with the best prospects for achieving independence and choice among those who study it. The airport bestseller certainly provides one kind of answer; the internet provides a host of others. What can universities *learn from them*?

The 'external shock' currently experienced by established institutions of knowledge production, whether in firms (i.e. journalism), 'public thought,' or universities, as a result of the competitive attractions and burgeoning capabilities offered by digital and online knowledge technologies, does mean that a phase of Schumpeterian 'creative destruction' – of existing paradigms, business models, and disciplines – is unstoppably under way.

Table 4.1 Mirroring, growing and extending the functions of the university online: distributed productivity and the growth of knowledge

Inlearning (institutional) versus	Outlearning (distributed)
The university as *teaching system* (know-how)	Web 2.0
The university as *research organization* (user-co-creation)	Crowdsourcing, open-source movement, SETI
The university as *searchable* (purposeful problem-solving)	Google
The university as *archive*[1] (library)	Google Books, Project Gutenberg, YouTube
The university as *realist documentary* (teaching by story)	e.g. BBC Online; NPR; independent producers
The university as *knowledge transfer* (knowledge shared)	Fan sites, Wikipedia, YouTube
The university as *game* (play)	Movies (models of comportment), serious games
The university as *coffee shop* (the meeting, talk)	The blogosphere, Twitter
The university as *audition* (talent scout and school)	The dance-off, the *Idol* franchise
The university as *festival* (convention)	Awards, online forums, spoofs, TED.com[2]

[1] See Chapter 7.

[2] See, for instance, http://www.ted.com/talks/ken_robinson_says_schools_kill_creativity.html.

Universities *actually provide* a 'puberty rite' (teaching) and a solution to the 'need to establish pecking orders without violence' (research) (Hartley 2008: 254), within an economy of credentialism. Instead of perpetuating this, what if we were to try to invent a *useful university*, based on what its affordances may be used *for*. Such functions include teaching, research, a searchable archive, stories about the real, knowledge transfer, intellectual play and experimentation, and a place where people can meet, exchange ideas, and prepare for a competitive future. This being so, is it already the case that *anything universities can do, the internet can do better* (Table 4.1)?

Is this the digital future, not only of 'public thought' but also of *social learning*? If so, the lesson is clear: it is not 'public thought' that has collapsed, but institutional monopoly. Universities are being driven further towards pecking-order credentialism, leaving the field of popular learning to self-organizing markets such as airport bookshops and the internet. Public institutions are drawing ever further away from engagement in public thought. If they are to prove useful to those who would benefit most from the growth of knowledge, they must be the ones to change, in order to find ways to bridge that gap.

Your reaction? Check one.[15]

- ☐ LOL
- ☐ OMG
- ☐ WTF
- ☐ Cute
- ☐ Geeky
- ☐ Trashy
- ☐ Old
- ☐ Ew

---

[15] Reaction code borrowed from http://www.buzzfeed.com/scott/crayola-color-chart-1903-2010.

5

Television Goes Online

KEN BARLOW [WILLIAM ROACHE] *(wearing a kimono): OK. Come on.
Let's have it. You've got a problem with this, I should imagine?*
BLANCHE: *A grown man, dressed as a Geisha? Have you gone stark
staring mad?*
KEN: *It is no different to a dressing gown. I mean what. Is there a rule?
'Thou shalt wear terry towelling in the North West of England'?*
BLANCHE: *There should be. . . .*
BLANCHE: *(Turns back to Ken) But Ken! Always got to be different.
Always sniffing out controversy. Does Tennessee Williams wear a
kimono?*
KEN: *Tennessee Williams is dead!*
BLANCHE: *I'm not surprised!*

(*Coronation Street* February 20, 2009)

Cultural Climate Change

The central cultural experience of modernity has been *change*, both the
'creative destruction' of existing structures and the growth, often exponential, of new knowledge. During the twentieth century, the central cultural
platform for the collective experience of modernizing societies changed
too, from page and stage to the screen – from publishing, the press, and
radio to cinema, television, and latterly computer screens. Despite the successive dominance of new media, none has lasted long at the top. The
pattern for each was to give way to a successor platform in popularity but

Digital Futures for Cultural and Media Studies, First Edition. John Hartley.
© 2012 John Wiley & Sons, Ltd. Published 2012 by John Wiley & Sons, Ltd.

to continue as part of an increasingly crowded media menu. Modern media are supplemented not supplanted by their successors.

Broadcast television has proven to be no exception. What constitutes 'television' now is quite different from when its broadcast form emerged in the 1950s. As the internet, Web 2.0, and mobile devices shift from their open, 'generative' stage (Zittrain 2008) towards a stabilizing phase of adoption and retention through market-based 'affordances,' it has become clear that 'television' has been radically transformed. What counts as television is diversifying – across technology, mode of production, viewing experience, programming, production base, and geography.

- *Technologically*, television includes non-broadcast technologies (DVDs, TiVo, bit torrent files) and it can be viewed on computers (YouTube) and mobile devices (phones, iPods) as well as via traditional television sets, which have evolved to flat-screen technologies.
- Television has physically *migrated* out of the domestic living room and is now integrated into bedrooms, offices, shops, cars, clubs, and cafés. It is personalized and portable, integrated with clothes, phones, and music platforms.
- Its *mode of production* it is also transformed: the giant studios that were once the unarguable sign of a powerful broadcaster are now largely empty, industry production having migrated to naturalistic settings or just-in-time facilities.
- It is a different *viewing experience*. Broadcast television can be used as an adjunct to other activities (e.g. a television stream on the office computer). You can customize television by decoupling viewing from transmission (e.g. collecting DVDs or files and wallowing in a favorite series for a weekend).
- *Television entertainment* has evolved to take user participation into the heart of programming – plebiscitary television (Hartley 2008: 126–62). The fragmentation of platforms, many of them associated with a specific demographic segment, has fed back into the evolution of television forms, resulting in both format repetition (e.g. clones of a given format such as house-improvement shows) and creative innovation (repurposing a traditional genre for a specialized audience, e.g. *Skins*).
- Most radically, the *production base* has broadened to include, in principle if not (yet) in practice, everybody with access to a computer. You can make television yourself or with others, and you can 'redact' existing

content. Either way, you can publish your efforts to family and friends and to the world at large. And then, the restlessness of imaginative creativity being what it is, some bright spark can turn that DIY format into a brilliant new type of 'TV' drama (online internet video-log) – for example, *lonelygirl15* and *KateModern*.

- *Spatially*, television has diversified from its origins in national and city-based communications systems to overlapping personalized and social networks that may be next door or may be global. Migrants, taste-constituencies, communities of interest (around identities, sport, politics, pastimes), and enterprising creatives can exploit the 'long-tail' characteristics of the internet to find content or an audience from anywhere.

Broadcast television was always a mixed blessing, displaying at once the positive and negative aspects of a regime of semiotic and political representation (see Chapter 1) in which common, generalized experience was represented on screen and in legislatures by professional expert elites (actors and politicians, *mutatis mutandis*). So, *everyone was represented* – ordinary life and everyday choices were the real 'platform' of mass media – but simultaneously *no-one spoke for themselves*. Everything was realist but nothing was real.

On the plus side, television's domestic setting, live immediacy, leisure-time availability, casual continuity, operational simplicity (two knobs), and the human scale of its screen were all suited to the context in which it thrived best: private life and family-building in conditions of expanding consumer affluence, otherwise known as the suburban experience. On-screen, broadcast television excelled at head-to-head dramatic conflict, both fictional and factual – drama, comedy, kids' shows, news, and sport. While encouraging people to stay at home, it taught neighborly comportment and experiential and national togetherness, and continuously brought new information and experience to all sections of the public. It could also coordinate population-wide (sometimes planet-wide) attention to, and emotional investment in, periods of excitement and high uncertainty, as during sporting finals, end-of-season cliff-hangers, elections, and political crises. It was the bellwether of change for a population living through change.

But at the same time television was a worry. The high capital cost of production and highly regulated distribution networks resulted in an extreme 'division of labor' between corporate expertise and lay audiences,

who seemed to be at the mercy of powerful persuaders, commercial marketing, and political manipulation. 'Network' television came to mean the
universalization of corporate will, encapsulated in advertising that
reduced audiences to consumers, agency to behavior, and modernity to
an endless pipeline of products, carried from manufacturers and retailers
to waiting, willing, wanting housewives, whose job it was to buy the
things that were advertised, serve them to her family (slouched on the
couch watching television), then clean up the house and the bodies in it
using more television-advertised products. Broadcast television perfected
its role as the purveyor of what was needed to sustain domestic life by
reducing it to a flow of consumption – products came into the house,
went through the alimentary system, and then safely out again, chased by
cleansing agents from toothpaste to Toilet Duck. No wonder they called
it the Tube.

'That Sign Needs Changing'

Fifty years later and trillions of tissues down the toilet, some things have
changed: for instance, the mode of television production, the domestic
context, and the content (and the study) of television, not to mention
the identity, lives, and general outlook of all the people involved on both
sides of the screen. But there is continuity too. Some things have stayed
very much the same: for instance, the world's longest-running soap
opera, first broadcast (live) on December 9, 1960 and still going strong
50 years on – the UK's *Coronation Street*. Ena Sharples (Violet Carson)
uttered *Coronation Street*'s first line, 'That sign needs changing.' She was
referring to a shop sign (a new owner was moving into the corner
shop), but perhaps this was a prophetic assertion of semiotic futures
more generally. Either way, whether you were watching at the time or
not yet born, there is a recognizable sense of continuity in *Coronation
Street* from that day to this, and also in television more generally, as a
cultural form.

The essence of that continuity is in the *viewing experience* of broadcast
television, including generic realism on screen in news and serial drama,
which from the point of view of the audience is not about change or difference so much as stability and recognition, both at home on the couch
with the biscuits and sisters and in the diegetic world of the characters with
their unfolding dilemmas about relationships. Continuous over half a

century is a *representative model* of the *broadcasting relationship*, based on one-way transmission of narrative entertainment, from a centralized corporate industry to a receptive but unproductive domestic audience. Another, matching, continuity is that much of the disputation in television studies has pivoted about this relationship and how it should be explained or evaluated. While there were undoubtedly negative aspects to the 'powerful producer/purposeless consumer' model, there was also something positive in it for both sides:

- *Economically,* the media industries burgeoned and became influential beyond their scale during the century of mass media;
- *Culturally,* the 'imagined community' of very large populations was coordinated into semiotic unity when 'we' all watched the same programs; and
- *Individually,* the experience of television was cheap, open, sociable, and full of emotional immediacy.

Broadcast television proved to be better than the press, cinema, or even radio at *riveting* everyone to the same spot, at the same time, in fear, laughter, wonderment, thrill, or desire. Television's emblematic moments – the shooting of J.R. Ewing in *Dallas* or J.F. Kennedy in Dallas; the moon landings; the twin towers; princess Diana's wedding and funeral; the Olympics and football World Cup finals; the cliff-hangers, weddings, departures, and finales – gathered populations from across all demographic and hierarchical boundaries into fleetingly attained but nevertheless real moments of 'wedom,' a simultaneous commonalty of attention that could sometimes aggregate to the billions.

Less Popular?

Because audience choice is increasingly fragmented across more channels and platforms, it is unlikely that any single fictional television show will ever again achieve the audience numbers of *I Love Lucy*'s top-rating episode (1953), Elvis Presley's *Ed Sullivan* debut (1956), the 'Who Shot JR?' episode of *Dallas* (1980), or the series finale of *M*A*S*H* (1983). Even so, it is still possible to experience *live community* through television – *Survivor, Lost,* the various iterations of the *Idol* franchise, the Super Bowl, the Olympics, and occasionally the news. Sometimes television is still used to experience the *live polity*. For instance, according to the *New York Times' Media Decoder* blog, the telecast of Senator Obama's acceptance speech at the Democratic National Convention in August 2008 reached 38.3 million viewers (plus millions more on C-Span and PBS). This was the highest rating in history for a convention speech – until Senator McCain's 38.8 million the following week (Serjeant 2008). Both were also watched by unknown millions world-wide, many of them also tuning in to a live feed. For once, politics out-rated sport and reality television: 'Mr. Obama's speech reached more viewers than the Olympics opening ceremony in Beijing, the final "American Idol" or the Academy Awards this year' (Stelter 2008). Such a result is the more surprising when compared with the 'tiny' ratings achieved by routine network programming:

> Sen. Barack Obama may have earned record-breaking ratings for his accept-ance speech on Thursday […] but *network television attracted otherwise tiny audiences during prime time*. According to Nielsen's final ratings, CBS led the night with 'Big Brother,' which drew 6 million viewers at 8 p.m. […] CBS broadcast a rerun of 'CSI' at 9 p.m. (5.3 million). (Toff 2008, my emphasis)

Even more surprisingly, perhaps, during that Convention week the sub-scription news channel CNN out-rated all three free-to-air broadcast net-works (ABC, CBS, NBC) in head-to-head competition, again for the first time in history:

> In nearly three decades, CNN has never beat all three broadcast networks in viewership when competing directly. […] This year, CNN had 5.38 million viewers, while NBC had 5.36 million, ABC had 3.48 million, CBS had 3.46 million, Fox had 2.7 million and MSNBC had 2.3 million. (*New York Times* 2008).

Even as they show how television can still bind a nation around an exceptional event, these figures also record some epic changes. The ratings for regular US network entertainment, topped at a mere six million for *Big Brother*, are pitiful compared with television's heyday. By comparison, the 1994–2004 sitcom *Friends* routinely rated between 20 and 30 million viewers; its range was from a low of 15 million to a high of over 50 million (Ginsburg n.d.). Meanwhile, pay-television has begun to beat network broadcasting, albeit with figures lower even than those scored by *Big Brother*. Thus has the proliferation of platforms destroyed the unity of the imagined community. It is a long way from the finale of *M*A*S*H* in 1983, when 105 million Americans tuned in.[1]

However, it would not be entirely true to say that the millions are abandoning *television*, only that they are choosier about when they watch and what platform they watch 'TV' on. The audience has migrated to subscriber, online, and mobile platforms. As a result, global popularity may significantly outpace even US primetime audiences and yet not register in traditional broadcast ratings. For example: 'It is popularly believed that the British TV show *Top Gear* is one of the most watched shows around the world. It is [...] purportedly watched by up to one billion people.' Admittedly the evidence for one billion viewers is shaky, precisely because no ratings system can follow a show's multiplatform career, but nevertheless such global reach is possible. Let *AutoTrader* explain how:

> From Australia to Albania, Kazakhstan to Vietnam, travel abroad and you're never far from the show. It's licensed to 117 countries via BBC World and BBC Prime. [...] More than 1.3 million hotel rooms have access to the show, 37 airlines use it and you can watch it on 29 mobile phone platforms. [...] It's licensed to 48 cruise ships. Before it was wiped off, one Clarkson clip had received almost a million views on You Tube. [...] *Top Gear* magazine's Michael Harvey claims *the show is the planet's most pirated programme*. (Hearn 2007, my emphasis)

Top Gear remains a favored piratical prize. A September 2008 search of YouTube yielded 52,000 *Top Gear* videos, headed by Jeremy Clarkson's test drive of the Ariel Atom, with nearly four million views, 8000 ratings, 20 video responses, and 4000 text comments. A follow-up search in February 2011 yielded 784,000 results for *Top Gear* and more than 8.25 million views for the Ariel Atom clip, with 10,000 comments and 17,500 'likes.' Further discussion will be needed on the extent to which increasing decentralization – *distributed popularity* if you like – seems to entail increasing silliness, or at least dancing, for this may turn out to be an important theoretical or at least taxonomic principle of post-broadcast television.

---

[1] This statistic and that below for *Top Gear* taken from 'List of most-watched television broadcasts' (n.d.).

More Democratic?

But, before that, it is necessary to consider a couple of conceptual para-
doxes: first, what might be thought to be *democratic* about old-style popular
television, given the extreme asymmetry in a representative system between
the corporate, expert makers and the domestic viewers of broadcast communications; and, second, why the declining ratings of mainstream broadcast television might nevertheless entail a more democratic television
system. How on earth did we get from Ena Sharples to Jeremy Clarkson?
The answer lies in the model of the broadcasting relationship that has been
discussed already in this book (see Chapter 1 and Chapter 3). In the heyday
of live, broadcast, expert-made, choice-restricted television, the model is
that of representative representation (both semiotic and political). This is
what has changed. Now, with streamed, downloaded, mobile, and DIY/
DIWO or consumer co-created television, the model is that of productivity.
And to cap it all the increasingly democratic system of viewer choice and
participation seems also to require increasing silliness.

During the heyday of representational broadcasting, popular television
was hailed as democratic, both politically (it reached most people) and
semiotically (it represented ordinary folk on screen). What, for instance,
could be more democratic than *Coronation Street*? It was a popularization
of a radical spirit on the British left of the 1950s that sought authentic
expression for ordinary people's lives, in the spirit of Richard Hoggart's *The
Uses of Literacy* (1957), which included a sympathetic and influential portrait of working-class community in the back-to-back terraces of northern
industrial cities. *Coronation Street* was Richard Hoggart incarnate – the
British architectural critic Reyner Banham dubbed it 'Hoggartsborough'
at the time (1962; see also Whiteley 2003: 94ff; Turner 2003: 41). Richard
Dyer (1981) made the same point, as did Maroula Joannou more recently
(2000: 69).

Not only was *Coronation Street* enormously popular among working
families, it also represented their strongest character traits, sometimes
giving the show an emancipationist edge despite the street brawls and class
sentimentality. It was 'character-led' rather than 'issue-led'; its democratic
spirit lay in the overall representativeness of the drama, not in the demographic proportionality of the characters. Instead of finding a place for each
minority identity or social issue, its writers from Tony Warren onwards
have wanted to share good stories about ordinary life among ordinary

people. That they are consistently good at this has been recognized well beyond the reaches of any remaining working-class district, as for instance when Melvin Bragg's highbrow *South Bank Show* named *Coronation Street* the 'best drama' of 2005 (Henderson 2007: 32–3). *Coronation Street*'s model of democratic inclusion remains typical of broadcasting – not to identify separately but to enfold narratively; not to speak for but to speak to. It wants to encompass its audience and entertain them, but it doesn't want them to do very much in return, except watch.

From *Coronation Street* to *Corrie*

How things have changed! One look at '*Corrie*' on the web will suffice to illustrate how different is the *representative mode* of broadcasting from the *productivity mode* of broadband. Developments in technology, globalization, and consumer activism have challenged the broadcasting model of a nationally bounded, vertically integrated, monopolistic, expert-paradigm television industry dedicated to leisure entertainment. Instead, a new model is emerging, based on social networks, consumer-created content, multiplatform publication, and a semiotic long tail. These changes, wrought in and by media technologies and the uses of Web 2.0, have altered the way that television is produced, distributed, and consumed, even the way that it might be imagined. The medium has transformed from mass to DIY, from 'read-only' to 'read-and-write,' and from network television to social networks – from a regime of representation to one of productivity.

On the net, '*Corrie*' is quite a different animal from *Coronation Street*. For a start, it becomes what consumers want it to be, and, beyond that, the distinction between producer and consumer becomes very uncertain. So, for example, since 1999 Corrie.net has been 'a website *by* Coronation Street fans *for* Coronation Street fans'; its pages of profiles and updates are 'the work of many Coronation Street fans from all over the world.' It is distinct from the show's 'official' ITV website although it credits people from the production company. Corrie.net is information-rich and archival, a classic user co-created site. However, it is much less 'consumerist' than the show's own site.

Meanwhile, *Corrie Blog* is produced by Shiny Media, a commercial stable of technology, fashion, and lifestyle blogs. *Corrie Blog* is edited by Sue Haasler, herself a successful romance author. On the day I visited, she had posted a news item about a new *Coronation Street* scriptwriter, which prompted the following exchange of comments:

> I'd seriously love to write for Corrie. That's what i plan on doing when i am older. After completing my A levels i plan to head on up to Manchester uni and hopefully get a job doing anything at Corrie, just so i have my foot in the door. It's my dream :) *Posted by: clare*
>
> Clare – Good luck with your plans! It would be fantastic if you became a Corrie writer. Hope you achieve your ambitions. [Sue H] *Posted by: Sue*
>
> Thank you very much Sue, it's much appreciated. *Posted by: Clare* (Hassler 2008)

Although this is a commercial site, Sue Haasler responds directly to the wishful thinking of young, hopeful Clare. A quick Google search perhaps reveals why – fellow-feeling:

> Sue Haasler was born and brought up in Co. Durham and studied English Literature & Linguistics at Liverpool University. After graduating she moved to London and worked for three years as a residential social worker. (Johnson n.d.)

This bio is one of the success stories listed on the site of a professional authors' advice service, which seems to have assisted Haasler towards her own debut as a published author. This string of links is typical of what any internet search exposes: a *social network* of both fans and professionals, readers and authors, newbies and experts; people who are more than willing to share their stories with each other, using '*Corrie*' literally as a pretext for social networking in the name of what used to be called the 'republic of letters.' Over on YouTube, '*Corrie*' blossoms. Thousands of clips have been posted, in which fans classify 'The Street' according to their own tastes and interests, whether these are prompted by the show (vintage episodes, favorite scenes) or by external criteria ('Gay Coronation Street,' 'Coronation Street Babes Past & Present'). Spoofs abound, both DIY and pirated professional (e.g. Victoria Wood as Ena Sharples). Comments and tribute videos continue the conversation and extend the network.

There is no need to extend these examples further. The point is that 'television' online takes on the open and productive characteristics of the internet while maintaining intricate relations with its broadcast form and audience. There is one issue that should be mentioned, however, and that is that episodes of *Coronation Street* are highly protected properties, especially if you are using a computer located outside the UK. The clips available to UK viewers on the official site won't play; lawyers crawl across YouTube issuing take-down orders; you can't get whole episodes through torrent streaming. From the corporate perspective, knowledge shared is knowledge lost, so 'Corrie' is a treated by *Coronation Street*'s owners as a virus to be controlled, Viacom-style, not a mode of propagation to be encouraged, viral-style.

More Democratic . . . and Sillier?

Jonathan Gray, Jeffrey Jones, and Ethan Thompson introduce their book on *Satire TV* (2009: 12) by observing the 'unique ability of satire TV to speak truth to power,' and not only in the Anglophone countries – they cite examples from China and Iraq too. They conclude:

> Gradually satire TV has crept up on the news as one of the pre-eminent genres used to understand varied political realities, rendering it an ideal entry point for a study of politics, audiences, television, comedy, entertainment, and citizenship in the early twenty-first century. (Gray, Jones, and Thompson 2009: 47)

Now all this may be true – and it constitutes a substantial claim on behalf of 'damn funny' television (46) – but turning audiences into activists requires something stronger than old-style US network television. Shows such as *The Colbert Report* and *The Daily Show with Jon Stewart* know from the outset that the polity is partisan, the audience is fragmented, and the platforms have proliferated. They thrive on subscription television (Comedy Central); they rely on viral propagation (clips on YouTube, fansites such as ColbertNation);[2] and they relish a mainstream adversary, trading (mercilessly) on the failings of CNN and Fox News.

The success of 'satire television' is a measure of the extent of popular disaffection with both mainstream politics and mainstream television – political and semiotic representation alike. But such shows are only the tip of the iceberg. The extension of television's productive and distributive base via the internet reveals infinite demand for an alternative to the regime of

---

[2] http://www.colbertnation.com.

representation. The demand is for 'just anyone' if not everyone to do it themselves (or with others). Both DIY and DIWO give the population formerly known as the audience something to do; they make real what was meant to be a contradiction in terms – the 'productive consumer.'

However, concomitantly, it seems, the more productive 'we' get, the sillier we become. Elections are now marked not only by online citizen journalism (Bruns 2008: 69–99) but also by home-made spoofs, satire, parody, and take-offs, some of which out-rate the official campaigns, for instance Hugh Atkin in Australia and Obama Girl in the US (see Chapter 3). The collapse of long-held (but always wobbly) distinctions between public and private life, power and entertainment, politics and celebrity, television and viral video was spectacularly evidenced by the entry of Paris Hilton into the 2008 US Presidential Campaign. Posted on the Funny or Die site,[3] her reply to a negative comment by John McCain soon attracted over seven million views, 2000 responses, and 500 favorites. Tagged as both 'political ad, president' and 'hot swim suit photo,' the uncanny attraction of the parody was that, while it was knowing, sly, and funny, Paris' energy platform was also quite plausible: as a response by 'More Cowbell Girl' put it, 'She's right, though. The offshore drilling thing? Totally hot. Anyway, it's just funny that she's kinda right.'

Although the official presidential nominees did not take up the Paris challenge directly, it should be noted that much of Barack Obama's early appeal was credited to his easy competence in the protocols of online DIY television. For instance, in a video posted to 'Barack TV' on YouTube in June 2007, Senator Obama is taped on a handheld camera, in an informal setting with available light, talking directly and apparently unscripted to the camera. Instead of telling viewers what he thinks and wants, he appeals to viewers to 'send us your stories' and to share stories about ordinary people making a difference. Obama uses both the aesthetics and the participatory ethic of Web 2.0 to reach those who have 'turned away' from politics as usual.[4]

---

[3]   http://www.funnyordie.com.

[4]   The 'send us your stories' video is no longer accessible (and 'Barack TV' changed to 'barackobamadotcom' for 2012), but was reported in a blog news item entitled 'Obama groupies, image control and the veracity of viral video':

Obama's team is making its own YouTube play this week. A video featuring him talking into the camera for two minutes and asking for volunteers to send in recordings of their work was also one of the top-watched videos Thursday. 'Send us your

How many answered the call is unknown. But there were certainly competing attractions. When silly is 'hot,' the serious players get up and dance. One of the most dynamic and popular features of YouTube is dancing, from the original girls-in-the-bedroom miming to favorite songs, such as the classic 'Hey clip' (Tasha 2005), with more than 30 million views, to more elaborate dance competitions. These have become so popular that they have attracted the participation of celebrities. A good example is Miley Cyrus' M&M Cru – responsible for 'the biggest dance battle in YouTube history [...] an onslaught of videos packed with celebrity cameos, MTV parodies and more "WTF!?" moments than you can shake a tail feather at' (Watercutter 2008; see also LaMissDookie 2008). This was a competitive exchange of dance videos between serious celebrities: 'Pop wunderkind Miley Cyrus and the director and star [Adam Sevani] of *Step Up 2: The Streets* have officially taken the art of the YouTube smackdown to a whole other level' (Watercutter 2008). No matter that Miley and Adam were 15 and 16 at the time, these videos were 'hot,' good enough to attract the same number of viewers as *Big Brother* and CNN over on regular television – five to six million hits each and many thousands of comments. Naturally the whole thing ended up on primetime television as the 'dance-off' was decided at the MTV Teen Choice awards, which Miley Cyrus hosted (and won). Here was cyberdemocracy in full 'party' mode, all difference between user and celebrity erased and everyone enjoying both making and watching the show. Or, as Angela Watercutter (2008) put it, 'The sheer silliness of this exercise (and its overuse of the concept of stepping things up) notwithstanding, what say you?'

What Say You?

As television studies chases DIY television into its participatory reaches, will it too get silly? Academic and popular knowledge have always been uneasy in each other's company – and not just since Ratemyprofessors.com

stories,' Obama says on the video. 'And what we hope to do is over the next several months to stitch together these stories to illuminate for the entire country how this next generation wants to grab the baton and lead us forward.' (http://technology.wm-loto.com/?p=57878).

See also http://ezinearticles.com/?Barack-Obamas-Website-is-Web-2.0-at-Its-Best&id=1435744.

(ultimately owned by Viacom) has allowed students to check whether their teachers are 'helpful' as well as 'hot,' thereby integrating academic with popular culture to the discomfort of many professors.[5]

So what *does* academic expertise look like when it is 'rendered' in and as popular culture? This was a founding theme of *Coronation Street* itself. One of the original characters created by Tony Warren represented none other than Richard Hoggart (Joannou 2000: 69). Amazingly, Ken Barlow (Bill Roache) remained (at the time of writing) the only character still in the show from its first episode. Like Hoggart, Ken was a 'scholarship boy' who had gone to university, and on his return to the Street retained an uneasy ambiguity in his relationship with working-class culture. Was this an opportunity for decades of *cultural studies* on primetime soap? Not likely; but it did provide 'representative' dramatic conflict:

> In the soap's early years, Ken was frequently presented as resenting what he saw as the anti-intellectual, repressed climate around him. A scathing article he wrote for a newspaper led to clashes with his father Frank and a Rovers punch-up with Len Fairclough. ('Ken Barlow' n.d.)

The silly thing is that, although Ken Barlow was reputedly one of the most boring characters on the serial (actor Bill Roache once successfully sued the *Sun* for suggesting this), his character became one of the Street's most successful lovers. Wikipedia reports that since 1960 'he has been married four times, widowed twice, and divorced once, and has had 27 girlfriends.' So perhaps he was 'hot' after all. However, the conflict between popular experience and formal knowledge was never resolved on *Coronation Street* – Ken subsided into cardiganed obscurity, while Hoggart's intellectual 'project' for working-class culture was forgotten, except in universities. The question for television scholars, now, is how to engage with television in order to bring out the strengths in both academic and popular knowledge (without brawling in the pub), finding ways to share it across the democratic vistas of participatory productivity.

---

[5] I'm not rated on ratemyprofessors.com, but Henry Jenkins is (albeit for his MIT position, not the more recent USC one): see http://www.ratemyprofessors.com/ShowRatings.jsp?tid= 225676.

Implications for Media Studies

After a quiet period when everyone wanted to talk about new media, television studies is certainly resurgent; the quality, boldness, and interest of many new books are remarkable. Perhaps like cinema studies it will flower most luxuriantly just after the medium to which it is attached has ceased to be popular on the mass scale. At the same time, television studies has begun to taxonomize itself, with ever narrower specialisms. It seems at last to be emerging into a formal order as a discipline in its own right. However, this is no time for coalescence into orthodoxy, because television studies is subject to the same forces of change that beset its object of study. In television evolution some species are headed for extinction (e.g. network television, couch potatoes), some look forward to open futures (e.g. social network markets, distributed expertise), and, as old antagonisms decay (e.g. cultural versus scientific approaches), new political struggles emerge (e.g. corporate digital rights management and copyright-enforcement versus knowledge-sharing systems). The changes that affect television also have an impact on television studies. Only recently established and still a contested field, television studies is already being forced to recast some basic assumptions, metaphors, and methods. It needs to shift from explanations based on how content is based on structures of power to ones based on the agents, mechanics, and dynamics of change, in which 'content' is no longer the preserve of professionals but distributed throughout the system. Such a shift brings into sharp focus the most important innovation in television as the television industry migrates out of the boardroom and the television experience migrates out of the sitting room – the *democratization of productivity*.

The problem faced by television studies is not simply one of how to account for distributed expertise among the general population. Such an approach would only confine it further within the regime of representation, where the purpose of scholarship is to encompass the whole object of study and to represent it in knowledge. Rather, the problem is how to take the risk of releasing television studies itself into the evolving system of networked productivity, using the affordances of Web 2.0 in ways that were not available in the broadcast environment. Integrating scholarly and 'vernacular' knowledge systems is itself productive and can lead to new forms of professional expertise (e.g. 'redactional' or editing skills, quality assessment and regulatory tests, coordination of team or crowd-sourced initiatives), just as amateur efforts like the 'Hey clip' get recoded into M&M Cru's dance-off. But, as television studies chases DIY television into its participatory reaches, won't it too get silly? Can it survive the participatory turn? We may look pretty silly for a while, but that's the challenge: academic expertise will have to learn some nifty new steps if it doesn't want to end up looking like an Ena Sharples trying to do a Miley Cyrus.

6

Silly Citizenship

A man without a gun is a subject. A man with a gun is a citizen.
(Bumper sticker in Columbia, MI, cited in Pasley 1999: 15)

Citizenship: Child's Play?

'Citizenship' is a term of *association* among *strangers*. Access to it involves contested identities and symbolic meanings; differing power relations and strategies of inclusion, exclusion, and action; and unequal room for maneuver or productivity in the *uses* of citizenship for any given group or individual. In a discussion of children's rights and citizenship in Brazil, Leticia Veloso has put it this way:

> For some, citizenship and the forms of access to it are still determined by their marginalized, stratified, and racialized subject position. For others, responsible, active, participating, and 'radical democratic' citizenship can take place only in the context of the reproduction of privilege. [...] What remains to be seen is to what extent either group will be able to take action to counter this predicament. (2008: 56)

That question is a good one with which to launch a consideration of the evolution of contemporary citizenship. It makes clear that the chances for and experience of citizenship are (systematically) not equal for all, but it goes on to draw our attention to the *actions* taken by different groups to

Digital Futures for Cultural and Media Studies, First Edition. John Hartley.
© 2012 John Wiley & Sons, Ltd. Published 2012 by John Wiley & Sons, Ltd.

deal with their circumstances, and thence to the prospects for integrated access to and practice of citizenship for all. Veloso's focus on children is also important, for children are (by definition) *not* citizens . . . and yet they must *become* citizens if the reproduction of the system is to continue.

Thus, the actual process of citizenship-formation is 'carried' by children who – individually, collectively, and differentially – *produce* citizenship in their actions, forms of association, and thence identities. Children are thus at one and the same time both the least important component of institutionalized citizenship, since they remain non-citizens, and its most important 'subjects,' since they necessarily and continuously *constitute the practice of citizenship formation.* And, because they undertake that practice 'insensibly' (to use an eighteenth-century term favored by Edward Gibbon (1776–1788), expressing the unthinking relation between subjects and historical change), children are prime agents of change for citizenship, to the extent that their unconsidered actions and unselfconscious association may model new modes of citizenship.

The extension of 'new media,' including computer-based social networks, mobile telephony, and globally dispersed entertainment formats into the space and time of childhood has enabled children's discursive actions and choices to become 'relatively autonomous' (as the Althusserians would have put it). Certainly children are freer than via previous media technologies from surveillance and control by parental or other authoritative institutions. But at the same time their actions, choices, and discursive interactions are now objectively trackable, via clickstream data, instant messaging systems, internet forums, and the like. Thus, it is now unprecedentedly possible to isolate and observe the cultural practice of 'association among strangers' in relation to children's own actions as a 'class,' something that has attracted considerable attention from latter-day child savers (Platt 2009 [1969]) and 'correction and protection' activists (for whom 'citizenship' means making sure that children are *excluded from* online participation)[1] but not so much from those interested in the *propagation of* civic discourse. Towards the end of this chapter, I plan to show how certain 'under-age' mischief may give us a glimpse of citizenship-formation 'on the fly' – in the apparently unlikely context of spoofs, silliness, and the dance-off. I argue that such antics provide an important lesson for citizenship *theory*, which has focused too much on citizenship as

---

[1]   See 'Children's Internet Protection Act' (n.d.) and 'Child Online Protection Act' (n.d.) on Wikipedia, and see Flynn (2009) for Australian developments.

a static or definable condition, frequently understood as universal, when in fact it should be understood as a *relational identity*, inconstant, dynamic, and evolving.

In order to demonstrate my point, a short history of citizenship is in order – in which, it will be noted, children apparently play no part. It is intended to demonstrate not only historical shifts in the relationship between individuals and the state but also the extent to which citizenship is a *discursive practice*, at the heart of which is the continually challenging problem of how to reconcile self and stranger in modern associated life, a problem that resolves itself into the question of what ordinary people (as opposed to governing elites) can and do use for the purposes of *self-representation* within technologically enabled *social networks*. Here is where silliness – and children – prove to be more important than social theory has tended to admit.

History or Science?

The term 'citizenship' has come a long way since its first recorded use in English in 1611, when it translated an unremarkable French word: '*Citoyennerie*, a Citizenship, the freedome of a Citie' (*Oxford English Dictionary*). It has since lost any necessary reference to cities, although Holston and Appadurai (1996) argue for the restoration of the city's analytical primacy. But in order to achieve *informational* 'freedome,' the concept had to break free of real cities. In modern disciplinary knowledge systems, abstract, explicit knowledge displaces embodied, tacit know-how. In this context, 'citizenship' achieved the status of a concept only once it became an abstraction. Only then could it contribute to the growth of knowledge. Hence it is effectively a nineteenth-century invention, required by the rapidly expanding modern knowledge system (Wallerstein 2001: 66ff.) to describe the equally rapidly expanding modern polity, as the nation state and colonial empire took shape. Having escaped the ground of actual cities into the rarefied air of abstract metaphor, citizenship could become – like many professors of communication – a discursive 'frequent flyer.' It commutes around different disciplinary domains, with occasional stopovers in ordinary language. Like Raymond Williams' original 'keywords' (1976), it is inevitably accompanied by historical and conceptual baggage (see Ong 1999; Isin and Turner 2002, Barnett 2003: 81ff.), which, despite the long-haul process of abstraction, citizenship continues to lug around.

Part of that history is disciplinary. Thus, citizenship brings with it from political science and history a focus on the relations between a state and the individual, with connotations of mutual status: rights, duties, conduct, allegiance, obligation, powers, and protection. In the study of communication, on the other hand, there has been a greater emphasis on the identity of the citizen within cultural practices and sense-making systems. But, precisely because it is a migrant term, 'citizenship' cannot choose between *relational status* (mutual obligations) and *individual identity* (personal attributes) but holds these two conceptually distinct features in tension. The result is that the term can never quite escape from contextual contingency (past tense, specific place, documented usage) to become a scientific concept (present tense, generalizable, definitional). At the same time, it is never so completely captured by history that it loses its abstract, universalizing potential. That is what is interesting about it: 'citizenship' applies to whole populations, but who is included or excluded is contentious and unsettled, and thus the term *evolves*.

'Citizenship' carries with it an implied comparison with a constitutional predecessor, the feudal 'subject' (where 'subject' literally meant subjection to the will of a monarch or liege). I perhaps say 'predecessor' because I was born a subject but am now a citizen, not only as a migrant but also because citizenship law has been amended over decades of decolonization. But in fact these two constitutional types have co-existed uneasily since the eighteenth century. They clashed most significantly when the American and French Revolutions installed the modern citizen, armed with '*droits de l'Homme et du citoyen*,' as the founding agent of the constitution. These 'rights of Man and citizen' were designed to *usurp* the place of the feudal monarch, transferring *sovereignty* to 'the people' – even though *the state* retained the power to decide who among those people counted as citizens.

Thus, citizenship is at heart a combative (ideological, mythologizing) term, with a long history of bloodshed, struggle, resistance, hope, fear, and terror caught up in its train, as captured in the epigraph to this chapter. Nevertheless, it is also a term that has been recruited to the cause of science, and definitional accuracy and generalizable universality have been sought. As a result, wherever it is deployed, the concept retains part of its modernizing energy, *requiring* citizens to adopt the 'common substantive purpose' of the state, be that purpose profit, salvation, progress, or racial domination (Oakeshott 1975: 114, 319). Citizenship is therefore one of those products of Enlightenment philosophy that proved exorbitant in its reach because of its proponents' desire to extend the contingent struggle of a given place and time to convert the whole of humanity for all time – whether they liked it or not – into 'free' subjects with 'universal' rights.

This *purposive* citizenship is what Michael Oakeshott calls an 'enterprise association.' The 'sovereign' citizen is *perforce* an agent of the 'common substantive purpose' of the state. This is in contrast with a more skeptical 'civil association' that limits the role of the state to the administration of the rule of law among consenting subjects; an ideal type of '*civitas*' not (yet) fully achieved (Oakeshott 1975: 131).

Emanating from the Enlightenment, exported by the American War of Independence and Napoleonic Wars, and disseminated, sometimes by force, to many other modernizing polities in national struggles over the succeeding centuries, citizenship remains contentious in the very act of seeking normative neutrality. Like so many other attributes of modernity, it manages to be democratic and imperial, scientific and political, all at once. The very idea of it is refuted in some jurisdictions; for example, in theocratic states such as Iran and Saudi Arabia where sovereignty is said to reside in the deity not the citizen; in Party-controlled states such as China, which recognize 'nationality' not 'citizenship'; and in some philosophies, such as Marxism and feminism, where subjectivity is determined by class or identity not ethno-territorial descent.

Thus, the term cannot simply be adopted in the communication sciences as a defined attribute of either civic relationship or individual identity. Nor can the relationships among citizens or between them and the state be taken for granted. There is no essence. Indeed, the history of the term's absorption into social science is itself a matter for analysis, because historical specificity and political force over-determine abstract categorization and neutral description. In other words, the capture of citizenship by science is itself a political or governmental act (Foucault 1984; Barnett 2003: 81–107). The *production* of a seemingly neutral category properly belongs to the *object of study* – that is, 'regimes of knowledge' in the administration of populations rather than to the *framework of explanation*. It may therefore be no accident that some of the best recent work on cities and citizenship has come from ethnographic approaches rather than from political science or liberal philosophy as such.

In practice, this means that 'citizenship' has no positive content that is not tied to an ideologically driven 'common substantive purpose' and that it has no boundaries that are not exclusionary. It may bring with it a connotative word-cloud, bringing to mind expectations of ethno-territorial descent and rights of abode; political representation and electoral rights; military or civic service obligations; and submission to specific national taxation and legal codes. But none of these is *essential*. Instead, during the career of modernity, the concept of citizenship has been successively adapted and extended to cover more and emergent 'relational identities.'

The 'Good Citizen'

In his account of the American 'good citizen,' Michael Schudson (1999) combines historical with categorical analysis. He recounts the vicissitudes of citizenship since the foundation of the Republic and uses that history to produce a dynamic typology of citizenship, thus:

- *Patrician* – In and following the colonial period, citizenship was expressed through male property-owners – the only electors – and thus formed part of the influence and patronage wielded by leading families, to whom others (non-citizens) needed to show deference. Thus, the US was founded not on a democratic but a patrician notion of citizenship.
- *Partisan* – During the nineteenth century, political partisanship coalesced into party-political competition, where citizenship was expressed through allegiance to parties, which continued elite control of politics even as they diffused political influence out to popular associations. The result was graft plus theatre: party politics combined venal competition for power (jobs, money, and influence) with the mobilization of mass support through techniques of showmanship, spectacle, and mediated entertainment, seeking a fervently partisan citizen. Although the partisan party system did recruit a mass voting public into (periodic) political activism, there arose a pressing reason for 'getting rid of the massive institutionalized venality and racial and sexual exclusionism that characterized nineteenth-century party politics,' as Jeffrey Pasley (1999: 2) argues: 'Little of significance would ever have been done to address the most pressing moral issue in American life, slavery, had that matter been left strictly to the party system.'
- *Informed* – According to Schudson, between the 1880s and 1920s there emerged a third type, the 'informed citizen,' whereby citizenship is expressed as an individualized, private, rational calculus, based on objective information conveyed by a dispassionate press to a reading public that is also the Republic. The 'informed citizen' was an ideal type,

invented by elite observers who despaired of the partisan system. In fact, actual voter turnout decreased compared with the showbiz and bribery of the previous phase. And, a surprisingly high proportion of citizens remained stubbornly *uninformed*, as the new science of public opinion rapidly discovered. Thus a situation emerged where *governance* was increasingly the domain of expert, specialist professional occupations, including objective journalism and public-opinion science, while many *citizens* were increasingly detached from daily participation in the deliberative process. The 'informed citizen' turned out to be a ruse to power for expert knowledge professionals, leading to the 'paradox' of a functioning democracy with seemingly couldn't-care-less citizens (Delli Carpini 2000: 548), whose 'behavior' was increasingly seen as non-rational and manipulatable, subject to emotional influences. These in turn could be rendered explicit ('scientific') by the psy-complex disciplines, and thence 'managed' (manipulated) for both political and commercial ends by the communication sciences.

- *Rights* – Citizenship evolved once again, according to Schudson, in a 'rights revolution,' associated with the new social movements of the 1960s. Civil rights, the peace movement, feminism, ecological activism, and identity politics (and pop culture) coalesced into countercultural pressure for change. Citizenship rights were claimed by individuals in the name of identity.

Given strong privatizing forces in government and the economy since the 1980s, an unforeseen consequence of the 'citizenship of rights' is the danger that multiple competing identity groups will fragment the nation. To counter this tendency, and also to bridge the gap between private citizens and public experts, Schudson proposes *monitorial citizenship*, where individuals are 'poised for action' (199: 311–12). In the age of the internet, Schudson wants to recruit the networked 'monitorial' citizen (as manifest in the blogosphere, for instance) to the public cause: 'we should have in view plausible aims that integrate citizenry competence with specialized expert resources.'

Evolving Citizenship

Schudson's evolving 'good citizen' remains a *national* figure, albeit from an unusually influential nation. An earlier theorist who sought to convert national history into general social theory was T. H. Marshall (1963). Marshall was looking for *sociological* generalities to identify what constitutes a complex but analyzable 'social system.' In a Europe of post-World War II reconstruction and Cold War ideological stand-off, his purpose was also to propose an accommodation between capitalistic (individualist citizenship) and socialistic (collectivist class) frameworks of explanation, at a time when these were at political and industrial as well as theoretical loggerheads, in order to demonstrate that capitalist enterprise might be compatible with social policy (Marshall 1963; Bulmer and Rees 1996).

Marshall proposed three successive stages of modern citizenship:

- *Civic* – the 'rights of man' and of the Enlightenment: personal liberty, freedom of speech, property rights, access to justice (rights claimed in the courts).
- *Political* – the right of elective representation, the vote, and the right to hold public office (rights claimed in representative decision-making bodies).
- *Social* – the 'welfare state,' where education, employment, and welfare benefits are *rights of citizenship* rather than private or economic arrangements at the level of the family or firm (rights claimed through social services and schools) (Marshall 1963; see also Qvortrup 2004: 8–10).

Marshall's citizenship may be seen as European, just as Schudson's is American. Certainly, a theory based on *social* rights was unlikely to have evolved in the US, where free-market policies led to a 'denuded and unprestigious conception of social citizenship' (Rees 1996: 14); that is, not Marshall's sonorous 'right to share to the full in social heritage and to live the life of a civilised being according to the standards prevailing in society' (1963: 72), but, instead, *food stamps.* Nevertheless, as the US still struggles with the politics of social citizenship, for instance through healthcare reform, employment rights after the global financial crisis, and the welfare rights of immigrant workers, it is clear that the category applies more widely than to the national context of its first articulation.

Another criticism of Marshall's schema is that it is progressivist, with a prescriptive, teleological ambition; a Whiggish view of history; and patrician, top-down expectations of reform. It under-emphasizes the extent to which each step 'forward' was resisted, denied, or compromised, and the very different historical experience of those whose struggle for full citizenship continues. But, for exactly these reasons, Marshall's normative model has political as well as conceptual value. It relies on – and also provokes – what would later be called the 'principle of democratic equivalence' (Laclau and Mouffe 2001 [1985]: 183–5), in which claims established as rights by one group (urban, white, working, heterosexual men) could be leveraged by the concerted action of unenfranchized others (women, people of color, and other groups) for their own emancipationist claims. Of course, even in 'welfare states,' social citizenship is susceptible to attempted roll-back (notably under Reaganism-Thatcherism). Nevertheless, it has proven resilient, if unevenly distributed, over two long generations, as a practical compromise between liberal-capitalist free-market wealth-creation values and social-democratic public-culture communitarian values.

Cultural Citizenship

Since Marshall, there have been numerous candidates for additional categories. Among others, Toby Miller proposes *cultural citizenship* ('the right to know and speak'), which he adds to political citizenship ('the right to reside and vote') and economic citizenship ('the right to work and prosper') (2006: 35).

In fact, 'cultural citizenship' is both an extension of and a challenge to Marshall's tripartite schema. Extending citizenship from public participation to social entitlements enjoyed in the family (in private) exposes the concept to challenge by its traditional opposite – the *consumer*. Here things get conceptually messy. Social theory has persistently valorized the difference between 'public' and 'private' domains: public institutions versus private markets, collective action versus individualism, emancipation versus exploitation. However, this ingrained opposition misses the everyday fact that most people in affluent societies experience themselves as citizens and consumers, publics and audiences, workers and traders, all at once. Further, it is now possible to express relational and identity associations, and to take actions and participate in collective decisions, through global commercial consumer culture. So, citizenship *as* consumption is startling to social theory but lived by millions.

To make things even messier, the emergent notion of 'cultural citizenship' can refer to different phenomena. First, overlapping Schudson's 'citizenship of rights,' it refers to claims made under the banner of 'identity politics' relating to (among others):

- Age groups, including children (Jans 2004) and 'seniors';
- Class and subculture;
- Disability (Morris 2005);
- Gender;
- Indigenous peoples (e.g. Nunavut);[2]
- Postcolonialism and multiculturalism;
- Race and ethnicity;
- Sexual orientation (Walker 1998); and
- Subnational minorities (e.g. Wales; see Drakeford et al. 2009) and micronations.[3]

A second type of 'cultural citizenship' is based less on descent or corporeal identity than on mediated affiliation and voluntarist (choice-based) communities, or what Michael Warner (2005) calls 'discourse publics.' Here the model might be the spectacular subcultures that featured so prominently in early cultural studies, where communities of affect, affiliation, place, and taste gave rise to full-time 'lifestyles.' These displayed strong semiotic markers of difference ('style') in youth subcultures (e.g. Ted, Mod, Punk, Goth), graduating to alternative food, housing, and family arrangements among countercultural experimental societies (e.g. hippies, new-age and religious cults and communes, eco-citizens). Such movements sometimes gain quasi-citizenship status (e.g. Freetown Christiania in Copenhagen), but they also interact vigorously with mainstream taste and commercial fashions. This type of cultural citizenship can just as easily be expressed in *markets* as in 'intentional communities' or 'counterpublics' (Warner 2005). Thus, cultural citizenship – the expression of relational identity – is mainstreamed via style, media, and markets.

---

[2] See http://www.gov.nu.ca/en/Home.aspx for further information.

[3] The Wikipedia entry on micronations makes it clear that the internet, social networks, and citizenship are inextricably interlinked: 'The advent of the Internet provided the means for the creation of many new micronations, whose members are scattered all over the world and interact mostly by electronic means. The difference between such Internet micronations, other kinds of social networking groups, and role playing games is often hard to define' ('Micronation' n.d.).

Media Citizenship

The pursuit of self-organizing, reflexive, common purpose among voluntary co-subjects, who learn about each other and about the state of play of their interests through the media, has led some commentators, myself included, to posit the emergence of *media citizenship* (Hartley 1996: 57–72; 1999: 162–5). This is based on the *use* of popular media by lay audiences for identity formation, associative relations, and even for periodic actions that reverse 'consumer demand' from a corporate strategy to a popular movement. The very people who have most keenly felt excluded from classic citizenship – groups who uncannily reproduce the Classical exclusion of women, slaves (read: workers), strangers (immigrants and ethnic others), and minors (children) – are most likely to engage in 'citizenship of media.'

These 'active audiences' and fans use leisure entertainment to inform themselves and to connect with co-subjects. They learn civic virtues (neighborly comportment and care for the community) from *Clueless* or *Twilight*. Civic engagement is *modeled* in the competitive and plebiscitary elements of reality television (Hartley 2008: 126–60). In the very process of consumption of commercial pop culture, 'citizens of media' also act as *producers* of 'imagined communities' – and real associations – that cut across formal citizenship. Despite the corporate provenance of the platform, 'media citizenship' is bottom-up, self-organizing, voluntarist, tolerant of diversity, and also a good deal more fun for participants than the modernist minimalism of the Habermasian public sphere. Despite the categorical messiness, people are not fazed by entertainment and comedy formats alongside informative and decision-making ones – and in this they have Athenian antecedents.

Productive Citizens

The era of the internet has made the extension of citizenship into the market more visible, and also given a technological boost to the phenomenon of *consumer productivity*. This seeming contradiction in terms (if you're a modernist) fits only awkwardly into available causal models that confine *productivity* to capitalist firms and their army of experts. In such powerful company, the informal use by private citizens of systems that they don't own, to make themselves up as they go along and to connect with like-purposed others, probably seems inconsequential. But now the analytic lens has refocused. The growth of digital media networks has prompted both critical and corporate attention to consumer productivity (Uricchio 2004; Jenkins 2006; Burgess and Green 2009).

There is a civic element to this. Digital connectivity evolved outside of the market, is driven by user-led innovation, and retains communitarian values. These remain important, albeit contested, even as the system matures from generative emergence to marketized adoption and retention (Zittrain 2008). Despite the pitfalls, consumer productivity can be modeled on the *growth of knowledge* (Beinhocker 2006), in a process that joins the anthropological ubiquity of cultural systems such as language, storytelling, and social networking with the technological scalability of computer-based connectivity and global media. That combination of population-wide participation with technological productivity allows *everyone in the system* – not just professional experts and competitive elites – to contribute to the generation of new meanings, new systems, and ideas. This is what Henry Jenkins (2006) calls 'participatory culture,' where users co-create content and propagate 'spreadable media' (Jenkins 2009). I call it 'DIY citizenship' (Hartley 1999: 179), borrowing the term from 'DIY (do it yourself) culture,' where citizenship was playfully defined by George McKay (1998: 37) as 'the right to protest and the right to dance.' DIY culture of the 1990s had a strongly analogue, 'lo-fi' (even 'countryside') feel to it, as perhaps the last pre-internet countercultural social-network movement. By that token, it demonstrates once again that the 'active audience' of media citizenship was just that, long before it migrated to the Net.

Even so, DIY activists were early adopters of the internet, soon resulting in the concept of 'DIWO' (do it with others):

> *DIWO* means exploring the potential to share visions, resources and agency, through collaboration and negotiation, across physical and virtual networks – maintaining a critical consciousness and hopefully, somehow having a decent life at the same time. (Catlow and Garrett 2007: 27–8)

DIY/DIWO *citizenship* is more individuated and privatized than previous types, because it is driven by voluntarist choices and affiliations, but at the same time it has an activist and communitarian ethic, where 'knowledge shared is knowledge gained.' It is a 'connect–collaborate–create' model of 'contributory' citizenship, with gift-economy characteristics. It has yet to establish effective legal recognition, although the Creative Commons copyright licensing movement is a weathervane for possibilities in this direction.[4] However, precisely because of its innovative, future-modeling characteristics – it is emergent, bottom-up, self-organizing, ephemeral, and reliant upon technological platforms and affordances that are typically owned by established corporations with their own agendas – DIY citizenship is not protected in legislation or even custom, and is easily corrupted, manipulated, rescinded, or ignored.

Silly Citizenship

As the internet has prospered, an important change has been recorded in the *representative status* of popular media. Throughout the twentieth century, the press, cinema, radio, and television operated as if their audiences were coterminous with 'the nation.' The 'mass' media felt they could speak both *to* and *for* the entire citizenry, and media theory followed suit. But that long-assumed status can no longer be claimed. Declining ratings and multiplying platforms mean that the audience – 'the public' – is revealed as fragmented, diverse, and internally conflicted. Thus, 'media citizenship' is changing from *representative* status to the more modest but active status of *productivity*, where much smaller groups can self-organize and self-represent, and act both culturally and politically, without bearing the weight of 'standing for' the whole society. As a result, 'DIY citizenship' is arguably becoming *more democratic* as individual media (content platforms) become *less popular*.

But, at the same time, mediated citizenship seems to be getting *sillier*. This can be observed in both mainstream media and in DIY/DIWO activism. In mainstream media the rise of 'satire TV' (Gray, Jones, and Thompson 2009), notably *The Daily Show* and *Colbert Report*, has propelled comedy, send-ups, and spoofs to the centre of the political process. Comedy is becoming a more trusted source of political information for the 'monitorial' citizen than partisan commentators in 'mainstream' news. For example, during 2009, a far-right campaign by so-called 'birthers' sought to cast doubt on the US citizenship of Barack Obama – thus challenging his right to be president. Despite its clear partisan origins and the fact that it had been widely debunked, the story persisted in various mainstream news

---

[4] See http://creativecommons.org/about/history and http://www.creativecommons.org.au.

outlets (Stelter 2009). CNN's Lou Dobbs pushed it even after it had been refuted on his own show.[5] The whole sorry saga was ridiculed on John Stewart's *Daily Show* (July 22, 2009),[6] which in turn became part of the news coverage (*The Week* July 23, 2009).[7] In this way, the role of 'wise counselor' defaults to 'the fool' – as it has in Western drama from Aristophanes to Shakespeare. Comedy is the go-to source for civic understanding.

The collapse of industrial-era distinctions between public and private life, power and entertainment, politics and celebrity, television and viral video, are never more in evidence than at election time. Here DIY/DIWO activism comes into its own. Elections are marked by homemade spoofs, parody, and send-ups, some of which out-rate official campaigns and themselves become the news. A good example was Hugh Atkin's (2007) amateur spoof for the 2007 election in Australia (see Chapter 3). Silly citizenship was also well to the fore in the 2008 US presidential campaign (see Kurtzman 2008). Here it connected with 'the right to dance.'

One of the most dynamic and popular features of YouTube is dancing, from teenage amateurs covering favorite songs, such as the classic 'Hey clip' (Tasha 2005), to more elaborate dance competitions that feature professionals and celebrities. Fifteen-year-old Miley Cyrus, for instance, won the 2008 MTV Teen Choice Award with her 'M&M Cru' dance-off (see Chapter 5). But 'defeated' opponent Jon M. Chu, director of *Step Up 2: The Streets*, immediately went one better, taking the dance-off into politics with his 'Official Rep. vs Dem. Dance Off!!' where the 'Obaminators' battled the 'McCainiacs' (Jonmchu 2008). This was answered by Minimoviechannel's (2008) brilliant 'Obama and McCain – Dance Off,' attracting multi-million viewers.

This kind of silly citizenship has become part of the mediated political landscape, with both professional and amateur creativity expended in the

---

[5] Story by Ruth Maddow on MSNBC, July 11, 2009 (since removed).

[6] See http://www.thedailyshow.com/watch/wed-july-22-2009/the-born-identity (since removed).

[7] This strange sideshow was not closed down until April 2011, when President Obama released the 'long form' of his birth certificate, for which GOP hopeful Donald Trump, a real-estate billionaire, took the credit (see http://www.washingtonpost.com/politics/trump-to-meet-with-gop-officials-in-new-hampshire/2011/04/26/AF9V2awE_story.html), at which point Trump's 'silliness' palled for the voting public and his ratings plummeted (see http://www.washingtonpost.com/politics/in_return_to_new_hampshire_trump_focuses_on_foreign_policy/2011/05/11/AF5NOMrG_story.html?wprss=rss_homepage).

cause of political agency. While it may not look very much like the Habermasian public sphere, it is clearly attracting the attention of those who are notoriously hard to reach by traditional technologies of citizenship: the very same teens and children who, according to Jens Qvortrup (2004: 1–2), are 'the single remaining group which has not yet been recognised as claims-makers on current political and societal resources' and who, therefore, 'politically and economically, are still part of a feudal system.' He adds: 'It remains to be doubted that children have economic and political rights as autonomous citizens.' True – except that in the case of cultural and DIY/ media citizenship minors are prominent among those who are developing new forms of associative agency. Still more weirdly for social theory, although not for its Classical antecedents, the *stage* for citizenship is literally that. It is as much dramatic and performative as it is deliberative. The play's the thing, as DIY citizens, many of them children, perform their own identities and relations.

Discursive Citizenship in the Era of New Media

Thus, we can extend Marshall's three-stage schema by two further types of citizenship (Hartley 1999: 163, 179), each stage increasingly reliant on *communication* and less on *the state*, although some aspects of cultural citizenship have gained statutory status, most obviously in 'identity' politics, where equal rights for women, sexual orientations, and ethnic or first peoples' rights have been legislated. Here is the extended list in full:

- *Civic* – the 'rights of man' and of the Enlightenment: personal liberty, freedom of speech, property rights, access to justice (rights claimed in the courts).
- *Political* – the right of elective representation, the vote, and the right to hold public office (rights claimed in representative decision-making bodies).
- *Social* – the 'welfare state,' where education, employment and welfare benefits are *rights of citizenship* rather than private or economic arrangements at the level of the family or firm (rights claimed through social services and schools).
- *Cultural* – identity-based rights; 'media citizenship' (rights claimed in direct activism and in the 'attention economy' (Lanham 2006; Boyd 2009), thence via legislation).

- *DIY/DIWO* – 'consumer productivity,' choice-based affiliation, and self-organized associations: 'silly citizenship' (rights claimed in social-network markets (Bollier 2008) and in the 'gift economy' (Benkler 2006: 122–7)).

Although the promulgation and establishment of each of these phases has succeeded the previous one historically, all five are now experienced simultaneously, and not only in developed countries. Those most open to such experience are not the people with the heaviest investment in civic, political, or social institutions but those most exposed to popular culture and media, prominent among them children. The 'tipping point' between the earlier and later senses – between 'social' and 'cultural' citizenship, where 'social' rights connected with family security and education transmogrify into 'cultural' rights connected with identity and participation in socially networked meaning formation – is *also* the transition phase between childhood and adulthood. In short, it is the place of the teenager.

This is why the conjunction between childhood and citizenship is so interesting, despite the fact that children are by most formal definitions *not* citizens (that's what makes them children). At the same time, the participation of children in public life (and in publicity) has become so familiar that it is now commonplace to claim that children *are* citizens (in the present tense); for instance, the Children's Commissioner for England, Professor Sir Albert Aynsley-Green, who cites the United Nations Convention on the Rights of the Child to say that 'children are people of today and are citizens with rights to be respected' (Aynsley-Green, n.d.). Among the rights claimed for children is that of participation, which means initiating, directing, and sharing projects and decisions for themselves (Hart 1997). If such a claim is to be taken seriously, then it must extend to projects that young people actually do initiate, direct, and share, including activities that under other definitional regimes are dismissed as teenage antics and child's play. I'm not trying to be perverse here; this is not just the logic of the argument but also the situation on the ground. If 'citizenship theory' and 'young people's associative identities' turn out to be one and the same, then these activities can be seen as the 'generative edge' of new senses of citizenship.

At the end of 2009, Kate Vale, head of YouTube Australia and New Zealand, posted YouTube's 'first official' most-watched lists for the year (Vale 2009). 2009 was unarguably the year of 'SuBo' – Susan Boyle (who 'Dreamed a Dream' on *Britain's Got Talent*). After her, number two among the 'instant celebrities thanks to YouTube,' and also number three of the 'most watched YouTube videos globally,' was 'JK Wedding Entrance Dance' (headed 'Jill and Kevin's Big Day'). Within six months (by January 2010), it had achieved nearly 40 million views, 144,000 ratings, and 130,000 comments. The 'civic' element to this is a real marriage ceremony; the 'silly' element an extravagant dance routine by the wedding party, including the groom and bride dancing up the aisle.

Instant genre! Not only was this wedding dance-off challenged by many 'related' videos, but it was soon answered by a skilful and very funny spoof, 'JK Divorce Entrance Dance' (headed 'Jill and Kevin's Last Day'), which transposed the scene to the divorce court and substituted high-stepping lawyers, break-dancing security men, and of course the decidedly *un*happy couple (this being a whole 'six months later' . . .).[8] Elsewhere on the most-watched lists were several party videos from by-now 16-year-old Miley Cyrus (two in the top five music videos, two in the top five overall), sure evidence of the online power of teenage viewers. Topping the category of 'top five most watched Australian user-generated content' were two videos by a less familiar name: Mychonny, whose 'My Crazy Sister' soon scored one million views, and 'Asian and White Parents' scored 900,000 views. Mychonny is described on WikiTubia as follows:

> John Luc, also known as mychonny by his fans, is an 18 Year Old Vietnamese-Chinese Australian who lives in Melbourne. [...] He makes 'Asianese' videos of himself, friends, and family. ('Mychonny' n.d.)

On the day the 'most watched' list was released, several Australian television news programs featured Mychonny. On Channel 7's high-rating *Today Tonight* show, clips of 'My Crazy Sister' and 'Asian and White Parents' were broadcast with this introduction from the host: 'In the world of just-add-water celebrity, anyone can now be a star at the click of a button' (LOOOLuhhs 2009). As of January 2010, teenager Mychonny's YouTube channel boasted 140,000 subscribers, 15 million total upload views, and three million channel views. In other words, it compares favorably with

---

[8]   See Vale (2009) for links to all of the 'most-watched' videos discussed. When accessed in January 2010, 'JK Divorce Entrance Dance' had 4.7 million views and over 7000 comments. It was made by a professional video production company (Indigo Productions, New York; see http://www.indigoprod.com). Here it is worth noting another strong characteristic of 'silly citizenship': among the very first of the 'early adopters' of user-generated content are professionals, especially comics and entertainers, who pick up very quickly on youthful self-representation and turn it into instant genre.

Today Tonight's own viewer base of 2.5 million.[9] Despite this, *Today Tonight* called him an '*unknown* Australian comedian' – indicating the extent to which DIY/DIWO citizens are invisible to mainstream media, with their 'just add water' view of such citizens.

These song-and-dance routines and comedic spoofs are a good example of 'life, Jim, but not as we know it' – the figures are impressive but the denizens of Planet YouTube are just as alien to social theory as they are to tabloid television. Their fan base is likely to be predominantly young, certainly including a much higher proportion of children than mainstream news media can hope to reach. But it is equally clear that their uploads address the most important aspects of 'civil society' – marriage (Jill and Kevin), relationships (Miley Cyrus' party songs), and family (Mychonny's hilarious 'analysis' of his sister and parents) – albeit in a form that prioritizes *jokes* over *journalism*, *moves* over *motives*, and *steps* over *statements*. But there they are: *practicing* citizenship. As if to prove it, Jill and Kevin Heinz, the couple at the centre of 'JK Wedding Entrance Dance,' invited viewers to donate to a charity involved in preventing domestic violence to women and children. They chose this particular good cause because of 'circumstances surrounding the song in our wedding video' – the 'circumstances' being that the dance music was Chris Brown's 'forever.' Brown had recently faced domestic abuse allegations in relation to his own partner, the singer Rihanna. Within six months Jill and Kevin Heinz had collected 26,000 US dollars from over 1000 individual donors.[10]

Ordinary Publics, New Media, and Cultural Citizenship

Thus, in the continuing work of updating our analysis of cultural citizenship for the digital era, we can learn something from the dance-off:

- *Purposeful play* – Citizenship is not simply the cerebral exercise of monitorial scrutiny; it is both a whole-of-body and a body-to-body experi-

---

[9]   Figures from http://www.youtube.com/user/mychonny (January 2010). On the same day Mychonny had over 30,000 fans on Facebook. On the day it broadcast Mychonny (December 17, 2009), *Today Tonight* topped the Australian ratings with 2,778,000 viewers (www.tvtonight.com.au/2009/12/week-51-3.html); the *content* of that show was of course a further 'rating' for Mychonny.
[10]   See http://www.jkweddingdance.com. See also Vihrachoff (2009) and Weiner (2009).

ence, comedic and competitive, entertaining and festive, in the very *performance* of political deliberation and participation. It is 'communicative action' that includes but is not reducible to Habermasian rationality. It entails recognizing that civic participation is also – and needs to be analyzed by means of – play. Play is routinely associated with childhood; but to imagine that it ceases when children turn into adults is clearly absurd – play is an element of human relational identity, even though it may be observable in 'purest' form among children. Thus, habitual thought renders the play element of citizenship as the converse of the citizenship element of childhood (children play but are not citizens; adults are citizens but do not play). The lesson to be drawn from this is that it is important to recognize the extent to which childhood infects adulthood and play infects citizenship, and thus to investigate how both childhood and play are constitutive of citizenship and especially of changes in self-organizing, bottom-up associative relations among strangers in mediated societies, where play may *model* new civic possibilities.

• *Discursive practices* – Citizenship's bottom-up, self-organized, self-representing practice of constructing, conducting, and comprehending 'associative relations among strangers,' leading to 'relational identity' for individuals, is *discursive* but not *narrative*. It is a signifying practice but not a story. It is textual but not wholly or necessarily verbal. The dance-off or spoof video needs to be recognized as part of discourse without being reduced to 'language' in the usual sense. However, it can be accepted into the discursive realm on the same terms as other elaborated signifying systems such as poetry, literature, music, and drama, of which it is a subspecies.

• *Dynamic change* – Citizenship's *emergent* features and uses may seem the most fleeting and inconsequential aspects. But in an open-future environment it may be the childish experiment or adolescent dance-off that models and predicts a new form. Citizenship *evolves* by producing variation (both national and functional), selection (cumulative change, e.g. from civic and political to social and cultural citizenship), and adoption (e.g. the struggle to give legislative force to identity). This means attending to the 'generative edge' of citizenship, even where, as in the case of media, DIY, and DIWO versions, it fails to present a serious or rationalist face.

• *Relational identity* – Citizenship cannot be reduced to individual identity, even when identity rights are its declared end purpose ('enterprise' in Oakeshott's terms). Individual identity is *produced* through changing but patterned relationships within communication systems. Thus, identity is not a matter of *essence*, or self-originated Cartesian *cogito*; instead it is *external*, a matter of relational *probabilities*. Citizenship is an attribute of populations not persons, but at the same time these external relations produce personal identity.

- *New conflicts* – New sites of conflict arise in the formation and expression of relational identities, often in the context of privately owned networks. Conflict emerges for instance in a persistent tension between *expertise* and its others ('amateur,' 'consumer,' etc.), leading to long-term low-level warfare between copyright enforcement agencies and 'pirates' of various kinds. At stake here is the openness of the system as a whole to bottom-up agency and diversity and, thence, the freedom of all agents to construct and share relational identities in globally extensible associative networks. This entails addressing the digital divide, understanding how civic comportment challenges copyright and how *distributed expertise* redefines citizenship through new kinds of electronic 'commons.'

- *Disciplinary knowledge* – Communication research is itself an *active agent* in the conceptual development of citizenship. This is to acknowledge the productive tension between micro-level corporeal 'knowing subjects' and macro-level global knowledge-systems. The history of mediated communication since the nineteenth century shows how completely civic engagement itself is 'abstracted' from local and personal realities, to be *represented* in global media. But the same media technologies are increasingly available for citizen-consumers to use *productively* for their own associative purposes. This means linking these 'micro' and 'macro' levels, bringing popular productivity and representative knowledge into active mutual relations; reconnecting dancing and democracy.

Arty-Farty Citizenship?

For too long, educated taste has refused to admit that the civic and the silly are in intimate physical contact. However, these reflections on citizenship in the light of the dance-off ultimately return citizenship to its Classical roots. Until recently, even the most authoritative translations of Classical texts systematically toned down any mention of bodily parts, functions, and congress. But following the release of new editions of Harvard's Loeb Classical Library, public attention has returned to the connection between serious democratic purpose and silly comic play. Thus *The Australian*, News Ltd.'s flagship newspaper, noted that 'the Athenian citizenry made an art form of what we now call smut, dirt, or soft porn.' As for Aristophanes:

> His plays are crammed with fart, phallus and bum jokes, and scorn is his metier, while his theatrical language is a blend of the lofty and the vulgar. But Aristophanic subversion had a rational end, as social critique essential for healthy democratic functioning. (Slattery 2009)

Unfortunately (for the democratic process), *The Australian*'s way of applying 'smut, dirt, or soft porn' to the maintenance of 'healthy democratic functioning' leaves quite a bit to be desired. One example is a news report from 2009, apparently from *US Magazine* in the US, criticizing Noah Cyrus, nine-year-old sister of Miley, for wearing a 'dominatrix' costume for Halloween. On closer inspection, it appears that the 'dominatrix' criticism appears to have been imported to the American site from Australia, where it was picked up from *The Australian*.[11] Most of the 'outrage' appears to come from News Ltd. papers – even their own readers, for the most part, didn't agree with the 'dominatrix' inference.[12] And, of course, it shouldn't need to be pointed out that *The Australian* reports 'outrage' while (a) showing the picture that caused it and (b) associating that picture with adult sexuality by juxtaposing it with adult dominatrix costumes: they do what they report as 'outrageous.'[13] Meanwhile, it seems pretty clear from the pictures of Ms Cyrus Jr. that here is an instance of 'silly citizenship' – a public outing by a nine-year-old with a newsworthy surname where 'partying' is of the fancy-dress and dance-off variety.

---

[11] The article in *US Magazine* headlined the 'dominatrix' gibe, which it sourced from an 'Australian newspaper,' with a link to the News Ltd. story. See: http://www.usmagazine.com/celebritynews/news/miley-cyrus-sister-slammed-for-wearing-dominatrix-halloween-costume-20092910.

[12] See http://www.news.com.au/entertainment/comments/0,26700,26261156-5013560,00.html.

[13] See http://www.news.com.au/entertainment/celebrity/noah-cyrus-9-causes-outrage-in-dominatrix-halloween-costume/story-e6frfmqi-1225791423053.

Silly Citizenship

Importing that world directly into the adversarial arena of the political news cycle may have dire and unforeseen consequences, stoking the fires of populist wowserism in relation to the supposed 'sexualization of children' in popular culture. The *politics* of this kind of editorial adventurism is not to keep democracy healthy with vulgarity as 'social critique' but to oxygenate calls for further 'protection' of youngsters *from* 'exposure' to or by the media, and so to soften up the public domain for the imposition of official regulations or internet 'filtering' (censorship) legislation – which was official government policy in Australia at the time this story ran. Clearly the mainstream media have a lot of catching up to do if they are to 'represent' the next generation of citizens.

Recognition of what is needed for 'healthy democratic functioning' requires renewed attention to these 'demotic' aspects of citizenship (Turner 2010a). Concealed beneath teenage mischief and YouTube antics is a classical 'right to dance.' Here is a new model of citizenship based on self-representation of, by, and for 'ordinary' people, using 'new' media to produce discursive associative relations, superseding the modernist 'man with a gun.' Now, we need to change our bumper stickers.

7

The Probability Archive

'A system can be making itself up as it goes along,' said Hiram. 'The weather is like that. Evolution is like that. Economies, if they aren't inert and stagnant, are like that. Since they make themselves up as they proceed, they aren't predestined. Not being predestined, they aren't predictable.' 'That may be a novel idea for meteorologists, but it's old news to linguists,' said Armbruster. [...] 'Language makes itself up as it goes along.' (Jane Jacobs 2000: 137)

This chapter began life in rather the same way that the universe did. It was initiated by a singular event, which was immediately followed by a burst of inflationary expansion.[1] The singular event occurred in the course of an Australian Research Council-funded Discovery project that I am conducting with colleagues, on the topic of 'Australian television and popular memory.'[2] We set up a project website that included links to clips on YouTube.[3] Some of these featured archival footage of early television. But I had miscalculated, forgetting that intellectual property rights trump 'national heritage,' never mind 'popular memory,' every time. Our plans to

---

[1] 'Inflation is a general term for models of the very early Universe which involve a short period of extremely rapid (exponential) expansion, blowing the size of what is now the observable Universe up from a region far smaller than a proton to about the size of a grape fruit (or even bigger) in a small fraction of a second' (Gribbin 1996).

[2] John Hartley, Graeme Turner, Alan McKee, Sue Turnbull, and Chris Healy (2008–12), *Australian Television and Popular Memory: New Approaches to the Cultural History of the Media in the Project of Nation-Building*. ARC Discovery Project DP0879596.

[3] http://www.TVLandAustralia.com.

---

upload and discuss archival footage as part of the project were duly thwarted when one of the clips we'd linked to was suddenly deleted by YouTube, owing to (unstated) 'terms of use violations.'[4]

That annoying 'singularity' led very quickly to an exponential 'inflation' of the problem. The *unreliability* of one clip got me thinking about archives as a whole; specifically, what sort of an archive 'popular memory' might use, or indeed be, in its digital form at least. The idea that 'popular memory' exists only inside the heads of the population, such that it can be accessed only by such techniques as oral history, was already under challenge, because so much of it can be found in – or reconstructed from – various existing archives, public and private, analogue and online, including those that we planned to mine for our project, namely:

- *Cultural institutions* (including archives, museums, galleries, and university collections);
- *Published works* (not just academic titles but also 'trade' publishing and popular ephemera such as weekly television guides);
- *Industry accounts* (interviews and oral histories conducted by researchers and others; published memoirs of industry personnel);
- *Television programs* (specifically the genre of television specials celebrating television history, plus station idents and logos that associate television with national values); and
- *Fan and pro-am[5] memorializations* (amateur and individual collections and celebrations, usually but not only on websites and personal collections).

In our project, these 'resource locations' were initially seen as essentially separate and distinct phenomena. Some of them were self-described as archives, some were not; but all could nevertheless be used *as* archives by

---

[4] It was a newsreel clip relating to a discussion about the claims of The Old Windmill in Brisbane to have been the site of the first experimental television broadcast in Australia. The Brisbane transmission occurred in April 1934, but Chris Keating has tracked down an earlier event, at the Menzies Hotel in Melbourne, in September 1929. See http://www.tvlandaustralia.com/uploadmemories/?p=43.

[5] 'Pro-am' refers to the blurring of the distinction between professionals and amateurs. It originated in reference to sport but was taken up widely to describe consumer co-created content where expertise is distributed beyond traditional professionalism, and people pursue amateur activities to professional standards; see http://www.demos.co.uk/publications/proameconomy.

us. Or so we thought. But the failure of our attempt to construct an archive of our own, by borrowing from or linking and adding to others online, raised a much more general question: *what exactly is an archive*, in the era of the internet? Suddenly, a singular question (where's my clip?) was inflated to a universal one (what is an archive?).

Institutions of Memory

If you want to *find something out*, what do you do? Or, more precisely, *where do you go*? This is of course a time-based or historical question, closely correlated with communications technologies. In the analogue era, you could, for instance, go to:

- *Oral social networks* (your parents or peers or priesthoods);
- *Media networks* – publishing, journalism, and works of the imagination in the broadcast or screen media (a good book, article, or show);
- *Privately held knowledge* (from shop windows and markets to corporate databases and copyrighted research);
- *Public institutions* charged with collecting, preserving, and making accessible various types of cultural and heritage material (galleries, libraries, archives, and museums); or
- *Disciplinary sciences* and *experts* (schools, universities, and specialist professions).

Without extending it any further, this partial list already covers a wide spectrum of knowledge sources, ranging from informal (although not unorganized) types in oral and visual culture up to some of the most august institutions on earth. Each type has its own long history, some stretching back to pre-modern times, which may include tensions and conflicts with other types. All of them rely on particular communications technologies, from speech or visual display to publishing and broadcasting. By such means, knowledge, including memory, has long since escaped the confines of the individual knowing subject. It is produced and archived exo-somatically – externally to the individual – by various *institutions of memory*.

Since the emergence of the internet, these institutional forms have also become increasingly available online. In the process, they have become part of a gigantic global (or globalizing) archive, their various types of knowledge linked and searchable by individual users, who thus gain unprecedented access to information on a previously unimaginable scale. This is as much an archive of memory (subjective) as it is of knowledge (objective). The same materials can serve both ends; and, as everyone knows, it is not always clear at first glance whether a given nugget of online information belongs to one end of that gradient or the other. 'Finding out' (or, negatively, 'being found out') in such a context is reordering established relationships of trust: *authority* is not automatically accorded to august institutions with classical porticos – that is, to previous generations' investment in authority.

At the same time, the distinctions between different types of knowledge institution are eroded. To take just one example from the list above, each type of public institution – galleries (artworks), libraries (books), archives (documents), and museums (artifacts) – has its own tradition of collection, curation, display and preservation, literally in different buildings in different parts of town, each with its own purposes, users, and social networks. Such knowledge was analogue, and not 'interoperable' with others. But these historic differences were compromised as soon as public and cultural institutions began to put their collections online. Artworks, publications, documents, and artifacts 'converged' (in Henry Jenkins' sense) as digital information. Before long, the institutions themselves began to converge too, consolidating previously autonomous structures into one 'industry sector' – soon dubbed GLAM (galleries, libraries, archives, museums).[6]

Once online, even such a broad sector is but one of many competing attractions for the user. Informal social networks, the media, commercial markets, and public-sector providers, as well as myriad educational agencies, are all present online. Despite their manifold differences, however, from the point of view of the user they are all equally just one thing: potential *information resources*. Thus, whether or not this was their intention or their corporate mission, they have become part of a gigantic *archive* of exo-somatic knowledge, both objective and subjective.

What kind of archive is this? The internet has transformed the very idea of what an archive can be, and with it how knowledge can be stored, shared, grown, and lost. Because of the scale of information available online, because the traditional boundaries between different types of knowledge

[6] See Wikipedia's 'GLAM' (n.d.), where the Australian Society of Archivists is credited with a GLAM Annual Conference in 2003.

are no longer reliable, and because of the ways that users can now navigate through multiple systems, I argue that we need a new conceptual framework to comprehend the nature of the archive; a framework that I suggest should be derived from *probability theory*. Learning from it, we may need to shift our disciplinary settings from inherited *modernist determinism* (linear or mechanical causal order) towards *quantum probability* (chaos, complexity, uncertainty). We may need to rethink the opposition between 'objective' and 'subjective' knowledge by integrating them with other kinds of distinction – between static and dynamic, fixed and iterative, residual and emergent, authoritative and uncertain. At that point we may need also to reconsider the ingrained habit that values one side of such polarities over the other.

From Objectivity to Quantum Theory

Meanwhile, probability's time has certainly come in the archive business. Changes can be observed in the organization of knowledge by looking at differences in archiving and display systems in the most prominent cultural institutions – institutions of knowledge – of successive periods. Thus, put simply, the *modern* period (roughly, the nineteenth century) was characterized by the museum; the *post-modern* (the twentieth century) by broadcasting; and the emergent (twenty-first century) *global network* system by the internet. Each type of archive is organized according to different principles. Thus:

* *Modern archives* (museums, galleries) were organized around the concept of *objectivity*. They were located in physical space, contained physical objects, and proposed a *mechanical* relation between the real and its representation. The *visitor* observed not a representation of the real but the real itself. The modern archive aspired to universal but coherently disciplined *knowledge*. I call these 'essence archives.'
* *Postmodern archives* (broadcast television systems) were organized around the concept of *mediation*. They were time-based, contained 'intangible' objects, and proposed – at least at the outset – a *realistic* relation between the sign and its referent. The *viewer* observed a representation that was motivated by a trace of the real within the sign. The archive aimed for indiscriminate but universal *audiences*. I call this an interim or 'transitional phase.'

- *Network archives* (YouTube, the internet) are organized around the concept of *probability*. They are digital, contain virtual objects, and propose an *uncertain* relation between what you see and what you get. The *user* co-creates content that may or may not be real. The archive aims for universally accessible and (re-)usable *content*. I call these 'probability archives.'

The shift from Newtonian (mechanical) to quantum (probability) knowledge has been cumulative and historical, and the boundaries between the different types are not as clear-cut as the categorization above implies. Indeed, some of the terms used, such as 'universal' and 'transitional,' demonstrate in their own unstable mutability the unpredictable nature of the categories I have described. Thus, I suggested that the 'postmodern' archive aimed for 'universal audiences' while the network archive aims for 'universal content.' But along the way the horizon has opened out, such that the term 'universal' has expanded from what it meant for broadcast television, 'everyone in a nation,' to 'everything known on earth' (Google's business plan). 'Population-wide' has expanded from a Foucauldian, governmental population (again, usually national) to a Darwinian, biological population (species-wide). Similarly, 'transitional' in my schema simply implies a transition phase between 'essence' and 'probability' archives, partaking of the properties of both. Of course, at the scale of *longue-durée* history and evolutionary change, 'transitions' will include the unpredictable transformation of all three phases.

Nevertheless, I am claiming that a transformation in the status of knowledge can be observed in the difference between what I am calling 'essence' and 'probability' archives respectively. 'Essence' archives are *object*-based; 'probability' archives are *user*-based. In an 'essence archive' such as a museum or gallery, each displayed object is collected and selected by experts for its intrinsic properties, which are themselves scientifically verified. There are elaborate systems in place to manage both the collection and its curators, with the emphasis on accuracy and expertise. But in a 'probability archive' like the internet, you don't know what you will find or who put it there. The status or even existence of individual objects is uncertain. They may be real or unreal, true or false, fact or fiction, original or copy. The *productivity* of the overall archive is *unmanaged* – knowledge is uploaded, archived, organized, debated, and deleted by myriad users, not by minority expertise.

Essence archives dominated *modern culture*, by which I mean Enlightenment-based industrializing countries of the modernizing West. They were associated with the rise of mutually competitive nation states during and following the nineteenth century. Probability archives are coming to dominate *global culture* and are a product of the collaborative network. They are associated with both global corporate culture (Google, Facebook, YouTube) and self-organized consumer co-created communities (such as Wikipedia) or what Charles Leadbeater (2010) has dubbed 'cloud culture.'

For their part, broadcasting (cultural technology) and post-modernism (artistic-intellectual movement) may be seen (in hindsight) as *transitional* rather than transformational. They form an interim phase – rather like the so-called 'Gutenberg parenthesis' (Pettit 2007) – between these two archival systems; a period of excess/collapse or what Yuri Lotman (2009) calls 'culture and explosion,' presaging more fundamental rearrangements. Thus, broadcasting clearly contributed to the development of the network age, preparing the way for globally distributed hypertext in the separation of the sign from the referent, leading to 'semiotic excess' (where signification is no longer anchored to 'the real') and rehearsing, via media-connected 'imagined' if not 'virtual' communities, the type of social networks that would later dominate the internet. But, at the same time, broadcast television relied on the same industrial-era mode of corporate organization as other kinds of modern archive. It was a closed expert system where producers (collectors and curators) were radically separated from consumers, and where control over what was gathered or produced, and how it was presented, remained at all times with the professionals. I argue that that the transformation of archival systems, relations, and practices (taking place over the past century or so) can be characterized as a change in underlying *theories of causation*. Modern or 'essence' archives were organized according to *objectivity theory*, where the intrinsic properties of an object directly *cause* what it 'means.' Network or 'probability' archives are founded on the principle of uncertainty, where meanings may vary according to their position, momentum, and a version of the 'observer effect.' They are organized according to *quantum theory*.

With the internet, suddenly we are slap bang in the middle of a universe of quantum indeterminacy and stochastic random probabilities, a place where Bayesian inference (Wolframmathematica 2009), Heisenberg's uncertainty principle (Acorvettes 2007), and Schrödinger's cat (Elpaw74165764 2007) rule the waves (and the particles): where you can exist (or not) everywhere (and nowhere) at once (Brooks 2010).

Here is where we encounter the emergent *probability archive*. It has taken a century or more for quantum theory to ripple out from physics and mathematics to media and the market. Physics (realism) shifted from Newtonian mechanics to quantum uncertainty around the time of World War I. The well-known names are Niels Bohr, Werner Heisenberg, and Max Planck. Language (post-modernism) went uncertain in the 1960s and 1970s. The well-known names are Roland Barthes, Jean Baudrillard, Jacques Derrida, and Michel Foucault. But commercial investment in probabilistic technology did not catch up until the internet was at last able to accommodate video, a moment best marked by the launch of YouTube in 2005.

Modernity's Essence Archive

The *essence archive* is a *deterministic* type of store, based on a Newtonian, mechanical, or linear theory of causation. The cultural institutions whose emergence accompanied the rise of the nation state in the nineteenth century (Bennett 1995) are nowadays collectively known as the GLAM sector. They are all essence archives. They collect, catalogue, conserve, and curate individual objects whose value is intrinsic to the object: this Rembrandt is not a fake; that book is not plagiarized; those manuscripts are original; our artifact is not a plaster cast. Each object is objective; its properties can be determined by empirical observation. 'Essence theory' requires that every object is explicable by its intrinsic properties.

A good example of an essence archive is the British Museum. The whole point about the artifacts in the British Museum is that they are what they appear to be – all real, no sign. For instance, the oldest object in the museum, the first known technological invention, and therefore earliest precursor of the internet, is the Olduvai stone chopping tool. The important thing about this bit of basalt is its *essence* – it alone, and not any other thing, is the oldest wrought object, so old that it pre-dates our species. It was made nearly two million years ago by the earliest hominin, *Homo habilis* (Leakey, Tobias, and Napier 1964). This claim is based on its *essential* or intrinsic properties, established by various scientific tests, whose importance is emphasized in the British Museum's online catalogue.[7]

---

[7] 'Olduvai stone chopping tool, from Olduvai Gorge, Tanzania, 1.8–2 million years old. Made nearly two million years ago, stone tools such as this are the first known technological invention. This one is the oldest object in the British Museum' (British Museum n.d. a).

Broadcast Television as Essence Archive

The difference between 'public culture' and 'private entertainment' has been a continuing rift throughout the modernist era, making it seem that there is little in common between national GLAM cultural institutions and commercial pop-culture media. But I argue that *broadcasting* too is an *essence archive*, even though it is time-based rather than bricks and mortar, not so much a store as a stream, and not *purposed* as an archive at all in its own estimation. It only becomes an archive in the hands of audiences, whose desire to use broadcast television as an archive was demonstrated as soon as they were technologically able to use it as one, first in the analogue form of video-rental stores such as Blockbuster Video; then online via Hulu, Tivo, etc.; and finally by being able to archive broadcast content for themselves by uploading, editing, and commenting on clips.

However much the audience's 'will to archive' was thwarted by broadcasting organizations, I am arguing nonetheless that broadcasting was (and still is) an essence archive in the sense that its 'collection' is 'displayed' on the same terms as are artifacts in a museum or artworks in a gallery. Broadcast television, as a 'business model', traded in individual shows, owned by the exhibiting institution (television channel) not by private collectors. Each program had its own intrinsic value, merit, or generic properties, and although viewers could choose among different channels each show was produced, paid for, and watched on the basis of its essential (or immanent) merits, via content that viewers could only experience one item at a time. The 'business model' required a kind of connoisseurship on the part of audiences, who were encouraged to choose *this* rather than *that* timeslot, station, and show according to their estimation of the intrinsic qualities of whatever was on air at a given moment.

For example, one of the most-praised episodes of the evergreen sci-fi series *Dr Who* in recent years was *Blink* (2007).[8] It co-starred Oscar-nominated Carey Mulligan alongside David Tennant and featured some of the scariest 'stone chopping tools' you could ever meet – aliens that look like marble statues of angels, that move when you're not looking, and kill

---

[8]   See http://en.wikipedia.org/wiki/Blink_%28Doctor_Who%29.

you if you blink.[9] Like the Olduvai stone chopping tool, *Blink* was valued *as such*. Fans loved it,[10] it won industry prizes,[11] and the 'weeping angels' were revived in series 5 (starring Matt Smith/Karen Gillan) (see Doctor-WhoCenter2010 2010). These accolades were won for the program's essential, intrinsic qualities as an individual episode, albeit in a series that goes back 40 years, in a crowded television schedule, with myriad competing attractions.

I am trying to suggest that, despite their different technologies and histories, and their sometimes daggers-drawn mutual relationship, the *value proposition* of the broadcasting system is the same as that of GLAM archives. Like artworks, books, documents, and artifacts, television shows are exhibited on the basis of the intrinsic merit and attractiveness of the individual item. Further, like GLAM collections, broadcast television is *provider-driven*. Experts in production (collecting), programming (curating), and promotion (audience maximization) are hired and fired on the basis of their value to the production process, which is corporately controlled and often vertically integrated. The same organization owns and controls each step of the process from inception to transmission, and that includes corporate control of a 'catalogue' of shows, series, movies, or presenters amounting to an evolving archive. Like museums, where most of what is collected remains in drawers and stores, and only a sample is displayed for viewing at any one time, broadcasters restrict access to their archive, releasing items on a schedule that suits their own purposes, not necessarily those of viewers, although they employ yet more (marketing) experts to keep these divergent desires in some sort of alignment.

Thus, broadcast television and cultural institutions are both 'essence' storehouses from which viewer-visitors can choose among 'contents' that are already created, collected, curated, verified, valued, and publicly released by experts. The first loyalty of these professionals is to the corporate

---

[9] See http://www.thewhoshop.com/weeping-angel-cutout-p-3224.html. The 'weeping angels' are themselves a victim of Eisenberg's uncertainty principle and the so-called 'observer effect.' They are 'quantum locked' – their speed is infinite when unobserved, but they cannot move when watched (see Xxnapoleonsolo 2010 and 'Quantum zeno effect' n.d.). The end of the episode suggests that viewers might want to be careful about blinking in front of some famous statues (see http://www.flickr.com/photos/8047619@N08/544264972).

[10] See, for instance, http://www.therpf.com/showthread.php?t=49264 and the reviews on Amazon.com: http://www.amazon.com/Doctor-Who-Complete-David-Tennant/dp/B000UVV2GA.

[11] See http://www.bbc.co.uk/doctorwho/s4/news/080512_news_01.

provider or sponsor, not directly to the viewer-visitor. But the broadcasting organization prospers only to the extent that its range of experts and its repertoire of items are wide enough to persuade a sufficient number of casual visitors to stop by – here, and now – for what even the blurb writers call 'essential' viewing.

From the point of view of the audience, broadcast television's attraction is also similar to that of a museum. If you think this idea is far-fetched, remember that, despite their high-culture tone, museums and art galleries are themselves among the most popular tourist attractions in world cities, attracting much the same mixed demographic as does television, to say nothing of the internet.[12] The experience of the 'content' from the perspective of the visitor-viewer is also comparable. To access what one wants it is necessary to visit the institution (in time for television; in place for the GLAM sector).[13] Each visit is competitive, because there is always the option of going elsewhere. But once the decision is made, whether in favor of the British Museum or the BBC, it is time-bound. Viewers can choose to spend their time with old favorites or interesting new possibilities in a way that is idiosyncratic but nevertheless part of a large-scale popular experience. The 'venue' is full of other people, unknown to and minimally interacting with each other, as each makes their chosen pathway through the content. In both cases enjoyment is centered about an object that cannot be 'consumed' in the literal sense because the viewer-visitor never owns it. The motivation is the same in both cases: *this* object (or show, or any other choice) is preferred over *that* one, in an experience that is nevertheless casual, non-committal, and non-instrumental.

The Probability Archive

I have argued that the GLAM sector and broadcasting are modern and post-modern, respectively, but that both are still based on the concept of

---

[12] The Visit London site lists the British Museum, Tate Modern, National Gallery, Natural History Museum, London Eye, Science Museum, Victoria and Albert Museum, Madame Tussauds, Tower of London, and National Maritime Museum as London's 'top 10 attractions […] in order of popularity based on visitor numbers' (http://www.visitlondon.com/attractions/culture/top-ten-attractions). Only of them (the Eye) is unequivocally not a 'GLAM' attraction.

[13] This is to leave out of account for the time being the question of online 'visits,' via websites or Second Life, for instance.

objective or intrinsic essence. It is only with the emergence of the internet that we can begin to speak of *probability*. The archive evolved too. The 'holotype' or first-described specimen of a *probability archive* was YouTube, of which the first book-length analysis appeared in 2009, by Jean Burgess and Joshua Green. Although YouTube's content is random and chaotic (no-one plans or manages what is uploaded), the probability is high that you will find something related to what you are looking for, including the thing itself, often uploaded multiple times by different users. For instance, you can find out quite a lot about the examples mentioned so far – the stone chopping tools from Olduvai and *Blink*, including chunks of the episode itself, uploaded by fans.[14] You will also find lots of other things, such as tribute videos, 'related' content, reviews, links, and users' comments.[15] Here emerges a different *philosophy* of collecting and keeping. Where the essence archive is devoted to an ideology of the coherent object, YouTube is organized around '*found objects*' (i.e. the results of search functions or tags) – the probability of finding a specimen of a certain class rather than the certainty or essence of individual identity aspired to by museums and broadcasting. Further, 'objects' may not retain the bodily integrity planned for them by their original creators. Fans will edit shows to foreground their favorite character, or re-edit clips to fit a favorite musical track, or simply 'snip' clips to illustrate something else. Online 'objects' have no essence.

YouTube is a dynamic and evolutionary environment. Clips are not only added but they are also constantly removed, as for instance when the corporate lawyers for a particular property trawl through the archive issuing take-down notices. Under pressure from the copyright enforcement lobby, YouTube introduced automatic detection and removal technologies in 2010. Whereas previously it was possible for copyright material to be uploaded by anyone and to remain accessible unless YouTube ordered it to be taken down, now the onus is on users to inform YouTube that automatically deleted material may be covered by 'fair use' provisions and should therefore be restored. Thus uncertainty is structured into the very process

---

[14] For example 'start of dr who blink': http://www.youtube.com/watch?v=wvp1Y7SZVhA (since deleted for copyright reasons – which is where this chapter came in . . .).
[15] One tribute video used *Blink* and Robbie Williams' song 'Angels': http://www.youtube.com/watch?v=O-WkhGwIGo4 (since deleted for copyright reasons); one of the comments it provoked was from a frustrated seeker of essence: 'im getting so pissed off every1 says that its real creepy but i can only find things like this with music i want the actual episode!!!'

of archiving. No-one – not the uploader, the copyright-holder, or the platform owner – knows whether a given item will survive to be seen by others – as we found out when 'our' clip on TVLandAustralia.com[16] was unceremoniously deleted.

Thus, YouTube is an *unreliable* archive. You never know what you'll find or not find, and the archive changes constantly. A probability archive is random, complex, uncertain, indeterminate, and evolving as to its contents at any given moment. But it is also contains *much* more information than a regular archive can manage: by YouTube's fifth birthday, it was estimated that 24 hours of footage were being uploaded each minute, and the site was receiving two billion views a day (Delahunty 2010). Such productivity is only possible because it is *not* managed at the level of the individual item. So little were YouTube's founders concerned with 'essence' that they didn't initially know *what* the site as a whole was for – they let *users decide on its purposes* for themselves. As a result, while YouTube was neutral about itself, it was able to *accommodate* myriad purposes among its users. It is therefore not trading on the 'essence' of its content, but on the 'probability' that users will find – or make – what they want independently of the will of the 'provider.'

This results in a self-organizing system of increasing but self-managed complexity (Jacobs 2000; Zittrain 2008). The archive is a mixture of user-uploaded content, often copied from television or music videos; corporately uploaded content seeking an audience; and user-created content – which is itself often a hybrid of copied and creative elements, typically using video from television and music from a commercial playlist, mixed and edited to produce something new by 'vidders' who may themselves attract large followings for their work.

Uniquely for a 'mass medium' (if that is what it is), YouTube has prospered by allowing professional and amateur content to co-habit. Non-professional users may upload clips of favorite television shows or music videos, both to *signal* their personal taste, socio-political affiliations, or sense of identity and also to *share* with others a sense of community or relationship, often by posting clips that comment on news events (politics, disasters, sport), thereby using 'content' that is formally the property of corporate media firms (who regard its reuse as theft) to signal, share, and save – to *archive* – their own private lives, loves, and loathings. Then there are the more active users who make their own content, whether it is

---

[16] http://www.tvlandaustralia.com.

air-guitar sessions in the teenage bedroom, such as the classic 'Hey clip' (Tasha 2005),[17] or hilarious home-made comedy from someone like Mychonny.[18] Some of this stuff is so popular that it out-rates commercial (i.e. broadcast) entertainment. Commercial interests themselves use YouTube directly for various purposes, including profiling, branding, audience-building, long-tail or niche marketing, education, community service initiatives, or campaigning. Recently, led by Britain's Channel 4 Television, broadcasters have started to make revenue-share deals with YouTube to allow free access to popular shows – this is called 'catch-up TV' or 'VOD' (video on demand) – making YouTube an *archive* for broadcasting itself. Reliability of content is gained, but only by ceding control over what is uploaded (and why) to the copyright-holding corporate provider (Barnett 2009).

Another important function for YouTube is the distribution of not-for-profit content. Neither consumerist nor commercial, this may range from highly professional educational or public-service material such as TED.com to localized community-building by non-professionals and activists.

Plenitude of the Sign

Going back in time to the essence archive, it is easy to see – now that we're all familiar with an alternative, although it wasn't so obvious during modernism's monopolistic heyday – that *essence* is not what it appears to be. Bizarrely, given the effort to achieve authoritative authenticity and objectivity, it turns out that *appearance* plays a determining role in producing something we may have to start calling 'the essence effect' rather than actual essence – an effect of *display*. In fact, once we've been alerted to the vagaries of the probability archive, it seems increasingly doubtful whether it has ever been possible to be sure that such a thing as 'this object' *really exists* in the essential or deterministic way that motivates the very idea of the modernist archive.

For it was right here, inside the museum itself – the archetypal essence archive – that *what it is* (the real) began to part company from *what it*

---

[17]   As a star video of YouTube, there is little likelihood that the 'Hey clip' will ever be deleted. It had enjoyed 31.5 million views when I last looked (October 2010).

[18]   See http://www.youtube.com/user/mychonny. Total upload views as of October 2010 were 36.7 million.

means (the sign). This happened as soon as the object – that stone chopping tool, for instance – was put on display. The questions 'how do we know?' and 'how can you find out?' took communicative form. The piece of stone became a signal, ceasing to be what it was (essence) and becoming something else: a sign.

> Semiotics is in principle the discipline studying everything *which can be used in order to lie*. If something cannot be used to tell as lie, conversely it cannot be used to tell the truth: it cannot in fact be used 'to tell' at all. (Eco 1976: 7)

In a real sense, it's lying to us (Eco 1976; Hyde 1998: 58–61; and see Chapter 9).

The Olduvai stone's 'essence' is not enough to guarantee its unique status as a sign. That has to be *signaled* by means of theatrical isolation in a large display case. It has to be *narrated* in order that it can be known.[19] Its essence is guaranteed by *story*. But, it turns out, this *ur-text* or holotype of all technology is far from unique. In fact, the British Museum itself has several.[20] I have also seen the 'same' stones in the National Museum of Denmark and the Museum of Anatolian Civilizations in Turkey,[21] and doubtless you can find them elsewhere too (check your local museum or department of anthropology). In the end, then, the intrinsic properties of an individual item are not what make it important. What counts is *our experience of it* as unique and original.

Museums are location-based and analogue archives, so if enough people around the world are going to be able to experience an object it has to be multiplied and distributed, rather as chunks of moon rock were chopped up and sent around the world – to universal wonder – in the 1970s.[22] But, if enough examples of a certain object are found, the individual essence of each item is compromised. The museum display itself begins to signify *plenitude*. There is evidently a law of diminishing returns in relation to the

---

[19]   See http://www.bbc.co.uk/ahistoryoftheworld/objects/ykHw5-oqQEGFnvat1gavxA.

[20]   'In these early artefacts it is possible to see the first spark of creative genius that set humans apart from other animals and gradually enabled us to adapt to different, often changing conditions all over the world' (see British Museum (n.d. b).

[21]   http://www.natmus.dk/sw20374.asp and 'Museum of Anatolian civilizations' (n.d.).

[22]   For an example in Wales see http://www.amgueddfacymru.ac.uk/cy/Rhagor/erthygl/carregllauad or http://www.museumwales.ac.uk/en/Rhagor/article/moonrock.

signifying power of the individual object. Hence, when one museum has lots of examples of a stone chopping tool, the display starts to signify 'pattern' rather than 'essence.' Similarly, moon rock drew round-the-block crowds when it was first displayed. But now it has become banal. You can buy it online for 40 bucks,[23] and NASA gives chunks of it away – for example to Neil Armstrong, who named his sample 'Bok.'[24]

The trick, then – the professional expertise of the GLAM archive – is not to collect, conserve, and curate *essence*, but to find ways to *signal* it. The combined weight of expert skill and corporate organization is devoted to providing the visitor with a feeling *about* essence. The 'preferred reading' of the 'motivated sign,' as media scholars used to say (Chandler 2002: 235), is not the authority of objective essence at all. It is feelings of awe that may well up if, in a competitive semiotic environment (a 'society of the spectacle,' as it were), you (dear viewer) are willing to imagine this item *as if* it is the first human tool.

The Internet as a Probability Machine (Or, How to 'Cast' the First Stone)

One way to increase the semiotic energy of objects is to release them online. Here, you can begin to feel the incredible power of probability. Stone chopping tools abound; and what you can find out about them is unbounded. Here is an example found on Flickr: someone has taken a picture of the 'Homo Ergaster' exhibit in the Spitzer Hall of Human Origins at the American Natural History Museum in New York. The exhibit is a *dramatization* or re-enactment of the Olduvai stone chopping tool, showing an early hominin holding it. Someone else has uploaded the same picture, and put a 'lolcats'-type[25] caption on it: 'Homo Ergaster couple *hailing a cab*' (my emphasis).[26] Meanwhile, if you are interested in the actual place where this scene is imagined to have occurred, Olduvai Gorge in Tanzania, where the stone chopping tools were found, there are several videos taken by tourists who captured both pictures of the setting

---

[23] See http://www.meteorites-for-sale.com/catalog/moon-boxes.html.
[24] See Pearlman (2006).
[25] See http://www.lolcats.com.
[26] See http://www.flickr.com/photos/ggnyc/657464514, and http://www.flickr.com/photos/wallyg/404063706 for the exhibit shown 'straight.'

and audio of their guide's commentary (see Cokeeorg 2007; Rahornerl 2008). You can gain a better understanding of the import of these discoveries, some of the science involved in finding them, and the cumulative theory-building process to which their discovery has contributed if you listen to Louise Leakey, descendant of their discoverer, giving a TED Talk (Leakey 2007).

In keeping with the shift from essence to experience, real to sign, original to reproduction, expertise to DIY, you can learn how to make your own stone chopping tool, guided by several YouTube videos (see e.g. Expertvillage 2008; Sourswithhawk 2009). Here the audio-visual internet has a clear advantage over print-based or static-display museums. It is much easier to follow the actions of a practised flint-knapper on YouTube than to follow written instructions. But, if you're still not confident about your own flint-knapping abilities, you can buy an authentic cast of an Olduvai stone tool, costing 14 US dollars.[27] The firm that supplies the casts also provides an accompanying web page that explains the story of the stones.[28]

The internet archives 'meta' information about the stones, and one source of this information is of course Wikipedia, which has numerous relevant entries, including one on the 'Olduvai imperative,' an anthropological term for 'the human desire or need to create tools.' Elsewhere, on YouTube, you can find bits of the history of storytelling about the stones – the *historiography* of DIY toolmaking – such as a 1947 film made for the Wellcome Foundation, called 'Stone age tools: Prehistoric stoneworking techniques' (WellcomeFilm 2009). It is billed as:

> A demonstration by M. Leon Coutier, archaeologist and former President of the Societe Prehistorique Francaise, of his technique for making replicas of Palaeolithic tools and weapons, including hand-axes, scrapers, gravers and flint arrowheads. Filmed at the former Institute of Archaeology, Regent's Park, London in June 1947. An important archaeological record.[29]

[27]   See http://lithiccastinglab.com/cast-page/oldowanflaketoolcast.htm.
[28]   See http://lithiccastinglab.com/index.htm. The illustrations are credited to the University of California-Berkeley, Department of Anthropology Collection. The site claims to have received nearly 40 million hits in a little over seven years. Its credits charmingly read: 'written, designed & the images are credited & copyrighted to Peter A. Bostrom. Technical advisor for all computer software and equipment is Linda Hewitt (my sister).'
[29]   See also http://catalogue.wellcome.ac.uk/record=b1663578~S3.

Amazingly Unlikely

All of these flakes of information lie higgledy-piggledy about the internet, easily accessible via one of those stream-of-consciousness searches that can be so pleasurably time-consuming when you're looking for something else. The exercise makes you realize that Google isn't really a 'search engine'; it's a 'find engine' (on the search as 're-finding,' see Halavais 2009). It confirms the extent to which knowledge – even individual identity, whether that of an artifact or of the knowledge-seeking subject – is itself a 'found object,' rendered into coherence and meaningfulness not by inner essence but via the pathways of agency that shoot through the potentiality (or 'probability') of an impressively large system, such as the internet, social networks, or neuronal networks in the brain.[30]

When someone from a humanities background becomes aware of impressively large systems, such as the individual brain's billions of neurons, the billions of individuals in various populations (from bacteria to *Homo sapiens*), and of course the cosmos, where, in Eric Idle's immortal words, 'our galaxy is only one of millions of billions/In this amazing and expaynding universe,' then the sensation of improbability is hard to avoid. As Idle (1983) so memorably put it:

> So remember, when you're feeling very small and insecure,
> How amazingly unlikely is your birth,
> And pray that there's intelligent life somewhere up in space,
> 'Cause there's bugger all down here on Earth. (see Hartley 2007)

Note that these improbabilities – neurons, populations, galaxies – seem to be scale-free versions of each other, and note further that the internet is a technological version of the same complex systemic structure. It both enables and is made of individual but networked agency, such that 'identity' begins to look like nothing more essential than the 'firing' of an individual neuron. If you note all this, then the 'amazingly unlikely' probability of *any* individual existence, whether of an idea, a bacterium, a human, or a star, becomes imaginable; precisely *as* an improbability . . . of cosmic proportions.

---

[30] See Dan (2009) and http://www.medgadget.com/archives/img/neurons_firing.jpg.

The Veblen Question

The possibility that humanities scholars in particular might be fazed by cosmic-scale improbability arises because our discipline is driven by three things that don't 'scale up' very well:

- *Meaning* – we tend to prefer in-close investigation of the generative process of individual meanings, in textual analysis, including history and literature;
- *Identity* – we are always on the lookout for aspects of individual identity (gender, class, race, sexuality, etc.) in ethnographic observation and cultural theory alike; and
- *The human* – we are concerned with how 'the human' constitutes itself from within, by philosophy or 'critical theory.'

We observe meanings and both individual and collective identity from the perspective of the observer. We are the very product of our own 'observer effect.'[31] The challenge of the probability archive for humanities-based disciplinary domains (including cultural and media studies) is not simply a challenge to the status of objects or to our finding, gathering, and archiving practices. It is a challenge to our own *mode of knowing*.

We are, in this respect, in the very same position today that economics was in more than a century ago. As noted in Chapter 2, in 1898 the American economist Thorstein Veblen published a paper with a provocative question: 'Why is economics not an evolutionary science?' Veblen contrasted the 'archaic' or 'animistic' mode of thought, which sought to explain observed phenomena and causes from the point of view of the perception of the individual, with a 'materialistic' or 'modern impersonal method of knowledge,' based on a 'systematisation of facts' forced by large-scale technological and industrial processes (Veblen 1898).

Veblen made the point that the transition from one mode of thought to the other is uneven, and that even the 'classical tradition' of economic theory of his day retained aspects of archaic thought. But a shift from 'animistic' (i.e. humanist) to materialist (i.e. evolutionary) modes of knowledge was, he concluded, only a matter of time:

---

[31] 'In physics, the term "observer effect" refers to changes that the act of observation will make on the phenomenon being observed' ('Observer effect (physics)' n.d.).

Provided the practical exigencies of modern industrial life continue of the same character as they now are, and so continue to enforce the impersonal method of knowledge, it is only a question of time when that (substantially animistic) habit of mind which proceeds on the notion of a definitive normality shall be displaced in the field of economic inquiry by that (substantially materialistic) habit of mind which seeks a comprehension of facts in terms of a cumulative sequence. (Veblen 1898)

Veblen was aware that humanist perceptions were regarded as being on a 'higher' plane, or considered more worthy and of greater 'ceremonial or aesthetic effect,' but he was interested in 'cumulative sequence,' not values:

But all that is beside the present point. Under the stress of modern technological exigencies, men's everyday habits of thought are falling into the lines that in the sciences constitute the evolutionary method; and knowledge which proceeds on a higher, more archaic plain is becoming alien and meaningless to them. The social and political sciences must follow the drift, for they are already caught in it. (Veblen 1898)

One of those 'modern technological exigencies' is the probability archive. It tells us that the essence of objective, individual identity is a semiotic outcome of display and narrative, not a property of objects or of people. The probability archive teaches us that the achievement of any particular identity is almost infinitely improbable. Nonetheless, it is organized, systematic, and predictable – at least in terms of overall (population-wide) probabilities. There is even a machine that demonstrates how order does indeed emerge from such chaotic complexity. It is called the Probability Machine or Galton Board, after the mathematician Sir Francis Galton.[32]

If what Veblen calls 'men's everyday habits of thought' are better explained by probability theory and 'cumulative sequence,' then there is a disciplinary imperative for those who study communications and culture to move beyond our own habitual thinking and shift our disciplinary gaze from the critique of *essence* to the embrace of *probability,* including a 'quantum' understanding of uncertainty and risk, and an evolutionary

---

[32] For a 'real' probability machine see IndexFundsAdvisors (2009b) (this is the 'pedagogic' model). See also IndexFundsAdvisors (2009a) (this is the 'Hollywood/marketing' model) and IndexFundsAdvisors (2010) (this one shows what happens when you let Schrödinger's cat touch your iPad).

approach to the dynamics of change in our chosen domains of meaning, identity, and the human. These are the probabilities that hover around us in the 'cloud culture' of the internet when we use it to investigate the growth of knowledge.

The Olduvai Imperative

Having cleared that up, we can now return to our original research project and, following the 'Olduvai imperative,' which explains our compulsion to create tools, we can begin to tackle the problem of archiving popular memory using the unreliable but immense resources of the internet, which is itself the latest successor to the Olduvai stone chopping tool, in the evolution of technology that signifies even as it shapes the real. What our particular example of a probability archive will look like remains uncertain, as we try to collect 'popular memory' about television as part of the project of nation-building. It seems likely that the very actions of observing and compiling an archive that seeks to understand a modern phenomenon (broadcast television in a nation state) using the affordances of networked knowledge (YouTube and Wikipedia) will alter the object of our studies.

8

Messaging as Identity

The words of Mercury are harsh after the songs of Apollo. (*Love's Labour's Lost* V.ii.938)[1]

This chapter analyzes the history and application of the term 'the message' in communication, cultural, and media studies. It goes on to propose that conceptual coherence can only be achieved for it if this concept is considered historically and in evolutionary terms. The chapter then pursues recent changes in the status of 'the message' through four phases of semiotic history (first discussed in Chapter 1):

- The *representative* (modern);
- The *excessive* (postmodern);
- The *productive* (user-created); and
- The message as human identity (*Homo nuntius*).

Having arrived at a conceptualization of 'messaging' as constitutive of our species, the chapter's final section provides the example of fashion communication to show what is meant by the term '*Homo nuntius*' (messaging humanity).

---

[1] See Malcolm Evans (1975) on this intriguing line.

Digital Futures for Cultural and Media Studies, First Edition. John Hartley.
© 2012 John Wiley & Sons, Ltd. Published 2012 by John Wiley & Sons, Ltd.

Message – What Message?

In the study of popular communication, the term 'message' has become so familiar that it often eludes careful attention, featuring almost as a proper name, not unlike the equally peculiar term 'content.' It seems to have slid into the critical vocabulary via some unnoticed side door. Looking back at the literary and critical origins of contemporary cultural and media studies, 'the message' is largely absent as a concept. It does not appear in Raymond Williams' *Keywords* (1976), in the revisionist *New Keywords* (Bennett, Grossberg, and Morris 2005), nor in the *Sage Dictionary of Cultural Studies* (Barker 2004). Within media studies the term is not included in Horace Newcomb's *Encyclopedia of Television* (2004). It does feature as a short entry (by John Fiske) in the first two editions of Routledge's multi-authored *Key Concepts in Communication* (O'Sullivan et al. 1983) and *Key Concepts in Communication and Cultural Studies* (O'Sullivan et al. 1994), but the treatment is perfunctory and the reader is advised to 'see *text* for a fuller discussion.' And, when that book was taken under single authorship (Hartley 2002), the term was dropped.

Nevertheless, 'the message' was deemed sufficiently central to contemporary communication sciences to feature prominently at the 2009 International Communication Association annual conference, whose theme for the year was 'keywords.' Certain such words – regulation, the message, the public sphere, communication, and the city – were featured at plenary and 'mini-plenary' panels organized to facilitate communication *across* the interdisciplinary differences represented among the International Communication Association's aptly named 'divisions' (Zelizer 2009).[2]

The first problem that this chapter addresses, then, is where 'the message' came from, and whether the interdisciplinary borrowings from which it is made amount to a coherent conceptualization. It transpires that the 'method' of contemporary theory is coherent only in the way that Romanticism is coherent – it presents a Faustian agony where knowledge is both desired and fatal. The best recourse for method here, I argue, may be to go back to the beginning and take the 'evolutionary turn,' seeking to provide coherence by historicizing the term rather than valorizing it – that is, its

---

[2]   The paper out of which this chapter evolved was originally prepared for a mini-plenary session on 'The message' at ICA 2009, the annual conference of the International Communication Association.

status has changed over successive historical phases of cultural evolution. This move requires rethinking 'the message' not as a noun (a thing, belonging to reason, that can be *defined*) but as a verb (an action, constituting humanity, linking *reason* to the *imagination*) – one moreover that may now be seen as a defining characteristic of our species (see also Buckminster Fuller, Agel, and Fiore 1970). The last part of the chapter puts this evolutionary idea to work in the context of one of the contemporary world's most important social networks – fashion – concluding that individual identity is constituted by the externalist social networks that we produce and maintain through messaging. Therefore, it seems, communication scholars would do well to take messaging seriously, and not just on mobile phones.

Part I: Interdisciplinary Encounters

What is 'the Message'?

The answer to that question depends upon who is asking. Modernist literary theory was skeptical about the idea of 'the message.' At the micro level (the text) it was axiomatic that the intentions or 'message' of an author cannot be 'read' from textual evidence (Brooks 1947; Richards 2004 [1929]), while at the macro level of the art form as a whole (the textual system) the 'message' of literature *as such* was regarded as non-instrumental (Shklovsky 1965 [1917]) – anti-intentionalist, if anything. Thus, 'literariness' shied away from popular, commercial, and mundane 'messages' and the intentions of author-producers, whether artistic or commercial. Before long, 'the message' of a given text was relocated to the reader (Hoggart 1960; Iser 1980); it could be recovered not from 'reading' the text itself but only from a kind of plebiscitary count of what a given population made of it (Hartley 2008: Chapter 7).

1. Madison Avenue: Campaigning, Commercial and Political

For Madison Avenue, however, and its admirers in political campaign headquarters, 'the message' was saturated with intentionality – their own.[3] They

---

[3] See this quotation from 1925 in the *Oxford English Dictionary* under 'message': 'The advertising man knows that people will not listen to his messages unless they are entertaining as well as instructive.'

wanted to 'get the message across' in commercial or political campaigns. For them, 'the message' was not found in the textual details of an advertisement (e.g. the storyline, characters, poetics) but in its broad meaning and overall import (*Oxford English Dictionary*, sense 5). This was the message that – they wished – consumers and voters would reconstruct from textual cues in order to think and feel for themselves the power and allure of a product or party. The efficiency of 'the message' could be measured indirectly – in sales and votes.

As descendants of medieval rhetoricians, the 'hidden persuaders' (Packard 2007 [1957]) of Madison Avenue – the *Mad Men* of recent revival (see 'Mad Men' n.d.) – brought to a secular and democratic age some uses of the term that were derived not from literary but from Biblical or royal origins. Here 'the message' was sent 'from on high' – God or sovereign (*Oxford English Dictionary*, senses 3b and 4). You can see the attraction of this sense of the term for advertisers: it was the *duty* of mere mortals to heed such messages.

2. McLuhan: 'The Medium is the Message'

Then Marshall McLuhan popped up, using his modernist training in textual analysis to interpret, not literature for scholars, but recent cognitive psychology for some new-found friends . . . in Madison Avenue (Wolfe 1969). As a professor of English literature, McLuhan might have been expected to express the usual skepticism and hostility to the appropriation of communicative powers by commerce. But instead he let them take him out to lunch, and he said something new: 'the medium is the message' (McLuhan 1964: 8).[4]

This bold hypothesis challenged the integrity of the single text – but also the effectiveness of advertising's stock in trade, *spot ads* on television and *display ads* in the press, both of which were 'single text' messages. But – certainly in the way that Tom Wolfe (1969) tells the story – this only endeared McLuhan to the 'Mad Men,' extending the reach of marketing and publicity well beyond the 'genre' of advertising to encompass the entire media and thence contemporary culture as a whole. His aphorisms unexpectedly closed the gap between highbrow and popular culture, between Shakespeare and shopping, by insisting

---

[4] See also http://www.marshallmcluhan.com/main.html.

that the same theory (media are an extension of mind) could apply to both. From then on the study of the 'power' of contemporary media 'messages' became a legitimate branch of textual and literary scholarship. Here it encountered two very different intellectual traditions, pulling in different directions.

3. Marxism: The Message is Power

On the one hand, the study of communicative power took people interested in media messages away from the text 'in itself,' drawing attention instead to the *relations* between 'addresser' and 'addressee,' and conceptualizing these relations in terms of asymmetrical power. This is where Raymond Williams made his own mark, not least with *Keywords* (1976). His connections with the British New Left of the 1950s, in which Stuart Hall was also active, ensured that 'power' was thought of in Marxist terms: mediated messages were thought to exert power *over* their recipients.

This remains a default assumption in political-economy approaches to media power (e.g. Schiller 1989), even where overt Marxist theorizations about the capitalist appropriation of surplus labor power have been abandoned, or at least reworded . . . into 'precarity' for instance (Ross 2009).

4. Information Theory: The Message is Physics

Pulling in a different direction were information theory and cybernetics (Shannon 1948; Cherry 1957; Baran 1964) – mathematically modeled and often derived from military research – in which the message was something to be conveyed, intact if possible, through mediating channels that might themselves be compromised by noise, interference, or decay. So, for example, 'the message' might be understood as a radio signal, and later as bits or bytes of computer information.

Information theory is relatively indifferent to the cultural, social, or political value – or even the textual 'content' – of the message: it makes very little difference whether the signals (or packets of data) 'contain' speeches by Shakespeare, Stalin, or Schwarzenegger. The main thing is to understand how they can be physically transported, and what mechanisms are needed in order for the receiver to 'decode' accurately what has been 'encoded' by the transmitter. These machine-based questions quickly assumed a human dimension; for mere mortals, such requirements as redundancy and feedback need to be built in to ensure efficient communicability. Inevitably, 'encoding' and 'decoding' – originally machine actions (especially for military messages) – were metaphorically transposed to humans (Hall 1973).

The unreliability of humans as messengers is playfully proven by the game 'telephone' or 'Chinese whispers,' where, for instance, the (apocryphal) message 'send reinforcements, we're going to advance' is corrupted into 'send three-and-fourpence, we're going to a dance.' On the other hand, the reliability of humans over machines (for the time being) when it comes to meaning is demonstrated by the difficulty computers have in such artificial intelligence tasks as automated translation, for instance.

5. Cultural Studies: Method Deleted

It is evident that 'the message' is not a coherent object of study, but is itself context- and discipline-dependent. However, mutually untranslatable usages can be highly productive of new meanings (Lotman 1990). Combining them has been a feature of media/cultural studies. Thus, textual analysts from the literary tradition (Hoggart 1957), often with Marxist leanings (Williams 1977), turned to semiotics (Eco 1976), seeking a systematic and possibly scientific basis (de Saussure 1974; Lotman 1990, 2009; Vološinov 1973) for a theory of meaning-generation that went beyond intentionalism; one that could account equally for macro-scale cultural systems including popular media (code) and for micro-scale texts (performance). Here is where 'the message' decisively entered media studies – a moment perhaps best marked by Umberto Eco's influential essay 'Towards a semiotic inquiry into the television message' (written in Italian in 1965, published in English in 1972, and most recently anthologized in Abbas and Erni 2005: 237–52).

The resulting interdisciplinary amalgam is what we now call cultural studies. It came of age in Williams' (1973) 'base and superstructure' model of 'determination' (i.e. causation in the relations between structural elements of modern cultures); in Hall's (1973) 'encoding/decoding' model (politicizing textual influence); and – if I may – in Fiske and Hartley's (2003 [1978]) semiotic 'readings' of television (see also Newcomb 1974), arguing that 'the message' may be open rather than ideological for active audiences, even when the 'activity' is sense-making rather than decision-making or creative fabrication.

Did these heterogeneous elements, combining literary interpretation, semiotics, Marxism, McLuhanism, and information theory, amount to a coherent 'take' on 'the message'? Not really. From these early days onwards, cultural studies has tended to delete the *method* from its interdisciplinary borrowings. In this it remains true to its literary antecedents and to T. S. Eliot's notorious dictum: 'The only method is to be very intelligent.'[5] Thus, it deleted the *mathematics* from information theory, the *science* from semiotics, the *agit-prop* from Marxism, and the *commercial applications* from McLuhan.

Part II: Madness, or Method?

Critical and Romantic Tendencies

Instead of seeking scientific methods or even technical tools to analyze the message at both micro- and macro-levels, method-lite cultural studies has increasingly adopted a 'values' approach, whether 'critical' in the Williams/ Hall tradition or 'romantic' in the Fiske/Hartley one.[6] The critical branch is 'glass half empty' about the message, while the romantic branch is 'glass half full.'

Critical pessimists seek to counter what they see as the globalization of the corporate and political message by preaching a kind of refusalism – a stance that is increasingly evident in the leftist backlash against digital media and the 'creative' internet, criticizing their corporatization (*New Statesman* 2009; Zittrain 2008), their exploitation of labor (Ross 2009), or their physical/environmental wastefulness (Maxwell and Miller 2008). Meanwhile, the romantic optimists seek to propagate as widely as possible the emancipationist potential of participatory media such as the internet and digital social networks, seeing this as an extension of the drive to democratize the media that drew them to this field of study in the first place (Jenkins 2006).

The point about these oppositions is that cultural/media studies displays both of them, more or less all the time. They are not opposing sides of an argument that one side is expected to win; instead they amount to what can be recognized as the *real method* of cultural studies; that is, a rhetorical staging of the tension between modernity's promise (if 'the medium is the message' then the message is 'a share for all'), and its problems (if 'the

---

[5] From the preface to Eliot's *The Sacred Wood* (1920).
[6] Toby Miller has dubbed me a 'hitherto semiotic romantic' (2009: 187).

medium is the message' then anyone who buys it is duped, dumbed-down, or a dope). The stage is thus set for an especially unproductive game of internecine struggle among those who seek to understand 'the message.' Arguments assume political and moral dimensions, sometimes ahead of (or in place of) intellectual problems or research questions. The earlier promise of interdisciplinary attention to all aspects of the theory, technology, politics, and meaning of 'the message' sometimes slides towards a certain rhetoric of 'critical' disapproval (of its corporate intentions) or 'romantic' approval (of its popular potential).

Both 'sides' forget that criticism – of *anciens régimes* – is the founding move of Romanticism and that Romanticism's optimism is literally a Faustian bargain, hard-won to say the least.[7] Looking back at the history of modernity, it seems clear that critique is at least in part a form of Romanticism, while optimism is also a self-destructive problem for collective entities as well as individuals. As a result, it may be wiser to treat the current politicization of academic studies of culture, communication, and media as an extended play-out of the tensions *within* Romanticism; not a standoff between rational and irrational tendencies but a confirmation of their continuing co-presence.

The way out of this impasse, then, is not to *win the argument* between promise and problem, optimism and critique, Dorian Gray and his portrait, but to *change the method*. Here, I would argue, it is necessary for cultural studies to turn from 'critique' as a method to *evolution* as a methodological goal.

Back to the Beginning

To fulfil the interdisciplinary promise of early semiotic, cultural, and Marxist approaches to 'the message,' it is important to revisit the disciplinary history I have tried to sketch above, from which one clear lesson is that more attention needs to be paid to methodology, the unsolved problem of any interdisciplinary field. But it is even more important to understand that the debates and uncertainties about the status and explanation of 'the message' cannot be resolved internally (within disciplinary terms), because

---

[7] The attraction of the Faustian bargain for modern Romanticism began with Goethe's *Faust* (1808–32), which sparked a century and more of imaginative work in literature, drama, music, and criticism, including work by Coleridge, Berlioz, Gounod, Oscar Wilde, and Thomas Mann (see 'Works based on Faust' n.d.).

account also needs to be taken of change in the external environment, beyond scholarship – dynamic shifts in the systems, networks, and relationships that determine what any message might mean. In other words, first we need to return to history, and thence to scientific (methodological) questions.

In this context, I propose that a definite *historical* trend can be discerned, in which the status of 'the message' has transformed or evolved over the stretch of modernity (say, the last 200–400 years in the modernizing West). Thence, *methodologically*, since the field is characterized by dynamism and change, it might better be studied using evolutionary and complexity approaches than by relying on values (for instance, political preferences).

From this historical/evolutionary perspective, it seems that our species may be in evolutionary mid-step. Many writers have sought to identify the 'unique selling point' (as it were) of *Homo sapiens* by glossing the species as one that uses language or song – that is, messaging. The Shakespearean scholar Terence Hawkes (1973) has 'the talking animal.' The African-American literary theorist Henry Louis Gates (1988) has the 'signifying monkey' while the baritone Joseph Shore (n.d.) has the 'singing ape,' which would give *Homo dicens* and *Homo cantans*, respectively. The possibility of the co-evolution of cultural as well as biological traits that may define humanity has long been recognized.[8] The variety of new specific names proposed for *Homo sapiens* (the knowing hominin)[9] bears witness to a long-felt need to explain how the ways that we make sense and interact defines what we are:

- *Homo ludens*, Johan Huizinga (1949) – the playful hominin;
- *Homo sociologicus*, Ralf Dahrendorf (1973) – the social hominin;
- *Homo aestheticus*, Ellen Dissanayake (1992) – the artistic hominin; and
- *Homo œconomicus*, Kurt Dopfer (2004) – the economic hominin.

In the same spirit, I propose:

- *Homo nuntius* – the *messaging* hominin: humanity the messenger, or 'messaging humanity.'

---

[8] For instance the work of the Centre for the Coevolution of Biology and Culture at the University of Durham: http://www.dur.ac.uk/ccbc.

[9] For the shift from 'hominid' to 'hominin' see Hirst (n.d.).

I don't think any of the proponents of the varieties listed above are suggesting that *Homo sapiens* has speciated . . . yet. So these binomial scientific names should properly be given as *trinomials* (genus, species, and rank or subspecies); thus (strictly speaking), *H. sapiens nuntius.*

Part III: Evolution of *Homo Nuntius*

Where did the term '*Homo nuntius*' come from? As for the word 'nuntius' itself, although communication was traditionally personified in the figure of the god Mercury (Rome) or Hermes (Greece)[10] – as in the 'winged messenger' – the Latin term 'nuntius' for 'the message' is also occasionally found. The earliest English usage recorded by the *Oxford English Dictionary* is from Francis Bacon's *The Advancement of Learning* (1893 [1605]). The relevant passage reads as follows:

> The knowledge which respecteth the faculties of the mind of man is of two kinds – the one respecting his *understanding and reason,* and the other his *will, appetite, and affection*; whereof the former produceth *position or decree,* the latter *action or execution.* It is true that *the imagination is an agent or nuntius* in both provinces, both the judicial and the ministerial. For sense sendeth over to imagination before reason have judged, and reason sendeth over to imagination before the decree can be acted. For imagination ever precedeth voluntary motion. (Bacon 1605: Book II, section XII, my emphases)

Bacon took pains to explain that the status of the messenger is not neutral:

> Neither is the imagination simply and only a messenger; but is invested with, or at least wise usurpeth no small *authority in itself,* besides the duty of the message. For it was well said by Aristotle, 'That the mind hath over the body that commandment, which the lord hath over a bondman; but that reason hath over the imagination that commandment which a magistrate hath over a free citizen,' who may come also to rule in his turn. (Bacon 1605: Book II, section XII, my emphasis)

---

[10] For Mercury see Hilmes (2009); for Hermes see Hyde (1998). In both cases it is clear that the messenger god is a slippery customer; a duplicitous, thieving trickster. See also Chapter 9.

Thus, 'the message' entered modern philosophy as the imaginative *agency* that 'commands' the link between understanding and desire. Further, the messenger's 'authority' is that of *self*-government, in this case of imagination by reason. Here is the first hint that messaging may be more constitutive of human identity than has previously been allowed.

Fast-forwarding to the beginning of the 'ad age,' the word 'nuntius' provided the title for Gilbert Russell's (1926) book *Nuntius: Advertising and its Future*, in the 'To-day and To-morrow' series of pre-World War II popular futurology.[11] Russell defended 'the message' of advertising thus: 'Suppose all advertising were suppressed, what would happen? The cost of living would immediately rise. Unemployment would increase. All newspapers as we know them to-day would cease to exist. The work of Government would be hindered' (Russell 1926). Thus, according to Russell, *messaging* animates the entire economy; and the polity as well. More recently the term 'nuntius' has crossed the digital divide, turning up as the name of a proprietary software application for email messages, for instance.[12] Again, the implicit assumption is that messaging is the underlying purpose of the whole technology (hardware and software).

Four Evolutionary Phases

As for the underlying concept that might be expressed by the term '*Homo nuntius*,' it too is the product of historical changes in the status of 'messages' over the course of modernity (not to speak here of earlier periods), during which time, as outlined in Chapter 1, distinct phases can be observed:

- The *representative* (modern);
- The *excessive* (postmodern); and
- The *productive* (user-created).[13]

---

[11] *The Observer* reviewed *Nuntius* thus: 'Expresses the philosophy of advertising concisely and well' (see e.g. http://www.taylorandfrancis.com/books/details/9780415463348). For more on the 'To-day and To-morrow' series see http://airminded.org/bibliography/to-day-and-to-morrow.

[12] The app is called 'Nuntius-Leo': see http://www.softpedia.com/get/Internet/E-mail/E-mail-Clients/Nuntius-Leo.shtml, where 'The *Lion of the Messages* . . . might be the right translation of the Latin words Nuntius Leo.'

[13] These phases supplement each other, because cultural evolution does not display the same tendency towards extinction as does biological evolution. Cultural 'species' or knowledge may remain active even after new forms have emerged, and the cultural products of one era may be revived in later ones, unlike living creatures (Lotman 1990).

To which we can now add:

- *The message as identity – Homo nuntius.*

Phase 1: The representative message

'Getting the message across' is a general semiotic requirement of any communication system, whether mediated, organizational, or interpersonal. However, unlike dyadic communication – when two people talk to each other – the modern *mediated* message has been imagined not as dialogue but as one-way communication. In this context, 'getting the message across' is essentially a *pedagogic* procedure (Hartley 1999), implying the conveyance of something with substance that can be transmitted (ideally unchanged), *from* a sender, *via* a channel, *to* a receiver, *for a purpose.* As we have seen, this type of message was a feature of (mass) communication theory, and was thought to be a feature of mass society too: powerful agencies, using professional experts, sent messages through the mass media in order to influence the behavior of reputedly passive receivers (the audience-consumer).

Here is an aspect of 'the message' that we have not considered so far: its *representative* status, based on an absolute commitment to *realism.* This is how and why an entire system of communication can be transformed into a system of representation: it is scaled-up teaching, trying to *represent the real* by whatever generic means, on whatever technological platform, to (and on behalf of) a whole population.

In order to represent the real, mass-mediated messages were produced by professional experts, not by the population as a whole. Those who made messages (producers and performers) were a tiny minority in the communication system. These expert-professionals therefore *represented* the population, which was typically understood to be coterminous with 'the nation' or 'society' as a whole:

- *Statistically,* they were a 'representative sample' of the polity,
- *Semiotically,* they stood in for it in stories and the imagination; and
- *Politically,* they acted for it in decision-making – imaginary and real, sometimes by the same person, as when movie stars entered politics.

There were very few storytellers, and not that many story types, but there were potentially billions of individual people within the 'story circle' (Hartley and McWilliam 2009). In this communication network, using

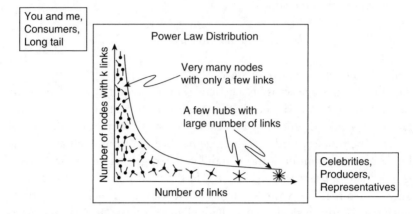

Figure 8.1   Barabási's 'scale-free' network, which grows by 'preferential attachment' where new 'nodes' tend to attach themselves to 'hubs' with many connections. This model shows how all the agents in a system are linked. Diagram modified from Barabási (2002: 71).

Albert-László Barabási's (2002) network terminology (and see Barabási and Bonabeau 2003), there were myriad 'nodes' organized by and among not many 'hubs,' which suggests that there may be a 'power law distribution' (long tail) between institutional hubs (the horizontal axis in Figure 8.1) and individual nodes (the vertical axis).

However, such a system was not necessarily *experienced* as dynamic and interconnected, especially by those ranged along the 'long tail.' To those 'nodes' with 'only a few links' (Figure 8.1), the system would seem much more stratified, hierarchical, and top-down than it may have been in mathematical point of fact. The 'long tail' *felt like* powerlessness. It seemed to be structurally opposed, sometimes antagonistically, to those 'hubs' with a 'large number of links'; a case of the semiotic 'have nots' versus the 'haves.' The *pedagogic* imperative of realist representation, coordinated by powerful state/corporate institutions ('hubs'), was to connect producers and consumers by means of one-way messages *from* one to the other, without acknowledging that the roles may be reversed.

Evidence for the realist system *not* being based on structured oppositions after all, but on dynamic change, is that, over the longer historical term, once-powerful corporate 'hubs' regularly become 'extinct' and are replaced by other agents whose own origins lie at some unremarkable point along the long tail. No matter how many connections a powerful 'hub' may possess, it is still part of the same system as the least-connected 'node' – thus, a corporate agency or media celebrity is *defined by their relationships with all the agents in the system*, not by their structural opposition to those agents. Or, as Rudyard Kipling once put it:

> Now this is the Law of the Jungle – as old and as true as the sky;
> And the Wolf that shall keep it may prosper, but the Wolf that shall break it must die.
> As the creeper that girdles the tree-trunk the Law runneth forward and back –
> For the strength of the Pack is the Wolf, and the strength of the Wolf is the Pack.
>
> (Kipling, 'Law of the Jungle,' 1895)

Note that Kipling's 'Law of the jungle' is decidedly *not* 'dog-eat-dog' or the Hobbesian 'war of each against all'; it is a *social network* where individual enterprise both determines and is determined by the choices of others, and where the actions of all determine individual outcomes. It follows that 'the law of the jungle' is a version of 'external' rationality (as in crowdsourcing) where reason is a *product* of the social networking process, not an a priori (Cartesian) *given* of individual identity. Here is where the much-maligned 'law of the jungle' improves upon neo-classical economics, in which methodological individualism requires the exercise of perfect reason, in advance of choice and action, by all individuals (see Herrmann-Pillath 2010). It is also clear that Kipling's law can only operate in circumstances where *open mutual messaging* is constitutive of the pack (or firm . . . or species), and the pack in turn can be understood as the *institutional* form taken by social networks in the lupine context.

For networked *Homo nuntius*, however, the institutional *asymmetry* between producers ('hubs' with myriad links) and consumers ('nodes' with few links) might be experienced by both 'sides' as a chalk-and-cheese distinction (where, as Kipling might have put it, 'never the twain shall meet'). This apparent 'alienation' of each from other was reified in (mass) communication theory by the linear model of communication, borrowed from information theory, which implied that there was a chain of causation going from producers to consumers, but not vice versa. The one-way model of communication mistakes *rhetoric* (persuasive pedagogy) for *logic* (causation). It forgets that 'the Law runneth forward *and back*.'

Thus, very quickly, consumers, citizens, the public, the audience (whatever guise 'the mass' took) came to be regarded as the *object*, an *effect* or destination of a realist *representational* system, not as the *subject*, cause, or origin of meaning. This model of communication is perfectly embodied in the realist mass media of the modern age – the press, broadcasting (radio and television), and cinema. None of these technologies could work without:

- An expert system of production;
- Representative status for the message;
- Pedagogic mode of address (in both entertainment and information formats);
- Linear causation of effects;
- Passive (or pacified) reception; and
- Belief that texts were referential (realist).

No wonder McLuhan said that 'the medium is the message,' because this was the powerful, pedagogic message sent by *representative* (mass) communication. It may be going too far to call it 'false consciousness,' but subsequent phases in the evolution of the message suggest that the linear, representative, mass-mediated model tended to drown out alternative models of how communication works among modern humans.

Phase 2: The excessive message – 'Il n'y a pas d'hors-texte'[14]
The realist system was already under intolerable strain by the 1960s, although that does not mean that the model or its adherents had or have since disappeared. But already then, and especially in environments influenced by continental philosophy and structuralist theory, trust in the referentiality of realist representation was in crisis, if not full flight. The crisis involved:

- The break-up of the nineteenth-century disciplines, leading to the 'new humanities' (Lee 2003);
- Disaffection with science in the context of the Cold War and 'military-industrial complex';
- The nascent consumer movement (Ralph Nader);

---

[14] 'There is no outside-the-text' (Jacques Derrida 1976: 158–9).

- 1960s-style countercultural hedonism (New Age); and
- Postmodernism, which was gaining ground among intellectuals both within and beyond the academy.

In the realm of ideas and in popular culture (which were in any case convergent), this period may be described as one of semiotic *excess*, based on the idea of 'the sign' breaking free of its referent, much as brain-work and design had already been *abstracted* from labor and artisanship during the industrializing era, to float – too freely for some – in a 'play of signifiers' that applies equally to advertising and philosophy. This period has lasted for much of my career and it has provoked much controversy. However, we don't need to go over that here. More to the present purpose is to note that this phase marked a massive expansion in the *productivity of the message systems of modernity*. Simply put, signs detached from realism are capable of *much more signification* than is mere realist reference. Meanings were also recognized to be more unstable – often duplicitous – and felt to be increasingly arbitrary, as the lines between fact, fiction, fabrication, and faking blurred – not least, on the nightly news.

Subjectivity (identity) re-entered the referential sphere in the form of the 'new social movements' – that is, politics organized not around the figure of the rational or 'informed citizen' (Schudson 1999) but around gender, ethnicity, sexual orientation, the peace movement, and the rest. This was the time of 'anything goes' post-modernism, at least in the eyes of opponents wedded to the strict referentiality of the sign (Sokal 1996).[15]

Phase 3: The productive message

Post-modernism in the 1960s to the 1980s was a kind of recalibration of the capacity of the meaning systems available for large-scale communication throughout modernized societies, setting the conditions for the further expansion and interconnectivity of these networks into abstracted or 'virtual' formats, boosted by technological developments associated with computing power.

The state of semiotic excess proved not to be terminal but transitional – an unstable phase where the *productivity of the sign* was a precursor of a more fundamental transformation, this time in the *productivity of the*

---

[15] And see the debates at Sokal's archive: http://www.physics.nyu.edu/faculty/sokal/#beyond_the_hoax.

user or agent. As is usual in such matters, this later kind of productivity *supplemented* the productivity of the sign; it did not *supplant* it. So, the true transformation was not in communication systems as technologies or even as texts, but in *agency* within them. Here is where the concept of the consumer derived from the industrial era transformed into its own opposite, from:

- Represented mass to direct participant;
- Receiver to transmitter;
- Passive to active;
- Object to subject; and
- Consumer to producer.

Here, in short, is where the *agency* of 'the message' flips from the professional expert to the population at large – now, in principle, *everyone* is a journalist, publisher, and creative artist.

Phase 4: The message as identity – Homo nuntius
Many things can be said about the status of 'the message' in the era of participatory culture, consumer co-creation, user-led innovation, social network markets, and Web 2.0 (Jenkins 2006). Here, I want to draw attention to just one aspect, which in my view fulfils the promise – the emancipationist desire – of early cultural studies. Now, at last, it is possible to imagine, although not yet to observe as a built structure or widespread practice, a communication system that is both population-wide and able to harness the creative and productive energies of every agent in the system. Such a prospect also returns to the forefront of the analytical agenda two of the founding problems of cultural studies: the question of *identity* (subjectivity) and the problem of *institutions*, both of which are caught up in the question of networked agency (Latour 2005).

Here's where *Homo nuntius* – 'messaging humanity' – seems like a useful concept, because it requires attention to population-wide human characteristics, rather than to partial (elite-driven) or private systems, however large (like the internet), and their technological peculiarities. At the same time, it requires an *externalist* definition of human identity (Herrmann-Pillath 2010), which is produced not by 'the brain' (Greenfield 2002) but by externally *networked* brains, linked primarily by language – dialogic, iterative, generative messaging in a coded system or semiosphere (Lotman 1990, 2009). Once it had evolved, language was causal of further productive change, which we may call culture. The species as a whole was permanently altered by these evolutionary shifts: *H. sapiens nuntius* is not quite the same animal as *H. sapiens* was *before* language and culture evolved.

Even though each individual must learn language, which means language is ontogenetic not phylogenetic, nevertheless all humans and all known human societies rely on language to externalize the process of knowledge reproduction, and adaptation. Language is able to *act on* individuals even as it is *produced by* them. Thus, although it returns attention to individual agency and identity, instead of focusing exclusively on industrial-scale systems and structures, the concept of *Homo nuntius* also allows for the agency of the network or networks used (i.e. for institutions) to be part of the species definition. Finally, since *Homo nuntius* is an evolved form of *Homo sapiens, Homo œconomicus, Homo ludens*, etc., it follows that language is an evolutionary concept too.

'Messaging humanity' allow us to think about 'the message' not as an external packet but as a *constitutive property of humanity*. This property is not new, although it has been precipitated into increased visibility recently because technological and scientific developments have allowed the messaging aspect to be observed more accurately. For instance, where once we could only talk metaphorically and abstractly about entities such as 'the reading public,' now we can observe and measure it directly at any given moment, for instance via clickstream and sales-tracking data.

Individuals in the species *Homo nuntius* don't just 'send' messages as an action ('message' as verb), they *are* a system of messages ('message' as collective noun); they are constituted by and productive through messages, which are the means by which reason emerges. Thus, in this model, rationality is the product or outcome of a 'social networking' process, not an input based on humans' big brains. Rather, the big brains are necessary to process the complexities of social networking.[16] This is what social networks such as Facebook have begun to codify, and where social network markets – the new term for the creative industries (Potts et al. 2008a) – are beginning to coordinate into self-organizing order.

---

[16] Recent observations suggest that the human brain may have been getting smaller over the last 20,000 years. One explanation is that increased sociality (following population increase, agriculture, settlements) allowed problem-solving by externally networked brains (like bonobos; unlike chimpanzees). See McAuliffe (2010).

Part IV: Fashion as 'the Message' of *Homo Nuntius*

From that perspective, then, what is 'the message' that *Homo nuntius* sends about itself? In order to illustrate how a 'messaging human' *produces* individual *identity* out of social-network *interaction*, consider the case of fashion.

'The Look': A Dialogic Message

A personal 'look' is a complex message, always evolving, never perfected, endlessly rehearsed, iterated over a lifetime. Using an infinite set of choices involving body, garments, make-up, hair, and accessories, not to mention a contextual location and venue, chosen or given, in which to strut one's stuff, each ensemble of elements is combined to communicate a single overall 'message' for the given moment. In this respect, as Roland Barthes (1967) observed, the 'fashion system' functions as a language, using intricate and dynamic rules to produce the visual equivalent of a poem or a lyric.

Yet, despite the complexity of the system, individuals of *Homo nuntius* are able to draw accurate conclusions about each other almost instantaneously, on sight. A given 'look' – whether that of the Mona Lisa, the latest supermodel, or a 14-year-old after an hour in the bathroom – will repay careful and detailed study. However, it can also be apprehended at a single glance. This is in fact the purpose for which such a 'look' is designed, often very artfully, but also quite spontaneously, as a dialogic message generating new meanings promiscuously from a system of infinite potential. For, like language, fashion is useless without an interlocutor, in this case the gaze of a real or imagined observer. Whether the 'dialogue' is with imagined critic ('does my bum look big in this?') or real friend, including professional stylists such as Trinny (Woodall) and Susannah (Constantine) or Rachel Zoe (Rosenzweig), the 'formative' elements of a look are submitted to their 'summative' – and instant – examination and judgment.[17]

In other words, there is nothing impoverished about a single glance. According to Aristotle's *Politics*, a democratic polity (i.e. a city state) ought

---

[17]   The difference between formative and summative assessment has been explained thus: 'When the cook tastes the soup, that's formative. When the guests taste the soup, that's summative' (Robert E. Stake, quoted in Scriven 1991: 19).

to comprise no more people 'than can be seen at a single glance' (see Peters 2001). This is the dialogic or messaging element of fashion language, the point of intelligibility towards which a given 'look' is intended; a point that always exists *outside* of the body whose look is communicated. What a dress ensemble *means* is therefore not as intended or predicted in the wearer's initial choice and arrangement of elements but in *how these are seen* by others. Meanings emerge and change in a socially networked system of active and evolving relationships identified by status-based signaling. That's the message.

Everyone continuously 'samples' this system to check their position, direction, status, links, mistakes, and scope for action, and we do this by constant looking, and constantly 'being looked at,' even when alone (Žižek 2002). The system is not merely complex, it is competitive, as Thomas Hobbes noticed in *Leviathan* (1651): 'the value of a man' consists in 'the esteem of others.' You cannot opt out, and it is always 'on.'

Consumer Productivity and Mediated Risk

Fashion is one of those areas where consumption is itself a form of production, and an essentially entrepreneurial form at that. People display on their own bodies the *risks* associated with aesthetic choice, constant innovation, dynamic change, and competitive status. Fashion is *risk culture in action* (Hartley and Montgomery 2009: 71).

For those inside the fashion scene, the right look at the right time is expressive not only of belonging to the scene (emulation), and not only of the riskiness of choices (originality), but also of a competitive social network in which dress is itself an *experiment* that others may emulate in turn. How you show up – wearing what, with whom, at what time, to what venue – becomes a move in a productive system where individual innovation is also a 'competitive advantage.' Indeed, everyone is on the lookout for just that. In this system, individual choices are determined, not by 'rational choice' or 'need' (as per *Homo œconomicus*), but *by the choices of others*; and this is a definition of *social network markets*, which constitute the creative industries (Potts et al. 2008 'Social network markets'). Even if you are just dressing for yourself (your own self-scrutinizing persona . . . an 'imagined community' of one) or your own private network, and not for public consumption, there is a continuum – not a structural opposition – between producers and consumers, even between celebrities and ordinary citizens, in a system that is always open to renewal from 'below.'

Conclusion: Messaging Humanity

This is because fashion, of all the art forms, is the one most integrated into everyday life; the one most open to aesthetic innovation by non-professionals ('street' fashion); and the one, of all the creative industries, that no one can escape (apparel choice is population-wide, even if high fashion is not). Thus, like language, fashion harnesses the energies of *everyone in the system*. Everyone is networked with everyone else, and there are surprisingly few degrees of separation between the 'top' (celebrity) and 'bottom' (street) players (witness the success of Kate Moss' brand at Topshop). That is how the system adapts and evolves. In Beinhocker's terms (2006: 15, emphasis in original), everyone's creativity and choices 'matter *as part of a larger evolutionary process.*'

Unlike language, however, fashion is not an evenly distributed human capability (even though dress is). Like literature, learning, and other *elaborate* arts that aestheticize ubiquitous activities (cooking, sewing, singing, playing music, dancing), fashion is a form of *knowledge*. And, by its very elaboration, it is also a teaching institution. In contrast to our hyper-specialist age, learning, literature, letters, and literacy were all of apiece during the emergence of the English language, nation, and state, as exemplified in the writings of King Alfred (around 887CE), who sought to improve the competence of his magistracy and at the same time to Anglicize the wisdom (*sapientia*) of the Latin tongue. 'Learning, literacy, language and literature become aspects of national and racial identity in . . . Alfred's own works' (Irvine 2006 [1994]: 416). Thus, the elaborate system of 'literature' was nothing less than 'wisdom' (or '*sapientia*'), required for the education of rulers, taking the ubiquitous native wit of the vernacular and conjoining it with the learning of the ancients. In the process of upgrading English learning, Alfred also created a persistent distinction between informal or tacit knowledge (English) and formal or explicit knowledge (Latin). Something of the same process is evident in fashion, where native 'dress' is disciplined and improved by French 'couture.' Thus there is a constant interaction ('*nuntius*') between '*Homo*' in general (language, dress) and '*sapiens*' in particular (learning, fashion), which over time results in a growth of knowledge among the whole population.

The professionalization of 'tacit' knowledge (Leadbeater 1999) is evident in 'haute' cuisine and couture (cooking and sewing); indeed, most arts take everyday or anthropological activities to a 'higher' or aestheticized level. Then, these expert variants become templates for population-wide emulation. Thus, fashion values are susceptible to growth and are improved by cumulative criticism and correction. Fashion adapts to change, but it also incorporates those adaptations to improve upon its own antecedents. Physically, textiles are better (more fit for purpose) than they were in the pre-modern era; socially, fashion allows women to transcend gender constraints (women can wear whatever they want) while simultaneously accentuating gender difference (fashion remains a 'portrait of a woman'). Such changes extend *choice* across vast populations, both quickly (this season) and historically (cumulative sequence). A difference emerges between costume as an anthropological fact and fashion as a historical one. The difference is that while *change* is 'intuitive' (*implicit* or tacit) in customary systems, it is an *explicit* value in fashion: fashion faces forward. Novelty is organized and coordinated into institutions and markets, themselves rapidly changing throughout the modern era. The rigor of change-driven 'messaging' is demonstrated best in the competitive turbulence of haute-couture seasonal collections – to retain competitive advantage, the high-end fashion houses must *completely change* their 'look' twice a year, while remaining *exactly the same* as a brand that is readily identifiable among the throng. The element of entrepreneurial risk could hardly be higher; this is the 'message' that fashion communicates as a representative system; it is the 'look' that individual wearers (users) *produce*.

Thus, fashion is a global teaching institution, propagating choices among hitherto unimaginably large populations. What is striking about contemporary fashion in fact is not the 'height' of haute couture but the 'width' of its influence – the extent of its reach, both demographic and geographical. Since its modern invention by aristocratic and mercantile elites in and following the European Renaissance (Welch 2005), it is remarkable how many 'ordinary' people are now involved in a given community, and how improved are general standards of dress, including standards of professionally advised choice within an ensemble, compared with the past, not least because of the tireless educative and competitive stimulation of the fashion media, from *Vogue* to *Project Runway*. In other words, like wealth and knowledge – and despite the occasional downturn or even 'mass extinction' – the fashion system is *growing* (one node at a time, as Barabási would say), as an integral part of modern entrepreneurial capitalism and as a globalizing 'message system' through which everyone expresses their identity, their relationships, and their knowledge. The fashion market (including fashion media) is a *coordinator* of choice, innovation, and replication within that culture.

This 'model' of choice does not follow the methodological individualism of *Homo œconomicus*, so beloved of neo-classical economics, where choices are based on 'rational' *self*-interest, a conceptual framework that requires that *rationality* itself be understood as a 'mentifact' – the Cartesian product of 'the' individual mind. Here, instead, we can literally visualize the *appeal* of creative innovation and of emergent knowledge within and about 'risk culture.' Fashion literally embodies the restlessness of capital (Metcalfe n.d.) and the sociality of choice on the bodies of 'entrepreneurial consumers' (Hartley and Montgomery 2009).

Here, then, rationality is a *product of the system* – it is an outcome of social networks. Each fashion 'message' – be it a person's 'look,' a designer's collection, or a photographer's set in *Vogue* – is therefore 'poetic' in the original sense of the word *poïesis* ('to make anew'). It both *transforms* and *continues* the world it *represents* (Lotman 2009). To get the message of fashion (the 'look') is to enter into dialogue (to *produce* a dynamic identity) with this *poetry of the age of risk*. Simultaneously it is to participate in the social network of competitive individual aesthetics, and thereby to become an active *agent in the growth of knowledge*. That is the 'message' of *Homo sapiens nuntius*.

9

Paradigm Shifters
Tricksters and Cultural Science

The past is a foreign country: they do things differently there.
(L. P. Hartley, *The Go-Between* 1953: 1)

This chapter draws the themes of the book as whole together by linking anthropological and economic treatments of the process of innovation and change, not only within a given 'complex system' (a cosmology; an industry) but also *between* systems, specifically cultural and economic systems. The role of the 'go-between' is considered, as both the anthropological figure of the Trickster (Hyde 1998) and the Schumpeterian entrepreneur. Both figures parlay appetite (economic wants) into meaning (cultural signs). Both practice a form of creativity based on deception or 'creative destruction' or renewal by the disruption and adaptation of existing systems. The disciplinary purpose of the chapter is to try to bridge two otherwise disconnected domains – cultural studies and evolutionary economics – by showing that the traditional methods of the humanities (e.g. anthropological, textual, and historical analysis) have explanatory force in the context of economic actions and complex-system evolutionary dynamics. The objective is to understand creative innovation as a general cultural attribute rather than one restricted only to accredited experts such as artists, and thus to theorize creativity as a form of *emergence* for dynamic systems. In this context, adaptive change is provoked by 'paradigm shifters' – tricksters and entrepreneurs who create new meanings out of the clash of difference, including the clash of incommensurable systems.

Digital Futures for Cultural and Media Studies, First Edition. John Hartley.
© 2012 John Wiley & Sons, Ltd. Published 2012 by John Wiley & Sons, Ltd.

Trickster the Entrepreneur

Lewis Hyde, in his book *Trickster Makes this World: How Disruptive Imagination Creates Culture* (1998), presents Coyote as the appetite-driven, deceiving, thieving, whatever-it-takes trickster, who steals from the gods, travels the open road, and plans to eat your children. How can such a character 'create culture'? For reasons that I hope will become clear, this scoundrel (and others of his type) makes a wonderful 'model' for an apparently very different figure that stalks the mythology of the creative industries; namely, the entrepreneur.

The word '*entrepreneur*' literally means 'between-taker' (in French); the English-language idiom would therefore be the 'go-between.' This is indeed the role of Coyote and other 'tricksters' across many mythologies, including the Greek god Hermes, who has been described thus:

> Hermes is the great messenger of the gods in Greek mythology and a guide to the Underworld. Hermes was [...] also the patron of boundaries and of the travelers who cross them, of shepherds and cowherds, of the cunning of thieves, of orators and wit, of literature and poets, of athletics and sports, of weights and measures, of invention, and of commerce in general. ('Hermes' n.d.)[1]

Hermes – or Mercury, as the Romans called him – was a deified trickster; the go-between creator and transgressor of boundaries; messenger-god of communication, whose gifts in translation and oratory were founded on deception, serving him well as the god of commerce, communication . . . and thieves.

Despite our modernity, we are still living in plain sight of this mythology. Our name for the boundary-defying shape-shifter liquid metal element is mercury. 'Mercury' signifies the open road (e.g. Mercury vehicles in the US). We call the interpretation of hidden meanings 'hermeneutics,' after Hermes. The 'winged messenger' remains a symbol of communication, and early newspapers were called mercuries (some still are; e.g. in Tasmania). After printing was invented, publishers soon appropriated the role of Hermes as he who waters the Tree of Knowledge.[2] Hermes harks back to

---

[1] And see http://home.vicnet.net.au/~hwaa/hermes.html.
[2] For an illustration see http://www.um.edu.mt/lib/onlinexhibitions/rare_books/Content.html (Origen's life, published by Christian Gensch, 1685).

Egyptian Thoth, god of writing and wisdom, forward to Roman Mercury, and thence to modern Europe. He is obviously a complex figure. The 'Hermetic' tradition claimed one version of him as the founder of magic and thence also science. It may be that this multiplicity of attributes indicates the chaos and irrationality of myth; but it may equally alert us to the possibility that such attributes are linked and have been since time immemorial. Here, I simply want to claim Hermes – and Coyote – as the archetypal model of the Schumpeterian entrepreneur – the bringer of the new and agent of the 'creative destruction' of old orders and existing rules. As Lewis Hyde puts it:

> I want to argue a paradox that the [trickster] myth asserts: that the origins, liveliness and durability of cultures require that there be a space for figures whose function is to uncover and disrupt the very things that cultures are based on. (1998: 9)

As far as Hyde is concerned, tricksters like Hermes and Coyote are agents of change, certainly, but change of a particular type, which ensures renewal and adaptation to new conditions: 'In spite of all their disruptive behaviour, tricksters are regularly honoured as the creators of culture' (1998: 8). In other words, the trickster is not a trivial figure, but one whose disruptions are fundamental to the system he disrupts. The trickster is not a mere con artist or venal politician: 'When he lies and steals, it isn't so much to get away with something or get rich as to disturb the established categories of truth and property and, by so doing, open the road to possible new worlds' (1998: 13).

Joseph Schumpeter's theory of entrepreneurship was based on exactly this principle:

> The typical entrepreneur is more self-centered than other types, because he relies less than they do on tradition and connection and because his characteristic task – theoretically as well as historically – consists precisely in breaking up old, and creating new, tradition [...] Our type seeks out difficulties, changes in order to change, delights in ventures.' (1934: 91–4)

Schumpeter's biographer Thomas McCraw comments on this passage:

> Breaking up old traditions and creating new ones could just as well describe what Schumpeter himself was doing to the discipline of economics. In passages such as these, he is defining the behavioral profile of the entrepreneur

as a type. He is arguing that the entrepreneur, in contrast to the ordinary manufacturer or merchant, is not merely overseeing the daily flow of production and consumption but is actually crafting the future. (2007: 71)

Schumpeter himself drew the parallel with science: 'The history of science is one great confirmation of the fact that we find it exceedingly difficult to adopt a new scientific point of view or method [...] So it is also in the economic world' (1934: 86). In short, the entrepreneur and trickster are no everyday *beneficiaries* of existing systems: they are *paradigm shifters*.

Cultural Science: System, Agency, Disruption, Change

What has this to do with 'cultural science'? The answer is that Coyote, Hermes, and other mythological tricksters give us material to think with, specifically about the relationship between *system* (e.g. the eternal order of the gods) and *agency* (e.g. the deceptions of the appetite-driven trickster) in order to theorize *change* (practical adaptations among both gods and humans). What is at stake in the struggle is not simply winnings (e.g. food) but the *rules* for winning and thus the survival – or otherwise – of both system and agent. Indeed, Hyde is at pains to point out that the proceeds of tricksters' larceny are not as important in themselves as is the discipline of delayed gratification. Hermes steals Apollo's cattle, but does not eat the meat: instead, he converts his appetite into knowledge, his winnings into signs, and his 'creative destruction' of the divine order into the conditions of possibility for renewal. The figure of the trickster allows us to think about the *abstract* or conceptual problem of how to *model* the relations among *systems, agency, change, and knowledge*, via an example that comes not from the scientific world or from contemporary economics and politics but from the most thoroughgoing and unrepentant tradition of the humanities, which is the study of human *meaningfulness* – that is, (a) anthropological observation of human cultural patterns over deep time and across wide geographical spaces and (b) astute discursive and textual analysis of cultural forms and stories (Hyde is exemplary in both of these endeavors). Here then is a mechanism for crossing another boundary – one that in various guises has bedeviled modern knowledge systems – namely, the distinction between arts and sciences as modes of knowing. If there is to be a 'cultural science,' then the nineteenth-century settlement of science as the realm of *facts* and humanities as the realm of *values* does not and cannot hold (Lee 2010: 47–53).

C. P. Snow's oft-cited but rarely investigated (with notable exceptions: Edgerton 2005; Kagan 2009) notion of 'two cultures' is itself in need of some 'creative destruction.' A go-between is needed to reformulate and renew the relations between science and culture. Of course we are not alone in such an endeavor, but the 'cultural science' group of researchers at the CCI (see Chapter 2, Part II) is an experimental start-up venture (as it were), seeking to change the rules about what counts as science and what counts as culture, in the study of system, agency, change, and knowledge in the realm of meaningfulness. It asks the 'Veblen question': why is cultural studies not an evolutionary science? Once asked, that question has proven to be a bit of a coyote, wandering in from the open road and gazing hungrily at our brain-children. It may cause us to question our own system:

- Why has cultural studies been content to remain a field of contestation and 'position'? Why do we so often refuse the option of cumulative elaboration, testing, and revision of knowledge claims that may result in a self-correcting 'science' in favor of studies dedicated to the justification of the political or moral stance of the investigator?
- How can cultural studies survive as a field when each new entrant can invent it anew, ignoring existing work?
- Why is cultural studies stuck on structures and oppositions (asymmetrical relations of power) rather than on process and change – or what Veblen calls 'causal sequence'?
- And why is cultural studies so deaf to the changes going on in other disciplines, notably economics itself, but also, perhaps even more challengingly, in the biosciences, neurosciences, and neo-Darwinian evolutionary theory?

When people in cultural studies hear the word 'science' – not to mention 'evolution' – they generally reach for their revolvers (Bérubé 2009). Instead of that, we thought we'd do some reading. The cultural science initiative at the CCI is based on a combination of three interdisciplinary inputs:

- *Evolutionary theory* – as elaborated in evolutionary or neo-Darwinian economics (Brian Arthur, Eric Beinhocker, Carsten Herrmann-Pillath, Jane Jacobs, Stan Metcalfe, Jason Potts);

- *Complexity theory* – that is, network theory (Santa Fe Institute, Albert-Laszlo Barabási, Alex Bentley, Paul Ormerod) and systems theory (Niklas Luhmann); and
- *Cultural studies* – notwithstanding its current eroded state, the reflexive tradition (CCCS, Birmingham) of in-close textual/contextual analysis of meaning and identity, using textual-discursive ideology-critique (literary/media cultural studies, feminism, etc.), ethnography (subculture/audience/fan studies), and language-based meaning systems (semiotics, Roland Barthes, Yuri Lotman, Umberto Eco).

The initiative is motivated by a desire to understand, and if possible to model, how change works in culture at the level of whole populations. We are motivated by the basic 'problem situation' of the humanities – what makes the human and how can we know? We cast that question across social networks of purposeful and meaningful action, and look to recent evolutionary and complexity theory to assist in the quest (of course, these fields have not been idle on the question of culture in the meantime). In fact, with Stephen Muecke (2009: 413), we aspire to 'a new cultural studies inspired by some scientific thought, a cultural science if you like,' which produces a 'new kind of subjectivity' among humanities scholars, one that is 'permanently networked and inter-species' (414). Thus, in relation to human sense-making, how is it possible to identify and track causal sequence, dynamic process, and rules of transformation, and even to ask to what extent the same 'algorithm' (an 'abstract series of steps'; Arthur 2009: 180) applies across seemingly disparate domains or activities (e.g. Alex Bentley's 'random copying' theory)?[3]

Such questions are in contradistinction to a by-now standard or every-day focus on structure, opposition, and the politics of difference in cultural studies; a perspective inherited from structuralism, semiotics, and

---

[3] 'Our first studies, published in 2003–2004 in *Proceedings of the Royal Society B*, showed how a simple model of random copying, with a small amount (i.e., <2%) of innovation, can explain many patterns of popular culture change at the national level, including "long-tail" distributions of popularity, discussed by Chris Anderson's book (2006). Our studies suggested that popular success does not necessarily require any inherent qualities – it can happen just by luck through the process of people randomly copying each other. What was amazing is that such a simple model could work so well – that at a population level, a model of random copying with occasional innovation can explain the data as well as anything else' (*Influx* 2007).

continental Marxism of the 1960s and 1970s and institutionalized as 'normal science' in the 'new humanities,' focusing on identity formation (individual and collective), discursive power, contextualized meaning, and the practices of ordinary life.

Our approach is also divergent from the rational choice and equilibrium states of neo-classical economics, a field that turns out to be just as turbulent as our own (see Lasn 2009). In other words, we do see cultural science as a 'paradigm shifter' for both cultural studies and economics. Perhaps this is why we became interested in *studying* as well as *attempting* disruption, renewal, and innovation of knowledge domains. In order to study culture itself more adequately, it is necessary to renew what can be meant by 'cultural studies.' For instance, cultural studies needs to include population-wide macro-systems as well as micro-descriptions, and to account for change from an evolutionary perspective rather than from an oppositional one, while at the same time not letting go of its interest in meaning, identity, situational context, textual and discursive forms and histories, and the politics of knowledge and culture.

New Firms

In part, this line of thinking was provoked by the CCI's practical need to engage with interlocutors in government, business, and technology, where the question of the moment – this was around 2004–5 – was not about resistant subjectivity, contextualized meaning, or orders of knowledge, but about *innovation*. This term is heavily accented by its usage in business literature, where it describes the hoped-for source of growth for knowledge-based economies, following the technological inventions associated with information and communication technologies, digital networks, and the internet.[4] When we were planning the CCI in 2004–5, 'national innovation systems' were imagined entirely within the confines of science and technology, including the biosciences but not the humanities. Creativity and culture were more likely to be accounted for as 'sticky' resistance to change or backward-looking 'suboptimal behaviour' (Bednar and Page 2007:

---

[4] 'The knowledge economy (KE) can be defined through analysis of four characteristic areas (the "four pillars" of the knowledge economy): (a) the policy and institutional framework; (b) an innovation system; (c) education and lifelong learning; and (d) information technology infrastructure and electronic development ("e-development")' (Goel et al. 2004: 1).

65–6)[5] than as part of a growing knowledge economy or national-competitive innovation system.

Could there be 'innovation' in culture? Is it possible to conceive of culture and the cultural as a domain of *emergence* rather than the 'heritage' of sticky, left-over, legacy systems? Here the term 'creativity' becomes crucial,[6] a go-between term to link business strategy (creativity as a key to wealth-creation in firms) to the humanities, where it has referred most readily to the creative and performing arts – that is, to *artistic* creativity. That is the question: How can the idea of the 'creative industries' harness both 'creativity' (individual talent) and 'industry' (commercial scale) in the pursuit of innovation (dynamic change), across local, national, and global contexts? Here an observation of Schumpeter proves prescient. He 'emphasizes the role of *new* companies in making innovations that interrupt the circular flow' (McCraw 2007: 74). In other words, the way to beat IBM is to found Microsoft; the way to beat Microsoft is to found Apple . . . etc. This truism of entrepreneurial innovation is also relevant to intellectual renewal in institutions of knowledge (e.g. disciplinary arrangements, university departments, etc.). You might be better off starting a new firm than seeking to reform the established dominant player. This is what we think about creativity and culture. To *rethink* them we have needed to get out of the modernist-humanist box. We recognize that the CCI is a 'new firm' – the odds are against it, but the need for renewal requires risky experimentation, and the chorus of criticism from those who thought we should know better (e.g. McGuigan 2006; O'Connor 2009) is predictable – almost a requirement.

The 'A' Word

The reason that the CCI needed to set up as a 'new firm' was not simply to escape the clutches of contrarian cultural studies; there was also the knotty problem of the 'A word': art. Over the past century and more, the notion of *artistic* creativity has been captured by the modernist discourse of the

---

[5] 'The hallmarks of cultural behavior include consistency within and across individuals, variance between populations, behavioral stickiness, and possibly suboptimal performance' (Bednar and Page 2007: 65–6).

[6] Crucial means 'of the crux' – that is, crossroads, the god of which is Hermes.

avant-garde, where 'the New,' as Barthes (1975, 1989) put it, contests the hegemony of 'repetition machines' in popular culture, media, education systems, and the like. Here, *originality* (associated with minority or 'difficult' art) takes precedence over *distribution* (associated with mass production, popular culture, and cheap goods) in the cultural value hierarchy. It may seem that this emphasis on originality is perfectly suited to the rhetoric of innovation. And indeed, the century-long insistence on the precedence of 'minority culture' over 'mass civilization' could easily be ventriloquized into the new discourse. It could even be claimed that the creative artist and the entrepreneur shared important qualities in common (Gu and O'Connor 2006). Before you know it, there is a master metaphor for the creative innovator of our age – 'the designer,' who takes over the mantle of progress from 'the engineer' of the industrial age. Designers can be both entrepreneurial and creative, providing value-added knowledge-based services to otherwise stagnating advanced economies, spreading innovation throughout the entire consumer economy.

However, there is a problem with this development. It keeps firmly in place the model of minority expertise, superimposing the creative artist onto the expert-pipeline model of industrial production, preserving the distinction between producers (active firms, and their *expertise*) and consumers (passive populations, and their *wants*). The way to scale up creativity for innovation systems, according to this model, is to fuse art with industry, which results in the 'copyright industries,' 'design labs,' and policies such as strong intellectual property regimes. But those nurtured on critical modernism see it as systematically impossible – the system does not allow it – to admit that the *creativity* of the artist can be scaled up in this way, because popularization, commercialization, and repetition at industrial scale is thought systematically to blunt the radical edge of 'the New.' The model does not allow that avant-garde critique, resistance, countercultural activism, and progressive politics can coexist with or emerge from commercial culture.

This worry has preoccupied the critics. But in my view a more serious problem remains unresolved. Substituting the artist-designer for the lab, and claiming the artist as entrepreneur, simply revamps the expert-system paradigm. This excludes the *majority of the population* from productivity in creative innovation. Art and commerce simply reinforce each other. Neither is transformed. A truly radical approach would be one that sought to explain and promote creative innovation among *whole populations* (using 'population' in a biological not Foucauldian sense, although the edges between these may need careful delineation in practice). The transformative change would be one that worked not to shore up the existing beneficiaries of expert systems but to extend the social base of creative productivity to – in principle – everyone. And, of course, this is exactly what the development of the internet and associated social network markets brings into the realm of practical possibility, perhaps for the first time. Now *everybody* is a producer of what Clay Shirky calls 'public thought' (see Chapter 4). This 'shock of inclusion' is most disruptive for existing interests:

> The beneficiaries of the system where making things public was a privileged activity, whether academics or politicians, reporters or doctors [and, we may add, artists], will complain about the way the new abundance of public thought upends the old order, but those complaints are like keening at a wake; the change they fear is already in the past. The real action is elsewhere (Shirky 2010).[7]

The way to move forward is not to insist that 'art as we know it' be included in the creative industries, as Kate Oakley (2009) among others has done, but to reform what we mean by art. Here is where you need 'cultural ratbags' such as Marcus Westbury, whose concept of 'not quite art' – where creativity meets digital networks – shows the way:

> *Not Quite Art* traces how our culture is shifting from the hierarchical, local and parochial structures to a global and networked world where Australian artists have audiences around the world, yet often remain relatively unknown in their local community. (http://www.abc.net.au/tv/notquiteart)[8]

Here we can glimpse the possibility of rethinking creativity for whole populations, and thinking about *distributed* art (not just 'original' work by accredited artists) as a game-changing disruption for whole systems. If we are to consider culture in evolutionary terms, this is a vital move: to get art, culture, creativity, and innovation away from their association with minorities, experts, the avant-garde, and firms, and to rethink them from first principles.

---

[7] See also http://www.edge.org/q2010/q10_index.html.
[8] *Not Quite Art* aired in two three-episode seasons in 2007 and 2008. For Westbury as 'cultural ratbag' see Oliver (2007). See also http://www.marcuswestbury.net.

Distributed Talent

This approach to creativity is by no means novel. It is part and parcel of the same democratic drive that resulted in modern representative government. One of the most successful popularizers of the idea of democratic government, based on the abilities of the whole population, was another radical ratbag – that is, an intellectual entrepreneur and political trickster – Thomas Paine, who played an active role in both the American and French Revolutions, and tried very hard to provoke one in Britain too. In *Rights of Man* (1906 [1792]) he wrote:

> It appears to general observation that revolutions create genius and talents; but those events do no more than bring them forward. There is existing in man [humanity] a mass of sense lying in a dormant state, and which, unless something excites to action, will descend to him, in that condition, to the grave. As it is to the advantage of society that the whole of its faculties should be employed, the construction of government ought to be such as to bring forward by quiet and regular operation, all that extent of capacity which never fails to appear in revolutions. (149)

Paine was convinced of the rightness of representative government because he thought 'mental powers' and wisdom were scattered, albeit unevenly, throughout society: 'there is always a sufficiency somewhere in the general mass of society for all purposes; but with respect to the parts of society, it is continually changing its place,' as is also the case for literature, where 'the republic of letters brings forward the best literary productions, by giving to genius a fair and universal chance' (148). In short, modern democratic theory, at its inception, conceptualized 'the mass of society' not as passive consumers but as a *resource* for both imagination and decision-making, because wisdom, like other talents, 'rises in one to-day, in another to-morrow, and has most probably visited in rotation every family of the earth, and again withdrawn' (148). Therefore, thought Paine, government should be conceived not as external control but, on a self-organizing principle, as 'some common centre, in which all the parts of society unite' that 'concentrates the knowledge necessary to the interest of the parts, and of the whole.' Thus, 'a nation is [...] like a body contained within a circle, having a common centre in which every radius meets' (154). Although he was no mathematician, Paine was imagining a *complex system* to explain how whole populations could be modeled in their interactions and mutual 'interests.' He also understood time-based dynamics: talents that lie in a 'dormant state' may be excited into action during times of revolution. Paine's writings demonstrate that there is nothing newfangled about an approach that not only seeks to incorporate the capacities of whole populations within large-scale systems that require some form of institutional coordination but also wants to mobilize the population in question and release their energies via self-organizing action.

Lying Worm and Cry Baby

However, although he demonstrated in his own career and ideas the steps Brian Arthur (2009: 176–80) describes as the 'core mechanism' of evolution – the evolution of the 'technology of democracy,' if you like – Paine himself did not have conscious access to appropriate theories to help him to model the replacement of *anciens régimes* by self-organizing population-wide systems that would release and harness the creative talents of all. We, on the other hand, do have access to such newfangled approaches (Santa Fe Institute, Arthur, Barabási, Beinhocker, Metcalfe, etc.).[9] The use of these approaches to date has largely been confined to digital networks and innovation economics; that is, to *technologies and firms* – the current beneficiaries of expert-pipeline invention. But the cat is out of the bag: the lessons available from such approaches may be applied for more general benefit. What is needed are 'new entrants [to] bring in new innovation' (Gay 2008: 79).[10] A go-between trickster-entrepreneur is needed to *change* the system as its performance declines, and to *preserve* the system from potential overall collapse. Or, as one of my Mambo t-shirts has it, 'to destroy the world we had to save it.'

Before I finish, I want to scale down to the micro level, and also to bring back the figure of the trickster, but this time in the guise of a lying worm and the human infant. Lewis Hyde (1998: 58–61) raises the issue of *deceit*

---

[9] 'The growth of knowledge cannot be formulated meaningfully as a constellation of equilibrating forces,' because knowledge maintains 'a potential for change that is ever present' (Metcalfe 2002: 9).

[10] 'The dynamics of knowledge diffusion and imitation will reduce variety among firms unless new innovation is created. Central firms thus have some degree of control over their market environment which, unless they seek new innovations, is eroded as specialized innovation is absorbed by others and new market innovation is brought in, mostly by new entrants inside or outside the industry' (Gay 2008: 79).

in his exposition of the nature of the trickster. He suggests that what we think of as consciousness – the mind – arises only when animal appetites are *not* pursued; when Hermes *does not* eat the meat of Apollo's cattle that he has just stolen on the day of his own birth, a self-imposed prohibition that allows mere meat (nature) to become a sign (culture). Hyde ascribes this move to Hermes' duplicity – 'only a thief' could have effected this shift. He invokes Umberto Eco's 'theory of the lie' to point out that such duplicity is the fundamental property of language itself:

> Semiotics is concerned with everything that can be taken as a sign. A sign is something which can be taken as significantly substituting for something else. [...] Thus semiotics is in principle the discipline studying everything *which can be used in order to lie*. If something cannot be used to tell as lie, conversely it cannot be used to tell the truth: it cannot in fact be used 'to tell' at all. (Eco 1976: 7)

Hyde explains this by reference to the trickster's earliest mythical exploit, the invention of bait to trap food:

> A worm with no hook in it [...] has [...] no significance, but the worm that says 'I'm harmless' when in fact it hides a hook tells a lie and by that lie worms begin to signify [...] Only when there's a possible Lying Worm can we begin to speak of a True Worm, and only then does Worm become a sign. (Hyde 1998: 60)

It may be counterintuitive but it should come as no surprise to find that lying Hermes is credited with the invention of language, not least by Plato (Hyde 1998: 75–6), and thence of oratory, in the form of Logios Hermes.

Hyde concludes that evolution itself relies on the trickster; or at least that the trickster is a figure for turning evolutionary process into instructive story. Citing the Nobel Laureate economist Jacques Monod, Hyde talks of two types of *chance* (1998: 118–21). One is path-dependent, the outcome of gradual cumulative sequence, whether this is evident or not. The other is a 'convergence of the twain' (*Titanic* meets iceberg) sort of chance, where independent chains of causation intersect, and random uncertainty produces something absolutely unpredictable and therefore new. This is the kind of chance that drives evolution – a random mutation and an 'opportunity niche' (as Arthur calls it) meet at the crossroads. And there sits Hermes. Thus, the trickster myth is a 'thinking machine' for telling how two (mutually incomprehensible) systems may intersect, and how new meaning may arise from that encounter – even as great destruction occurs: 'And consummation comes, and jars two hemispheres' (Hardy 1915). In short, the trickster is an anthropomorphic figure of *emergence*. Emergence is 'the process whereby the global behavior of a system results from the actions and interactions of agents' (Sawyer 2005: 2).

But if there are two types of chance there must be two types of emergence. One is endogenous, the evolution of complexity within a system. But the other type requires at least two systems to interact, and the agent of interaction is the trickster, entrepreneur, go-between. Here emergence is the product of the clash between systems. The concept of two systems intersecting in order for meaning to emerge is the basis for the theory of language developed by Yuri Lotman, based on his concept of the semiosphere. He says:

> A minimally functional structure requires the presence of at least two languages and their incapacity, each independently of the other, to embrace the world external to each of them. This incapacity is not a deficiency, but rather a condition of existence, as it dictates the necessity of the other (another person, another language, another culture). (Lotman 2009: 1–3)

Immediately, 'interaction' is a matter of interpretation, of *translation across difference*. Elsewhere, Lotman (1990) illustrates what he means by describing the 'language of smiles' by means of which a mother communicates with her infant baby. Neither knows the language of the other, but they work things out, as they must, both for the individual survival of the infant and the collective survival of the species. It may be added that every baby turns trickster almost at once. Their *first* cry may be a direct expression of an inner state – hunger, usually – but the *second* cry, cognisant that the first one attracted the mother, is a lie: it says 'I am hungry' but it means 'I want attention.' Only the second cry is communication. As Eco insists, this lie is the founding move of language and of any general theory of semiotics (1976: 7).

Structural Change

Lotman adds a new dimension, that of time, with his concept of 'culture and explosion.' Change, like chance, can be gradual and disruptive, and both types are necessary to explain this fundamental question: 'how can a system *develop* and yet remain *true to itself*?' (Lotman 2009: 1). How can a system cope with both *succession* (of the same) and *innovation* (of the new)? For cope it must, or it faces extinction. The answer is that cumulative or incremental change coexists with 'explosion,' or what Paine would have called revolution. Cumulative change is path-dependent; disruptive change is random chance. Both require openness to the possibilities of the future. Brian Arthur makes a similar point when he argues that our thinking about change is in need of paradigm-shifting, from the 'ad hoc, case-by-case basis' of historians (i.e. the humanities) towards 'a means to think abstractly about structural change' (i.e. the sciences) (Arthur 2009: 194–5). Once shifted, neither humanities nor science thinking would remain the same:

> The shift in thinking I am putting forward here is not large; it is subtle. It is like seeing the mind not as a container for its concepts and habitual thought processes but as something that emerges from these. (193–4)

For Arthur, structural change – evolution – is a 'sequence of problem and solution – of challenge and response' (196). The agent of challenge, the trickster-entrepreneur, may break the rules in order to renew the system, sitting at the boundaries between otherwise mutually unintelligible states, brokering the moment between past and future, when the infinite possibility of potential choice is reduced to the meaningfulness of present action. Or, as Arthur puts it, 'we hope in something we do not quite trust' (215). He writes: 'This way of thinking carries consequences. It means that the economy *emerges* – wells up – from its technologies' (193–4). Therefore it exists always in 'a perpetual openness of change – in perpetual novelty' (199), a situation of 'messy vitality' (213) that can nonetheless be subjected to algorithmic analysis. The 'two cultures' of culture and science can be brought into meaningful dialogue through the figure of the trickster, the agent of emergence, and the deceiver who provokes emergencies. The task facing cultural science is to think abstractly about creative destruction and renewal wrought by lying.

Bridging Culture and Science

The point is that culture itself is perfectly susceptible to analysis by means of the approaches that have been developing in complexity theory, systems theory, evolutionary theory, and the like. This is not the place to work through the contributions made by the writers from whom the cultural science group has drawn inspiration, but they include:

- Actor Network Theory (Latour 2005);
- Brian Arthur (2009) on the evolution of recombinant technologies (and thence, he argues, of the economy);
- Brian Boyd (2009) on the evolution of stories and Eric Beinhocker (2006) on the link between storytelling and population-wide reasoning;
- Carsten Herrmann-Pillath (2010) on the 'economics of identity and creativity,' which he situates in a naturalist, externalist, and neo-Darwinian framework;
- Michael Hutter on the cultural sources of newness (and economic sociology) (e.g. Hutter and Throsby 2008);
- Yuri Lotman (1990, 2009) on language as an evolving dynamic system, especially in *Culture and Explosion*; see also other writers on evolution and language, for example Deutscher (2005), Hurford (2007), MacNeilage (2008), Bickerton (2009), and Hrdy (2009);
- Niklas Luhmann on systems theory (e.g. see Cary Wolfe 2009 on how Luhmann may be reconciled with Derrida in the pursuit of post-humanism);
- Elinor Ostrom (1990) and Charlotte Hess (Hess and Ostrom 2006) on knowledge commons;
- W. G. Runciman's (2009) sociological theory of cultural evolution;
- Keith Sawyer (2005) on social emergence; and
- Numerous domain-based studies in the realms of fashion, games, intellectual property, and consumer co-creation.

It is certainly my view that these writers and others – the list is not infinite, but it is not short – are producing the conceptual tools by means of which we may be able to model and thence investigate the evolution of cultural systems.

Cultural science is a go-between, seeking the rules that underlie messy vitality. This is an appropriate enough task for Brisbanites, as in 2010 Brisbane witnessed the opening of the 'Go Between Bridge,' slightly misnamed after local band the Go-Betweens (see Hurst 2010). But beware the trickster, even as you cross. As Ian Paisley, former firebrand leader of Northern Ireland's Democratic Unionist Party (cited in Francis 2006: 19), once commented: 'A traitor and a bridge are very much alike, for they both go over to the other side.'

References

AAP (2007, November 20) Teen girl 'led pack of animals' in bashing cop. *Courier Mail*. Accessible at: http://www.news.com.au/couriermail/story/0,23739, 22796978-952,00.html

Abbas, A. and Erni, J. (Eds.) (2005) *Internationalising Cultural Studies: An Anthology*. Malden, MA: Blackwell.

Acorvettes (2007) Quantum mechanics the uncertainty principle light particle's [sic]. *YouTube*. Accessible at: http://www.youtube.com/watch?v=KT7xJ0tjB4A

Allan, S. (1999) *News Culture*. Buckingham, UK: Open University Press.

Anderson, C. (2006) *The Long Tail: How Endless Choice is Creating Unlimited Demand*. London: Random House.

Arnold, M. (1869) *Culture and Anarchy*. Accessible at: http://www.gutenberg.org/ebooks/4212

Arthur, B. (2009) *The Nature of Technology: What it is and How it Evolves*. London: Penguin; New York: Free Press.

Atkin, H. (2007) Kevin Rudd – Chinese propaganda video. *YouTube*. Accessible at: http://www.youtube.com/watch?v=ptccZze7VxQ

Aynsley-Green, A. (n.d.) Children and young people having their say. Presentation. Accessible at: http://www.4children.org.uk/uploads/information/AlAynsley-Green.pdf

Bacon, F. (1893 [1605]) *The Advancement of Learning*. London: Cassell & Company. Accessible at: http://ebooks.adelaide.edu.au/b/bacon/francis/b12a/complete.html

Bagehot, W. (1872 [1867]) *The English Constitution*. Accessible at: http://www.gutenberg.org/etext/4351

Baldwin, T. (2007, June 19) 'Obama girl' highlights senator's YouTube dilemma. *The Australian*. Accessible at: http://www.theaustralian.com.au/news/

Digital Futures for Cultural and Media Studies, First Edition. John Hartley.
© 2012 John Wiley & Sons, Ltd. Published 2012 by John Wiley & Sons, Ltd.

world/obama-girl-highlights-senators-youtube-dilemma/story-e6frg6so-1111113777590

Banham, R. (1962, February 9) Coronation Street, Hoggartsborough. *New Statesman*, 200–1.

Barabási, A.-L. (2002) *Linked: The New Science of Networks*. Cambridge, MA: Perseus Publishing.

Barabási, A.-L. and Bonabeau, E. (2003, May) Scale-free networks. *Scientific American*, 50–9. Accessible at: http://www.nd.edu/~networks/Publication%20 Categories/01%20Review%20Articles/ScaleFree_Scientific%20Ameri%20 288,%2060-69%20(2003).pdf

Baran, P. (1964) *On Distributed Communications: I. Introduction to Distributed Communications Networks*. Santa Monica, CA: Rand Corporation. Accessible at: http://www.rand.org/pubs/research_memoranda/2006/RM3420.pdf

Barker, C. (2004) *The Sage Dictionary of Cultural Studies*. London: Sage Publications.

Barnett, C. (2003) *Culture and Democracy: Media, Space and Representation*. Edinburgh: Edinburgh University Press.

Barnett, E. (2009, October 18) Is Channel 4's 'catch-up' TV deal with YouTube a new watershed? *Daily Telegraph*. Accessible at: http://www.telegraph.co.uk/ technology/google/6367931/Is-Channel-4s-catch-up-TV-deal-with-YouTube-a-new-watershed.html

Barthes, R. (1967) *Système de la Mode*. Paris: Editions du Seuil.

Barthes, R. (1975) *The Pleasure of the Text*. New York: Hill & Wang.

Barthes, R. (1989) The war of languages. In *The Rustle of Language* (R. Howard, trans.), 106–10. Berkley, CA: University of California Press.

Bednar, J. and Page, S. (2007) Can game(s) theory explain culture? The emergence of cultural behavior within multiple games. *Rationality and Society*, 19(1), 65–97.

Beinhocker, E. (2006) *The Origin of Wealth: Evolution, Complexity, and the Radical Remaking of Economics*. New York: Random House.

Benkler, Y. (2006) *The Wealth of Networks: How Social Production Transforms Markets and Freedom*. New Haven, CT: Yale University Press. Accessible at: http://www.benkler.org/Benkler_Wealth_Of_Networks.pdf

Bennett, T. (1992) Useful culture. *Cultural Studies*, 6(3), 385–99.

Bennett, T. (1995) *The Birth of the Museum: History, Theory, Politics*. London: Routledge.

Bennett, T., Grossberg, L., and Morris, M. (2005) *New Keywords: A Revised Vocabulary of Culture and Society*. Malden, MA: Blackwell.

Bennett, T., McFall, L., and Pryke, M. (2008) Culture/economy/social. *Journal of Cultural Economy*, 1(1), 1–7.

Bentley, R. A. (2009) Fashion versus reason in the creative industries. In M. O'Brien and S. Shennan (Eds.), *Innovation in Cultural Systems: Contributions from Evolutionary Anthropology*, 121–6. Boston, MA: MIT Press.

Bérubé, M. (2009, September 14) What's the matter with cultural studies? The popular discipline has lost its bearings. *Chronicle of Higher Education (Chronicle Review)*. Accessible at: http://chronicle.com/article/Whats-the-Matter-With/48334

Bethell, S. L. (1944) *Shakespeare and the Popular Dramatic Tradition*. London: Staples.

Bickerton, D. (2009) *Adam's Tongue: How Humans Made Language, How Language Made Humans*. New York: Hill & Wang.

Bird, S. E. (2003) *The Audience in Everyday Life: Living in a Media World*. New York: Routledge.

Blake, H. (2010, May 4) Digital universe to smash 'zettabyte' barrier for first time. *Daily Telegraph*. Accessible at: http://www.telegraph.co.uk/technology/news/7675214/Digital-universe-to-smash-zettabyte-barrier-for-first-time.html

Bohn, R. and Short, J. (2010) *How Much Information? 2009 Report on American Consumers*. San Diego, CA: Global Information Industry Center, University of California. Accessible at: http://hmi.ucsd.edu/pdf/HMI_2009_Consumer Report_Dec9_2009.pdf

Bollier, D. (2008) *Viral Spiral: How the Commoners Built a Digital Republic of Their Own*. New York: The New Press.

Boyd, B. (2009) *On the Origin of Stories: Evolution, Cognition, and Fiction*. Cambridge, MA: Harvard University Press.

British Museum (n.d. a) Olduvai stone chopping tool. *The British Museum*. Accessible at: http://www.britishmuseum.org/explore/highlights/highlight_objects/pe/s/olduvai_stone_chopping_tool.aspx

British Museum (n.d. b) Stone chopping tools. *The British Museum*. Accessible at: http://www.britishmuseum.org/explore/highlights/highlight_objects/pe/s/stone_chopping_tools.aspx

Brooks, C. (1947) *The Well Wrought Urn*. New York: Harcourt Brace.

Brooks, M. (2010, May 8) Weirdest of the weird: From undead cats to particles popping up out of nowhere, from watched pots not boiling – sometimes – to ghostly influences at a distance, quantum physics delights in demolishing our intuitions about how the world works. *New Scientist*, 36–42.

Bruns, A. (2005) *Gatewatching: Collaborative Online News Production*. New York: Peter Lang.

Bruns, A. (2008) *Blogs, Wikipedia, Second Life, and Beyond: From Production to Produsage*. New York: Peter Lang.

Brunsdon, C. (1997) Television studies. In H. Newcomb (Ed.), *The Encyclopedia of Television*. New York: Routledge. Accessible at: http://www.museum.tv/eotvsection.php?entrycode=televisionst

Buckminster Fuller, R., Agel, J., and Fiore, Q. (1970) *I Seem to be a Verb: Environment and Man's Future*. New York, NY: Bantam Books.

Bulkley, K. (2008, November 6). Movie star in the making: China's answer to YouTube. *The Guardian*. Accessible at: http://www.guardian.co.uk/technology/2008/nov/06/youtube-tudou-video

Bulmer, M. and Rees, A. (Eds.) (1996) *Citizenship Today*. London: University College London Press.

Burgess, J. and Green, J. (2009) *YouTube: Online Video and Participatory Culture*. Cambridge, UK: Polity Press.

Canning, S. (2007, October 25) Political ads mocked on YouTube. *The Australian*.

Carr, N. (2008) Is Google making us stupid? What the Internet is doing to our brains. *The Atlantic*. Accessible at: http://www.theatlantic.com/magazine/archive/2008/07/is-google-making-us-stupid/6868

Catlow, R. and Garrett, M. (2007) Do it with others (DIWO): Contributory media in the Furtherfield Neighbourhood. In *A Handbook for Coding Culture*, 22–9. Sydney, NSW: d/Lux/MediaArts. Accessible at: http://www.dlux.org.au/codingcultures/handbook.html

Caves, R. (2000) *Creative Industries: Contracts between Art and Commerce*. Cambridge, MA: Harvard University Press.

Chandler, D. (2002) *Semiotics: The Basics*. London: Routledge.

Cherry, C. (1957) *On Human Communication*. Cambridge, MA: MIT Press.

'Child Online Protection Act' (n.d.) *Wikipedia*. Accessible at: http://en.wikipedia.org/wiki/Child_Online_Protection_Act

'Children's Internet Protection Act' (n.d.) *Wikipedia*. Accessible at: http://en.wikipedia.org/wiki/Children%27s_Internet_Protection_Act

Cokeeorg (2007) Olduvai Gorge, Tanzania. *YouTube*. Accessible at: http://www.youtube.com/watch?v=vMrPJlt1CY8

Collini, S. (2009, November 13) Impact on humanities: Researchers must take a stand now or be judged and rewarded as salesmen. *Times Literary Supplement*. Accessible at: http://entertainment.timesonline.co.uk/tol/arts_and_entertainment/the_tls/article6915986.ece

Conboy, M. (2002) *The Press and Popular Culture*. London: Sage Publications.

Conboy, M. (2007) Permeation and profusion: Popular journalism in the new millennium. *Journalism Studies*, 8(1), 1–12.

Coultan, M. (2007, October 26) YouTube revolutionaries upstage the party machine. *Sydney Morning Herald*. Accessible at: http://www.smh.com.au/news/federalelection2007news/rudd-faces-youtube-revolution/2007/10/25/1192941243230.html?s_cid=rss_news

d'Argens, B. (attrib.) (1748) *Thérèse Philosophe, ou Mémoires pour Servir à l'Histoire du Père Dirrag et de Mademoiselle Éradice*. Accessible at: http://du.laurens.free.fr/auteurs/Boyer_Argens-Therese_philo.htm

Dahlgren, P. (1992) Introduction. In P. Dahlgren and C. Sparks (Eds.), *Journalism and Popular Culture*, 1–23. London: Sage Publications.

Dahrendorf, R. (1973) *Homo Sociologicus*. London: Routledge and Kegan Paul.

Dan, Y. (2009, April 30) Breaking the waves: A single neuron can change the activity of the whole brain. *Howard Hughes Medical Institute.* Accessible at: http://www.hhmi.org/news/dan20090430.html

Darnton, R. (1982) *The Literary Underground of the Old Regime.* Cambridge, MA: Harvard University Press.

Darnton, R. and Roche, D. (Eds.) (1989) *Revolution in Print: The Press in France 1775–1800.* Berkeley, CA: University of California Press.

Darwin, C. (1871) *The Descent of Man.* Accessible at: http://ebooks.adelaide.edu.au/d/darwin/charles/d22d/index.html

de Baecque, A. (1989) Pamphlets: Libel and political mythology. In R. Darnton and D. Roche (Eds.), *Revolution in Print: The Press in France 1775–1800,* 165–76. Berkeley, CA: University of California Press.

de Saussure, F. (1974) *A Course in General Linguistics.* London: Fontana.

Delahunty, J. (2010, May 17) YouTube celebrates 5th birthday, gets two billion views daily. *AfterDawn.* Accessible at: http://www.afterdawn.com/news/article.cfm/2010/05/18/youtube_celebrates_5th_birthday_gets_two_billion_views_daily

Delli Carpini, M. X. (2000) Review of Michael Schudson, *The Good Citizen: A History of American Civic Life. Public Opinion Quarterly,* 64, 546–9. Accessible at: http://repository.upenn.edu/asc_papers/15

Department for Culture Media and Sport (1998, revised 2001) *Creative Industries Mapping Document.* London: Her Majesty's Stationery Office.

Derbyshire, D. (2009, February 24) Social websites harm children's brains: Chilling warning to parents from top neuroscientist. *Mail Online.* Accessible at: http://www.dailymail.co.uk/news/article-1153583/Social-websites-harm-childrens-brains-Chilling-warning-parents-neuroscientist.html#ixzz0VVZ6nhK7

Derrida, J. (1976) *Of Grammatology.* Baltimore, MD: Johns Hopkins University Press.

Deutscher, G. (2005) *The Unfolding of Language: An Evolutionary Tour of Mankind's Greatest Invention.* New York: Metropolitan.

Disraeli, B. (1980 [1845]) *Sybil: Or The Two Nations.* London: Penguin Books.

Dissanayake, E. (1992) *Homo Aestheticus: Where Art Came from and Why.* New York: Free Press.

DoctorWhoCenter2010 (2010) Weeping angels in Doctor Who series 5! *YouTube.* Accessible at: http://www.youtube.com/watch?v=r_jxOx0CMKA

Donsbach, W. (2004) Psychology of news decisions: Factors behind journalists' professional behavior. *Journalism,* 5(2), 131–57.

Donsbach, W. (2007) *What professional journalists should know about communication research.* Keynote address presented at Harmonious Society, Civil Society and the Media, Beijing, China.

Dopfer, K. (2004) The economic agent as rule maker and rule user: Homo sapiens oeconomicus. *Journal of Evolutionary Economics,* 14(2), 177–95.

220 *References*

Drakeford, M., Scourfield, J., Holland, S., and Davies, A. (2009) Welsh children's views on government and participation. *Childhood*, 16(2), 247–64.

Dyer, R. (Ed.) (1981) *Coronation Street*. London: British Film Institute.

Eco, U. (1972) Towards a semiotic inquiry into the television message. *Working Papers in Cultural Studies*, 3, 103–21.

Eco, U. (1976) *A Theory of Semiotics*. Bloomington, IN: Indiana University Press.

Edgerton, D. (2005) *Warfare State: Britain, 1920–1970*. Cambridge, UK: Cambridge University Press.

eHow (n.d.) How to write a business best-seller. Accessible at: http://www.ehow.com/how_2055005_write-business-bestseller.html

Eliot, T. S. (1920) *The Sacred Wood*. London: Methuen.

Elpaw74165764 (2007) Schrodinger's cat for real. *YouTube*. Accessible at: http://www.youtube.com/watch?v=EN-jCuV7BoU

Evans, M. (1975, Spring) Mercury versus Apollo: A reading of *Love's Labor's Lost*. *Shakespeare Quarterly*, 26(2), 113–27. Accessible at: http://www.jstor.org/pss/2869241

Expertvillage (2008) Techniques for flintknapping: How to make Stone Age tools. *YouTube*. Accessible at: http://www.youtube.com/watch?v=-cHM8rfmQII

Fineran, L. (2009, January 24) Cop-bashing gang teen out on bail. *Gold Coast Bulletin*. Accessible at: http://www.goldcoast.com.au/article/2009/01/24/42335_gold-coast-news.html

Fiske, J. and Hartley, J. (2003 [1978]) *Reading Television*. London: Routledge.

Flynn, I. (2009, December 16) Our views on mandatory ISP filtering. *Official Google Australia Blog*. Blog. Accessible at: http://google-au.blogspot.com/2009/12/our-views-on-mandatory-isp-filtering.html

Forgacs, D. (1984) National-popular: Genealogy of a concept. In B. Schwartz et al. (Eds.), *Formations: Of Nations and Peoples*, 83–98. London: Routledge and Kegan Paul.

Foucault, M. (1977) *Discipline and Punish: The Birth of the Prison* (A. Sheridan, trans.). New York: Vintage.

Foucault, M. (1984) *The Foucault Reader* (P. Rabinow, Ed.). London: Penguin.

Francis, N. (2006) *Anatomy of the Conflict in Northern Ireland: From the Plantations to the Good Friday Agreement*. Accessible at: http://www.wcfia.harvard.edu/fellows/papers/2005-06/paper_Francis_NIreland.pdf

Fynes-Clinton, J. (2010, January 14) Girl fights show today's teens are not so sugar and spice. *Courier Mail*. Accessible at: http://www.news.com.au/couriermail/story/0,23739,26584444-5012473,00.html

Gantz, J. and Reinsel, D. (2010, May) *The Digital Universe Decade – Are You Ready?* Report. IDC. Accessible at: http://www.emc.com/digital_universe

Garnham, N. (1986) Contribution to a political economy of mass-communication. In R. Collins, J. Curran, N. Garnham, P. Scannell, P. Schlesinger, and C. Sparks (Eds.), *Media, Culture and Society: A Critical Reader* (pp. 9–32). London: Sage Publications.

Gates, H. L. Jr. (1988) *The Signifying Monkey: A Theory of African American Literary Criticism*. New York: Oxford University Press.

Gauntlett, D. (1998) Ten things wrong with the 'effects model.' In R. Dickinson, R. Harindranath, and O. Linné (Eds.), *Approaches to Audiences – A Reader*. London: Edward Arnold. Accessible at: http://www.theory.org.uk/david/effects.htm

Gauntlett, D. (2005) *Moving Experiences: Media Effects and Beyond* (2nd edn.). London: John Libbey.

Gay, B. (2008) Firm dynamic governance of global innovation by means of flexible networks of connections. *Journal of Innovation Economics*, 2(2), 63–83. Accessible at: http://www.cairn.info/revue-journal-of-innovation-economics-2008-2-page-63.htm

Gibbon, E. (1776–1788) *The History of the Decline and Fall of the Roman Empire* (six vols.). Accessible at: http://ebooks.adelaide.edu.au/g/gibbon/edward/g43d

Gibson, M. (2007) *Culture and Power: A History of Cultural Studies*. Oxford: Berg; Sydney, NSW: University of New South Wales Press.

Gilroy, P. (2006) Bold as love? On the moral economy of blackness in the 21st century. Presented at the W. E. B. du Bois Lectures, Harvard University, Cambridge, MA. Accessible at: http://www.news.harvard.edu/gazette/2006/10.12/09-gilroy.html

Ginsburg, D. (n.d.) *Friends* Nielson Ratings Archive: The only complete online *Friends* ratings archive! Accessible at: http://newmusicandmore.tripod.com/friendsratings.html

'GLAM' (n.d.) *Wikipedia*. Accessible at: http://en.wikipedia.org/wiki/GLAM_%28industry_sector%29

Goel, V., Koryukin, E., Bhatia, M., and Agarwal, P. (2004) *Innovation systems: World Bank support of science and technology development*. Working paper 32. Washington, DC: World Bank.

Gramsci, A. (1971) *Selections from the Prison Notebooks*. London: Lawrence & Wishart.

Gray, J. (2010) Entertainment and media/cultural/communication/etc. studies. *Continuum: Journal of Media & Cultural Studies*, 24(6), 811–17.

Gray, J., Jones, J. P., and Thompson, E. (Eds.) (2009) *Satire TV: Politics and Comedy in the Post-Network Era*. New York: New York University Press.

Grayling, A. C. (2005) *Descartes: The Life of René Descartes and its Place in His Times*. London: The Free Press/Pocket Books.

Greenfield, S. (2002) *The Private Life of the Brain*. London: Penguin Books.

Greenfield, S. (2008) *ID: The Quest for Identity in the 21st Century*. London: Sceptre.

Gribbin, J. (1996) Inflation for beginners. *Cosmology for Beginners*. Accessible at: http://www.lifesci.sussex.ac.uk/home/John_Gribbin/cosmo.htm

Grossberg, L. (1993) Can cultural studies find true happiness in communication? *Journal of Communication*, 43(4), 89–97.

Gu, X. and O'Connor, J. (2006) A new modernity? The arrival of 'creative industries' in China. *International Journal of Cultural Studies*, 9(3), 271–283.

Haasler, S. (Ed.) (2008, September 5) So you want to be a Corrie scriptwriter? *Corrie Blog*. Blog. Accessible at: http://www.corrieblog.tv

Hahn, M. (1997, August 26) Writing on the wall: An interview with Hunter S. Thompson. *The Atlantic Online*. Accessible at: http://www.theatlantic.com/past/docs/unbound/graffiti/hunter.htm

Halavais, A. (2009) *Search Engine Society*. Cambridge, UK: Polity Press.

Hall, S. (1973) *Encoding and decoding in the media discourse*. Stenciled Paper 7. Birmingham: Centre for Contemporary Cultural Studies.

Hall, S. (1981) Notes on deconstructing the popular. In R. Samuel (Ed.), *People's History and Socialist Theory*, 227–40. London: Routledge and Kegan Paul.

Hall, S., Critcher, C., Jefferson, T., Clarke, J., and Roberts, B. (1978) *Policing the Crisis: Mugging, the State and Law and Order*. London: Macmillan.

Halloran, J. D. (1981) The context of mass communication research. In E. McAnany, J. Schnitman, and N. Janus (Eds.), *Communication and Social Structure*, 21–57. New York: Praeger.

Hardy, T. (1915) The convergence of the twain: Lines on the loss of the 'Titanic.' Accessible at: http://rpo.library.utoronto.ca/poem/916.html

Hargreaves, I. (2003) *Journalism: Truth or Dare*. Oxford: Oxford University Press.

Hart, R. (1997) *Children's Participation: The Theory and Practice of Involving Young Citizens in Community Development and Environmental Care*. London: Earthscan; New York: UNICEF.

Hartley, J. (1992a) *Tele-ology: Studies in Television*. London: Routledge.

Hartley, J. (1992b) *The Politics of Pictures: The Creation of the Public in the Age of Popular Media*. London: Routledge.

Hartley, J. (1996) *Popular Reality: Journalism, Modernity, Popular Culture*. London: Edward Arnold.

Hartley, J. (1999) *Uses of Television*. London: Routledge.

Hartley, J. (2002) *Communication, Cultural and Media Studies: The Key Concepts*. London: Routledge.

Hartley, J. (2003) *A Short History of Cultural Studies*. London: Sage Publications.

Hartley, J. (Ed.) (2005) *Creative Industries*. Malden, MA: Wiley-Blackwell.

Hartley, J. (2007) A double drabble of bugger all: On Monty Python's galaxy song. *In Media Res*. Accessible at: http://mediacommons.futureofthebook.org/imr/2007/11/23/a-double-drabble-of-bugger-all-on-monty-python%E2%80%99s-galaxy-song

Hartley, J. (2008) *Television Truths: Forms of Knowledge in Popular Culture*. Oxford: Blackwell.

Hartley, J. (2009) *The Uses of Digital Literacy*. St. Lucia, QLD: University of Queensland Press; New Brunswick, NJ: Transaction Publishers.

Hartley, J. and McWilliam, K. (Eds.) (2009) *Story Circle: Digital Storytelling Around the World*. Oxford: Wiley-Blackwell.

Hartley, J. and Montgomery, L. (2009) Fashion as consumer entrepreneurship: Emergent risk culture, social network markets, and the launch of *Vogue* in China. *Chinese Journal of Communication*, 2(1), 61–76.

Hartley, L. P. (1953) *The Go-Between*. London: Hamish Hamilton.

Hawkes, T. (1973) *Shakespeare's Talking Animals*. London: Edward Arnold.

Hawkins, G. (2009) The politics of bottled water: Assembling bottled water as brand, waste and oil. *Journal of Cultural Economy*, 2(1–2), 183–95.

Haywood, I. (2004) *The Revolution in Popular Literature: Print, Politics and the People, 1790–1860*. Cambridge, UK: Cambridge University Press.

Hearn, A. (2007, March 16) *Top Gear* around the world. *AutoTrader*. Accessible at: http://www.autotrader.co.uk/EDITORIAL/CARS/FEATURES/33790.html

Hébert, L. (2011) The functions of language. *Signo*. Accessible at: http://www.signosemio.com/jakobson/a_fonctions.asp

Henderson, L. (2007) *Social Issues in Television Fiction*. Edinburgh: Edinburgh University Press.

'Hermes' (n.d.) *Wikipedia*. Accessible at: http://en.wikipedia.org/wiki/Hermes

Hermes, J. (2005) *Re-reading Popular Culture*. Oxford: Blackwell.

Herrmann-Pillath, C. (2010) *The Economics of Identity and Creativity: A Cultural Science Approach*. St Lucia, QLD: University of Queensland Press; New Brunswick, NJ: Transaction Publishers.

Hesmondhalgh, D. (2007) *The Cultural Industries*. London: Sage Publications.

Hess, C. and Ostrom, E. (Eds.) (2006) *Understanding Knowledge as a Commons: From Theory to Practice*. Cambridge, MA: MIT Press.

Higgs, P., Cunningham, S., and Bakhshi, H. (2008) *Beyond the Creative Industries: Mapping the Creative Economy in the UK*. Report. London: NESTA. Accessible at: http://www.nesta.org.uk/library/documents/beyond-creative-industries-report.pdf

Hilmes, M. (2009) Nailing mercury. The problem of media industry historiography. In J. Holt and A. Perren (Eds.), *Media Industries: History, Theory and Method*, 21–30. Malden, MA: Wiley-Blackwell.

Hirst, K. K. (n.d.) Hominin. *About.com*. Accessible at: http://archaeology.about.com/od/hterms/g/hominin.htm

Hobbes, T. (1651) *Leviathan*. Accessible at: http://www.gutenberg.org/etext/3207/

Hoggart, R. (1957) *The Uses of Literacy*. London: Chatto & Windus.

Hoggart, R. (1960) The uses of television. *Encounter*, 14(1), 38–45.

Hoggart, R. (Ed.) (1967) *Your Sunday Paper*. London: University of London Press.

Holston, J. and Appadurai, A. (1996) Cities and citizenship. *Public Culture*, 8(2), 187–204.

Howkins, J. (2001) *The Creative Economy: How People Make Money from Ideas*. London: Penguin.

Hrdy, S. (2009) *Mothers and Others: The Evolutionary Origins of Mutual Under-standing.* Cambridge, MA: Harvard University Press.

Hughes, R. (1992, February 3) The fraying of America. *Time*, 44–9.

Hughes, R. (1993) *The Culture of Complaint.* New York: Oxford University Press.

Huizinga, J. (1949) *Homo Ludens: A Study of the Play-Element in Culture.* London: Routledge and Kegan Paul.

Hurford, J. (2007) *The Origins of Meaning: Language in the Light of Evolution.* Oxford: Oxford University Press.

Hurst, D. (2010) Bridge honour: Go-Betweens consult legal, grammar people. *Brisbane Times.* Accessible at: http://www.brisbanetimes.com.au/queensland/bridge-honour-gobetweens-consult-legal-grammar-people-20100704-zvhq.html

Hutter, M. and Throsby, D. (Eds.) (2008) *Beyond Price: Value in Culture, Economics, and the Arts.* Cambridge, UK: Cambridge University Press.

Hyde, L. (1998) *Trickster Makes this World: How Disruptive Imagination Creates Culture.* New York: Farrar, Strauss and Giroux.

Idle, E. (1983) The galaxy song. In *Monty Python's The Meaning of Life* (T. Jones, Dir.). Accessible at: http://www.youtube.com/watch?v=JWVshkVF0SY

'Illuminati' (n.d.) *Wikipedia.* Accessible at: http://en.wikipedia.org/wiki/Illuminati

IndexFundsAdvisors (2009a) From chaos to order on the Galton Machine – Representing the returns of capitalism. *YouTube.* Accessible at: http://www.youtube.com/watch?v=9xUBhhM4vbM

IndexFundsAdvisors (2009b) IFA.com – Probability Machine, Galton Board, randomness and fair price simulator, Quincunx. *YouTube.* Accessible at: http://www.youtube.com/watch?v=AUSKTk9ENzg

IndexFundsAdvisors (2010) One year later: Lessons from the fall – IFA quote of the week #72 – iPad cat. *YouTube.* Accessible at: http://www.youtube.com/watch?v=oVt-LdF2BTU&feature=watch_response_rev

Influx (2007, May 15) Influx interview – dr. alex bentley [sic] – random copying and culture. *Influx.* Accessible at: http://influxinsights.com/2007/interviews/influx-interview-dr-alex-bentley-random-copying-and-culture

Inglis, F. (1995) *Raymond Williams.* London: Routledge.

'Invisible College' (n.d.) *Wikipedia.* Accessible at: http://en.wikipedia.org/wiki/Invisible_College

Ironside, R. (2010, January 12) Girl fight videos posted on internet amid violence surge. *Courier Mail.* Accessible at: http://www.news.com.au/couriermail/story/0,23739,26578386-952,00.html

Irvine, M. (2006 [1994]) *The Making of Textual Culture: 'Gramatica' and Literary Theory 350–1100.* Cambridge, UK: Cambridge University Press.

Iser, W. (1980) *The Act of Reading: A Theory of Aesthetic Response.* Baltimore, MD: Johns Hopkins University Press.

Isin, E. F. and Turner, B. S. (Eds.) (2002) *Handbook of Citizenship Studies*. London: Sage Publications.

Jacobs, J. (2000) *The Nature of Economies*. New York: Random House.

Jans, M. (2004) Children as citizens: Towards a contemporary notion of child participation. *Childhood*, 11(1), 27–44.

Jenkins, H. (2006) *Convergence Culture*. New York: New York University Press.

Jenkins, H. (2009) If it doesn't spread, it's dead. *Confessions of an Aca-Fan*. Blog. Accessible at: http://www.henryjenkins.org/2009/02/if_it_doesnt_spread_its_dead_p.html

Joannou, M. (2000) *Contemporary Women's Writing: From* The Golden Notebook *to* The Color Purple. Manchester, UK: Manchester University Press.

Johnson, H. (n.d.) 'Sue Haasler.' *The Hilary Johnson Authors' Advisory Service*. Accessible at: http://www.hilaryjohnson.demon.co.uk/SueHaasler.htm

Jonmchu (2008) The official Rep. vs Dem. dance off!! *YouTube*. Accessible at: http://www.youtube.com/watch?v=PvJuo2C7eS4

Josipovici, G. (2010, January 6) What are universities for? Letter to the *Times Literary Supplement*. Accessible at: http://entertainment.timesonline.co.uk/tol/arts_and_entertainment/the_tls/article6977577.ece

Joyce, H. (2001) Adam Smith and the invisible hand. *Plus Magazine*. Accessible at: http://plus.maths.org/content/os/issue14/features/smith/index

Kagan, J. (2009) *The Three Cultures: Natural Sciences, Social Sciences and the Humanities in the 21st Century*. Cambridge, UK: Cambridge University Press.

Keen, A. (2007) *The Cult of the Amateur: How Today's Internet is Killing our Culture*. New York: Doubleday.

Keen, A. (2009) Why culture isn't free. *DGA Quarterly*, Fall. Accessible at: http://www.dgaquarterly.org/BACKISSUES/Fall2009/ThePiracyProblemWhyCultureIsntFree.aspx

Kennedy-Cuomo, K. (2000) *Speak Truth to Power: Human Rights Defenders who are Changing our World*. New York: Crown Publishers.

'Ken Barlow' (n.d.) *Wikipedia*. Accessible at: http://en.wikipedia.org/wiki/Ken_Barlow

Kipling, R. (1895) *The Jungle Book*. London: Cassell. Accessible at: http://www.poetryloverspage.com/poets/kipling/law_of_jungle.html

Kipling, R. (1899) The white man's burden. Accessible at: http://www.online-literature.com/kipling/922

Kurtzman, D. (2008) The 25 funniest viral videos of Election 2008. *About.com*. Accessible at: http://politicalhumor.about.com/od/electionvideos/tp/top-election-web-videos.htm

Laclau, E. and Mouffe, C. (2001 [1985]) *Hegemony and Social Strategy: Towards a Radical Democratic Politics*. London: Verso.

LaMissDookie (2008) Dance Battle 2 w/Miley Cyrus, Adam Sandler, Chris Brown etc. *YouTube*. Accessible at: http://www.youtube.com/watch?v=zdapdkvs0FY

Langer, J. (1998) *Tabloid Television: Popular Journalism and the 'Other News.'* London: Routledge.

Lanham, R. A. (2006) *The Economics of Attention: Style and Substance in the Age of Information*. Chicago, IL: Chicago University Press.

Lasn, K. (Ed.) (2009) *Thought Control in Economics*. Special issue of *Adbusters*, 17(5).

Latour, B. (2005) *Reassembling the Social: An Introduction to Actor-Network-Theory*. Oxford: Oxford University Press.

Leadbeater, C. (1999) *Living on Thin Air: The New Economy*. London: Penguin.

Leadbeater, C. (2008) *We-Think. Mass Innovation, not Mass Production: The Power of Mass Creativity*. London: Profile Books. See also http://www.youtube.com/watch?v=qiP79vYsfbo

Leadbeater, C. (2010) *Cloud Culture: Promise and Danger*. Report. Counterpoint. Accessible at: http://www.counterpoint-online.org/cloud-culture-promise-and-danger

Leakey, L. (2007) Louise Leakey's TED talk. Accessible at: http://video.google.com/videoplay?docid=-3334028809823553219#

Leakey, L. S. B., Tobias, P., and Napier, J. (1964) A new species of the genus homo from Olduvai Gorge. *Nature*, 4927, 7–9.

Lee, R. E. (2000) The structures of knowledge and the future of the social sciences: Two postulates, two propositions and a closing remark. *Journal of World Systems Research*, 6(3), 786–7.

Lee, R. E. (2003) *Life and Times of Cultural Studies: The Politics and Transformation of the Structures of Knowledge*. Durham, NC: Duke University Press.

Lee, R. E. (2010) *Knowledge Matters: The Structures of Knowledge and the Crisis of the Modern World System*. St. Lucia, QLD: University of Queensland Press.

Lewis, J. (2005) *Language Wars: The Role of Media and Culture in Global Terror and Political Violence*. London: Pluto Books.

'List of most-watched television broadcasts' (n.d.) *Wikipedia*. Accessible at: http://en.wikipedia.org/wiki/List_of_most-watched_television_episodes

Loeffelholz, M. and Weaver, D. (Eds.) (2008) *Global Journalism Research: Theories, Methods, Findings, Future*. Malden, MA: Wiley-Blackwell.

LOOOLuhhs (2009) MYCHONNY- Most Famous Youtubers(Today Tonight) 17/12/09. *YouTube*. Accessible at: http://www.youtube.com/watch?v=5MXO1Uaentw

Lotman, Y. (1990) *Universe of the Mind: A Semiotic Theory of Culture*. Bloomington, IN: Indiana University Press.

Lotman, Y. (2009) *Culture and Explosion* (W. Clark, trans.). Berlin: Mouton de Gruyter.

Lumby, C. (1999) *Gotcha! Life in a Tabloid World*. Sydney, NSW: Allen & Unwin.

Maccoby, S. (2001) *English Radicalism: 1832–1852*. London: Routledge.

MacNeilage, P. (2008) *The Origin of Speech*. Oxford: Oxford University Press.

'Mad Men' (n.d.) *Wikipedia*. Accessible at: http://en.wikipedia.org/wiki/Mad_Men

Mao, Z. (1957) On the correct handling of contradictions among the people. In *Little Red Book*. Beijing: Foreign Languages Press.

Marshall, T. H. (1963) *Sociology at the Crossroads and Other Essays*. London: Heinemann.

Marx, K. (1845) *The German Ideology*. Accessible at: http://www.marxists.org/archive/marx/works/1845/german-ideology/ch01b.htm

Maurizi, S. (2008) The physicist who stood up to the pope. *New Scientist*, 2645, 48–9.

Maxwell, R. and Miller, T. (2008) Creative industries or wasteful ones? Accessible at: http://orgnets.net/urban_china/maxwell_miller

Mayhew, H. (1849) *London Labour and the London Poor*. Accessible at: http://etext.virginia.edu/toc/modeng/public/MayLond.html

McAuliffe, K. (2010, September) The incredible shrinking brain. *Discovery*, 54.

McCalman, I. D. (1992) Popular irreligion in early Victorian England: Infidel preachers and radical theatricality in 1830s London. In R. W. Davis and R. J. Helmstadter (Eds.), *Religion and Irreligion in Victorian Society: Essays in Honor of R. K. Webb*, 51–67. London: Routledge.

McCalman, I. D. (1993) *Radical Underworld: Prophets, Revolutionaries and Pornographers in London, 1795–1840*. Oxford: Clarendon Press.

McCraw, T. (2007) *Prophet of Innovation: Joseph Schumpeter and Creative Destruction*. Cambridge, MA: Harvard University Press.

McGregor, O. R. (1995) Rights, royals and regulation: The British Experience. Harold W. Andersen Lecture, World Press Freedom Committee. Accessible at: http://www.wpfc.org/AL1995.html

McGuigan, J. (2006) Book review: *Creative Industries*. *Global Media and Communication*, 3(2), 372–4.

McKay, G. (1998) DiY culture: Notes towards an intro. In G. McKay (Ed.), *DiY Culture*, 1–53. London: Verso.

McLuhan, M. (1964) *Understanding Media: The Extensions of Man*. New York: McGraw Hill.

Media International Australia (1999) Media wars. *Media International Australia*, 90, themed section.

Metcalfe, J. S. (2002) Knowledge of growth and the growth of knowledge. *Journal of Evolutionary Economics*, 12, 3–15.

Metcalfe, J. S. (n.d.) *Restless capitalism: Increasing returns and growth in enterprise economies*. Manchester, UK: ESRC Centre for Research on Innovation and Competition. Accessible at: http://www.cric.ac.uk/cric/staff/J_Stan_Metcalfe/pdfs/restcapit.pdf

'Micronation' (n.d.) *Wikipedia*. Accessible at: http://en.wikipedia.org/wiki/Micronation

Miller, T. (2006) *Cultural Citizenship*. Philadelphia, PA: Temple University Press.

Miller, T. (2009) Can natural Luddites make things explode or travel faster? The new humanities, cultural policy studies, and creative industries. In J. Holt and

A. Perren (Eds.), *Media Industries: History, Theory and Method*, 184–98. Malden, MA: Wiley-Blackwell.

Minimoviechannel (2008) Obama and McCain – Dance off! *YouTube*. Accessible at: http://www.youtube.com/watch?v=wzyT9-9lUyE

Mitchell, N. (2008, October 31) Computers and your head - Susan Greenfield on All in the Mind. *ABC Radio National*. Blog. Accessible at: http://blogs.abc.net.au/allinthemind/2008/10/computers-and-y.html

'Moore's law' (n.d.) *Wikipedia*. Accessible at: http://en.wikipedia.org/wiki/Moore's_law

Morgan, J. (2010, December 9) Appetite for education. *Times Higher Education*. Accessible at: http://www.timeshighereducation.co.uk/story.asp?storycode=414509.

Morris, J. (2005) *Citizenship and Disabled People*. Report. Leeds, UK: The Disability Rights Commission. Accessible at: http://www.leeds.ac.uk/disability-studies/archiveuk/morris/Citizenship_and_disabled_people_final.pdf

Muecke, S. (2009) Cultural science? *Cultural Studies*, 23(3), 404–16.

'Museum of Anatolian civilizations' (n.d.) Wikipedia. Accessible at: http://en.wikipedia.org/wiki/Museum_of_Anatolian_Civilizations

'Mychonny' (n.d.) *Wikitubia*. Accessible at: http://youtube.wikia.com/wiki/Mychonny

National Museum of Photography, Film and Television (2000) *The Daily Herald* newspaper and archive. Accessible at: http://www.nationalmediamuseum.org.uk/Collection/Photography/DailyHeraldArchive.aspx

New York Times (2008, August 29) Conventions: CNN claims ratings milestone. *New York Times: Media Decoder*. Blog. Accessible at: http://mediadecoder.blogs.nytimes.com/2008/08/29/conventions-cnn-claims-ratings-milestone

Newcomb, H. (1974) *Television: The Most Popular Art*. New York: Anchor Books.

Newcomb, H. (2004) *Encyclopedia of Television* (2nd edn.). New York, NY: Routledge.

New Statesman (2009, May 4) Technology special issue. Accessible at: http://www.newstatesman.com/world-affairs/2009/05/online-information-feedback and http://www.newstatesman.com/scitech/2009/05/technology-world-brave-stupid

Nice, L. (2007) Tabloidization and the teen market: Are teenage magazines dumberer than ever? *Journalism Studies*, 8(1), 117–36.

'Observer effect (physics)' (n.d.) *Wikipedia*. Accessible at: http://en.wikipedia.org/wiki/Observer_effect_(physics)

O'Connor, J. (2009) Creative industries: A new direction? *International Journal of Cultural Policy*, 15(4), 387–402.

O'Sullivan, T., Hartley, J., Saunders, D., and Fiske, J. (1983) *Key Concepts in Communication*. London: Methuen.

O'Sullivan, T., Hartley, J., Saunders, D., Montgomery, M., and Fiske, J. (1994) *Key Concepts in Communication and Cultural Studies*. London: Routledge.

Oakeshott, M. (1975) *On Human Conduct*. Oxford: Clarendon Press.

Oakley, K. (2009) The disappearing arts: Creativity and innovation after the creative industries. *International Journal of Cultural Policy*, 15(4), 403–13.

Obama Girl (2007) Crush on Obama. *YouTube*. Accessible at: http://www.youtube.com/watch?v=wKsoXHYICqU

Oliver, R. (2007, October 15) Not quite art. *The Age*. Accessible at: http://www.theage.com.au/news/tv-reviews/not-quite-art/2007/10/15/1192300666820.html

Ong, A. (1999) *Flexible Citizenship*. Durham, NC: Duke University Press.

Ong, W. (2004 [1958]) *Ramus: Method, and the Decay of Dialogue; from the Art of Discourse to the Art of Reason*. Chicago, IL: Chicago University Press.

Orwell, G. (1949) Appendix: The principles of newspeak. In *Nineteen Eighty-Four*, 241–51. Harmondsworth, UK: Penguin.

Ostrom, E. (1990) *Governing the Commons: The Evolution of Institutions for Collective Action*. Cambridge, UK: Cambridge University Press.

Packard, V. (2007 [1957]) *The Hidden Persuaders*. New York: Ig Publishing.

Page, S. E. (n.d.) Research on culture. *Scott E Page*. Accessible at: http://www.cscs.umich.edu/~spage/culture.html

Pain, S. (2005) Why the pharaohs never smiled. *New Scientist*. 2506, 36–9.

Paine, T. (1906 [1792]) *Rights of Man* (H. B. Bonner, Ed.). London: Watts & Co. Accessible at: http://www.ushistory.org/paine/rights

Pasley, J. (1999) Party politics, citizenship and collective action in nineteenth-century America. Paper presented at The Transformation of Civic Life, Middle Tennessee State University, Murfreesboro and Nashville, TN. Accessible at: http://frank.mtsu.edu/~seig/pdf/pdf_response_pasley.pdf

PCMag.com (n.d.) Definition of: digerati. Accessible at: http://www.pcmag.com/encyclopedia_term/0,2542,t=geekerati&i=41273,00.asp

Pearlman, R. Z. (2006, April 18) NASA honors Neil Armstrong with moon rock award. *Space.com*. Accessible at: http://www.space.com/2310-nasa-honors-neil-armstrong-moon-rock-award.html

Peters, J. D. (2001) 'The only proper scale of representation': The politics of statistics and stories. *Journal of Political Communication*, 18(4), 433–9.

Pettit, T. (2007) Before the Gutenberg parenthesis: Elizabethan-American compatibilities. *Media in Transition*, 5. Accessible at: http://web.mit.edu/comm-forum/mit5/papers/pettitt_plenary_gutenberg.pdf

Platt, A. (2009 [1969]) *The Child Savers*. Piscataway, NJ: Rutgers University Press.

Plunkett, J. (2003) *Queen Victoria: First Media Monarch*. Oxford: Oxford University Press.

Ponce de Leon, C. L. (2002) *Self-Exposure: Human Interest Journalism and the Emergence of Celebrity in America 1890–1940*. Chapel Hill, NC: University of North Carolina Press.

Popper, K. (1945) *The Open Society and its Enemies*. London: Routledge and Kegan Paul.

Porter, M. (1985) *Competitive Advantage: Creating and Sustaining Superior Performance*. New York: The Free Press.

Potts, J. (2010) Can behavioural biases explain innovation failures? Toward a behavioural innovation economics. *Prometheus*, 28(2), 133–48.

Potts, J., Cunningham, S., Hartley, J., and Ormerod, P. (2008a) Social network markets: A new definition of the creative industries. *Journal of Cultural Economics*, 32, 167–85.

Potts, J., Hartley, J., Banks, J., Burgess, J., Cobcroft, R., Cunningham, S., and Montgomery, L. (2008b) Consumer co-creation and situated creativity. *Industry and Innovation*, 15(5), 459–74.

Pratt, A. C. (2008) Cultural commodity chains, cultural clusters, or cultural production chains? *Growth and Change*, 39(1), 95–103.

'Quantum zeno effect' (n.d.) *Wikipedia*. Accessible at: http://en.wikipedia.org/wiki/Quantum_Zeno_Effect

Quiller-Couch, A. (1946 [1916]) *The Art of Writing*. London: Guild Books.

Qvortrup, J. (2004) *Children as Legitimate Claims Makers on Societal Resources*. Report. Leeds, UK: WELLCHI Network. Accessible at: http://www.ciimu.org/webs/wellchi/reports/workshop_1/w1_qvortrup.pdf

Rahorner1 (2008) The scoop on Olduvai. *YouTube*. Accessible at: http://www.youtube.com/watch?v=umwuqAljFVo

Rees, A. (1996) T. H. Marshall and the progress of citizenship. In M. Bulmer and A. Rees (Eds.), *Citizenship Today*, 1–25. London: University College London Press.

Rennie, E. (2006) *Community Media: A Global Introduction*. Lanham, MD: Rowman & Littlefield.

Richards, I. A. (2004 [1929]) *Practical Criticism*. Philadelphia, PA: Transaction.

Rojek, C. (2004) *Celebrity*. London: Reaktion Books.

Ross, A. (2009) *Nice Work if You can Get it: Life and Labor in Precarious Times*. New York: New York University Press.

Runciman, W. G. (2009) *The Theory of Cultural and Social Selection*. Cambridge, UK: Cambridge University Press.

Rusbridger, A. (2000, November 4) Versions of seriousness. *The Guardian*. Accessible at: http://www.guardian.co.uk/dumb/story/0,7369,391891,00.html

Russell, G. (1926) *Nuntius: Advertising and Its Future*. London: Kegan Paul, Trench, Trübner.

Ryan, A. (2001, March 26) The New Statesman essay – How we let more mean worse. *New Statesman*. Accessible at: http://www.newstatesman.com/200103260019

Sawyer, K. (2005) *Social Emergence: Societies as Complex Systems*. Cambridge, UK: Cambridge University Press.

Schiller, H. (1989) *Culture, Inc.: The Corporate Takeover of Public Expression*. New York: Oxford University Press.

Schudson, M. (1999) *The Good Citizen: A History of American Civic Life*. Cambridge, MA: Harvard University Press.

Schumpeter, J. (1934) *The Theory of Economic Development*. Cambridge, MA: Harvard University Press.

Schumpeter, J. (1942) *Capitalism, Socialism and Democracy*. New York: Harper & Bros.

Sconce, J. (2007) A vacancy at the Paris Hilton. In J. Gray, C. Sandvoss, and C. L. Harrington (Eds.), *Fandom: Identities and Communities in a Mediated World*, 328–43. New York: New York University Press.

Scriven, M. (1991) *Evaluation Thesaurus* (4th edn.). Newbury Park, CA: Sage Publications.

Serjeant, J. (2008, September 5) John McCain speech draws record TV ratings. *Reuters*. Accessible at: http://www.reuters.com/article/wtMostRead/idUSN 0439266820080905

Shannon, C. (1948) A mathematical theory of communication. *The Bell System Technical Journal*, 27, 379–423; 623–56. Accessible at: http://cm.bell-labs.com/cm/ms/what/shannonday/shannon1948.pdf

Shirky, C. (2006) *Here Comes Everybody: The Power of Organizing without Organizations*. New York: Penguin.

Shirky, C. (2010) The shock of inclusion. *The Edge*. Accessible at: http://www.edge.org/q2010/q10_1.html#shirky

Shklovsky, V. (1965 [1917]). Art as technique. In L. T. Lemon and M. Reis (Eds.), *Russian Formalist Criticism*, 3–24. Lincoln, NE: University of Nebraska Press.

Shore, J. (n.d.) What is singing talent? Accessible at: http://www.josephshore.com [click on 'Vocal Pedagogy Writings,' then on 'What is "Talent" in Singing?']

Shuttleworth, A. (1966) *Two working papers in cultural studies – A humane centre, and Max Weber and the 'cultural sciences.'* Occasional Paper 2. Birmingham, UK: Centre for Contemporary Cultural Studies, Birmingham University.

Simkin, J. (n.d.) Journalists. *Spartacus Educational*. Accessible at: http://www.spartacus.schoolnet.co.uk/journalists.htm

Slattery, L. (2009, August 19) The Greeks had a blue word for it. *The Australian*. Accessible at: http://www.theaustralian.news.com.au/story/0,25197,25948349-25192,00.html

Snoddy, R. (1992) *The Good, the Bad and the Unacceptable: The Hard News About the British Press*. London: Faber & Faber.

Sokal, A. (1996) Transgressing the boundaries: Toward a transformative hermeneutics of quantum gravity. *Social Text*, 46/47, 217–52. [*Caveat lector*]

Sojka, S. (2007) John Howard - Bennelong Time Since I Rock and Rolled. *YouTube*. Accessible at: http://www.youtube.com/watch?gl=AU&hl=en-GB&v=8_zulGddP6o

Sonwalkar, P. (2005) Banal journalism: The centrality of the 'us-them' binary in news discourse. In S. Allen (Ed.), *Journalism: Critical Issues*, 261–73. Maidenhead, UK: Open University Press.

Sourswithhawk (2009) Native ancestral skills: Stone tools from Franciscan chert. *YouTube*. Accessible at: http://www.youtube.com/watch?v=yBbjP9aCbG8

Stelter, B. (2008, August 29) 38 million view Obama's speech; Highest-rated convention in history. *New York Times: Media Decoder*. Blog. Accessible at: http://mediadecoder.blogs.nytimes.com/2008/08/29/conventions-38-million-view-obamas-speech

Stelter, B. (2009, July 24) On television and radio, talk of Obama's citizenship. *New York Times: Media Decoder*. Blog. Accessible at: http://mediadecoder.blogs.nytimes.com/2009/07/24/on-television-and-radio-talk-of-obamas-citizenship/?hp

Stolz, G. (2010, January 13) Re-offending gang leader Tiani Slockee escapes jail. *Courier Mail*. Accessible at: http://www.news.com.au/couriermail/story/0,1,26582270-952,00.html

Tasha (2005) Hey clip. *YouTube*. Accessible at: http://www.youtube.com/watch?v=-_CSo1gOd48

The Trials of Oz (1991) Film. S. Folkson (Dir.). United Kingdom: BBC.

The Week (2009, July 23) 'Jon Stewart vs. Lou Dobbs and "birthers."' *The Week*. Accessible at: http://theweek.com/article/index/98892/Jon_Stewart_vs_Lou_Dobbs_and_birthers

Thompson, D. (2001) The English republic. *The Republic*, 2, 72–80. Accessible at: http://www.republicjournal.com/02/contents002.html

Thompson, E. P. (1963) *The Making of the English Working Class*. London: Victor Gollancz.

Throsby, D. (2001) *Economics and Culture*. Cambridge, MA: Cambridge University Press.

Time (1942, March 23) The press: Hearst's third war. *Time*. Accessible at: http://www.time.com/time/magazine/article/0,9171,802309-1,00.html

Toff, B. (2008, August 29) Ratings: Barack Obama, and all the rest. *New York Times: Media Decoder*. Blog. Accessible at: http://mediadecoder.blogs.nytimes.com/2008/08/29/ratings-barack-obama-and-all-the-rest

'Truthiness' (n.d.) *Wikipedia*. Accessible at: http://en.wikipedia.org/wiki/Truthiness

Turner, G. (2003) *British Cultural Studies* (3rd edn.). London: Routledge.

Turner, G. (2004) *Understanding Celebrity*. London: Sage Publications.

Turner, G. (2005) *Ending the Affair: The Decline of Current Affairs in Australia*. Sydney, NSW: University of New South Wales Press.

Turner, G. (2010a) *Ordinary People and the Media: The Demotic Turn*. London: Sage Publications.

Turner, G. (2010b, October 13) In thrall purely to sciences. *The Australian.* Accessible at: http://www.theaustralian.com.au/higher-education/opinion-analysis/in-thrall-purely-to-sciences/story-e6frgcko-1225937840268

University of the West Indies (n.d.) Stuart Hall: Publications and papers. University of the West Indies at Mona, Jamaica. Accessible at: http://www.mona.uwi.edu/library/stuart_hall.html

Uricchio, W. (2004) Cultural citizenship in the age of P2P networks. In I. Bondebjerg and P. Golding (Eds.), *European Culture and the Media*, 139–63. Bristol, UK: Intellect Books.

Vale, K. (2009, December 17) Australia's most watched YouTube videos of 2009. *Official Google Australia Blog.* Blog. Accessible at: http://google-au.blogspot.com/2009/12/australias-most-watched-youtube-videos.html

Veblen, T. (1898) Why is economics not an evolutionary science? *Quarterly Journal of Economics*, 12. Accessible at: http://socserv.mcmaster.ca/econ/ugcm/3ll3/veblen/econevol.txt

Veblen, T. (1899) *The Theory of the Leisure Class.* Accessible at: http://xroads.virginia.edu/~hyper/VEBLEN/veblenhp.html

Veloso, L. (2008) Universal citizens, unequal childhoods: Children's perspectives on rights and citizenship in Brazil. *Latin American Perspectives*, 35(4), 45–59.

Vihrachoff, D. M. (2009, October 15) 28 million views, 900 donors, $23,000 dollars – and one fantastic couple. *Wellstone Action!* Accessible at: http://wellstone.org/blog/28-million-views-900-donors-23000-and-one-fantastic-couple

Vološinov, V. (1973) *Marxism and the Philosophy of Language.* London: Seminar Press.

von Hayek, F. (1944) *The Road to Serfdom.* London: Routledge and Kegan Paul.

Walker, B. (1998) Social movements as nationalisms or, on the very idea of a queer nation. *Canadian Journal of Philosophy*, Supplementary Volume 22, 505–47.

Wallerstein, I. (2001) *Unthinking Social Science: The Limits of Nineteenth-Century Paradigms* (2nd edn.). Philadelphia, PA: Temple University Press.

Wallerstein, I. (2004) *The Uncertainties of Knowledge.* Philadelphia, PA: Temple University Press.

Warner, M. (2005) *Publics and Counterpublics.* New York: Zone Books.

Watercutter, A. (2008, June 11) Miley Cyrus delivers latest blow in YouTube dance battle. *Underwire.* Blog. Accessible at: http://www.wired.com/underwire/2008/06/miley-cyrus-del

Webb, R. K. (1955) *The British Working Class Reader 1790–1848.* London: George Allen & Unwin.

Weiner, J. (2009, August 7) '"JK Wedding Dance" internet sensation directs buzz toward charity. *TheDailyTell.* Accessible at: http://www.thedailytell.com/2009/08/jk-wedding-dance-internet-sensation-directs-buzz-toward-charity

Welch, E. (2005) *Shopping in the Renaissance. Consumer Cultures in Italy 1400–1600*. New Haven, CT: Yale University Press.

WellcomeFilm (2009) Stone age tools: Prehistoric stoneworking techniques, part 1 (1947). *YouTube*. Accessible at: http://www.youtube.com/watch?v= Bu5eqBg5Lr4

Westbury, M. (2009, June 16) Creativity needs creative destruction. *The Age*. Accessible at: http://www.marcuswestbury.net/2009/06/16/creativity-need-creative-destruction

Whiteley, N. (2003) *Reyner Banham: Historian of the Immediate Future*. Cambridge, MA: MIT Press.

Williams, R. (Ed.) (1968) *May Day Manifesto*. Harmondsworth, UK: Penguin.

Williams, R. (1973) Base and superstructure in Marxist cultural theory. *New Left Review* I/82, 3–16.

Williams, R. (1974a) Communications as cultural science. *Journal of Communication*, 24(3), 17–25.

Williams, R. (1974b) *Television: Technology and Cultural Form*. London: Fontana.

Williams, R. (1976) *Keywords*. London: Fontana.

Williams, R. (1977) *Marxism and Literature*. Oxford: Oxford University Press.

Wilson, E. O. (1998) *Consilience: The Unity of Knowledge*. New York: Alfred A. Knopf.

Wilson, S. (1995, February 17) From the margins not the gutter (book review of *Cultural Politics – Queer Reading*). *Times Higher Education*. Accessible at: http://www.timeshighereducation.co.uk/story.asp?storyCode=161892&sectio ncode=6

Windschuttle, K. (1998) Journalism versus cultural studies. *Australian Studies in Journalism*, 7, 3–31.

Windschuttle, K. (2000) The poverty of cultural studies. *Journalism Studies*, 1(1), 145–59.

Wolfe, C. (2009) What is Posthumanism? Minneapolis, MN: University of Minnesota Press.

Wolfe, T. (1969) What if he is right? In *The Pump House Gang*, 105–33. New York: Bantam Books.

Wolframmathematica (2009) Bayes' theorem and inverse probability. *YouTube*. Accessible at: http://www.youtube.com/watch?v=_RLb58eoEco

'Works based on Faust' (n.d.) *Wikipedia*. Accessible at: http://en.wikipedia.org/ wiki/Works_based_on_Faust

Xxnapoleonsolo (2010, April 23) The weeping angels' Doctor Who return intrigues Blink star Finlay Robertson. *Scifylove*. Accessible at: http://scyfilove.com/ 2058/the-weeping-angels-doctor-who-return-intrigues-blink-star-finlay-robertson/

Zelizer, B. (2004) When facts, truth, and reality are God-terms: On journalism's uneasy place in cultural studies. *Communication and Critical/Cultural Studies*, 1(1), 100–19.

Zelizer, B. (2009) President's message. *ICA Newsletter*, 37(5). Accessible at: http://www.icahdq.org/publications/publicnewsletter/2009/6-7/JUNJULY09_PRESMSG.asp

Zittrain, J. (2008) *The Future of the Internet – and How to Stop it*. New Haven, CT: Yale University Press. Accessible at: http://yupnet.org/zittrain

Žižek, S. (2002) Big Brother, or, the triumph of the gaze over the eye. In T. Levin, U. Frohne, and P. Weibel (Eds.), *Ctrl [Space]: Rhetorics of Surveillance from Bentham to Big Brother*, 224–7. Cambridge, MA: MIT Press.

Acknowledgments

This book is based on research supported by the Australian Research Council, project numbers FF0561981 (Federation Fellowship) and DP0879596 (Discovery Project). I acknowledge the Federation Fellowship team at Queensland University of Technology, especially Jason Potts and post-docs John Banks, Jean Burgess, Lucy Montgomery, and Christine Schmidt. Far-flung colleagues on the 'cultural science' adventure have made all the difference, especially Carsten Herrmann-Pillath, Alex Bentley, Paul Ormerod, Alex Mesoudi. Many thanks go to Jonathan Gray for his generous critique of the draft manuscript, and to Jayne Fargnoli at Wiley-Blackwell for her wonderful support. As always, my principal debt of gratitude is to Tina Horton, to whom this book is dedicated.

I acknowledge the Chinese University of Hong Kong (Jack Qiu) for inviting me to give the paper on which Chapter 7 is based. I am grateful to the Communication University of China (Fan Zhou); Beijing Research Centre for Science of Science, Beijing Academy of Science & Technology (Zhang Shiyun); the Government of Thailand and the WIPO (Dimiter Gantchev); the UK Arts and Humanities Research Council (Shearer West and Gary Grubb); and London Metropolitan University (Pat Wood) for invitations to present the ideas about the creative economy summarized in Chapter 2. The ideas at the beginning of Chapter 4 were first presented at the University of Tallinn, Estonia (thanks to Indrek Ibrus), and those at the end of it at the Annenberg School for Communication, University of Pennsylvania, US (thanks to Barbie Zelizer). Other material herein has been revised from papers as follows:

- Chapter 1: Hartley, J. (2009) My media studies: The history and future of ideas. *TVNM*, 10(1), 69–71.
- Chapter 3. Hartley, J. (2008) 'The supremacy of ignorance over instruction and of numbers over knowledge': Journalism, popular culture, and the English constitution. *Journalism Studies*, 8(5), 679–91; and Hartley, J. (2009) Journalism and popular culture. In K. Wahl-Jorgensen and T. Hanitzsch (Eds.), *The Handbook of Journalism Studies*, 310–24. New York and Abingdon: Routledge.
- Chapter 5: Hartley, J. (2009) Less popular but more democratic? Corrie, Clarkson and the dancing *Cru*. In G. Turner and J. Tay (Eds.), *Television Studies after TV: Understanding Television in the Post-broadcast Era*, 20–30. London: Routledge.
- Chapter 6: Hartley, J. (2010) Silly citizenship. *Critical Discourse Studies*, 7(4): 233–48.
- Chapter 8: Hartley, J. (2010) *Homo nuntius* – Messaging humanity. *Popular Communication*, 8(4), 293–311.

Index

2001: A Space Odyssey   25
Abbas, M. Akbar   181
ABC (America)   122
ABC (Australian Broadcasting
   Corporation)   89, 90
abstraction   17–18, 20, 25, 33, 37,
   103, 136, 191
   of citizenship   135–6, 137, 152
   of knowledge   17, 19, 135
   of the sign, signification   20–1, 22,
   113
   of thought   202, 204, 213
Actor Network Theory (ANT)   53,
   214
Adbusters   57–8
airport bestseller   4, 13, 94, 108–12,
   115
   bookshop   94, 115
Alfred (the Great, king)   196
Allan, Stuart   79
Anderson, Benedict   39
Anderson, Chris   55, 204n
Apple (company)   14n, 206
archive   4, 12, 14, 15, 16, 55, 115–16
   essence   159, 160, 161, 162, 163,
   166, 168

modern   159, 161
network   160
postmodern   159, 160
probability   160–2, 165–8, 173, 174,
   175
Argens, Jean-Baptiste de Boyer,
   Marquis d'   62
Aristotle   185, 194–5
Armstrong, Neil   170
Arnold, Matthew   29, 30n
Arthur, Brian   203, 204, 210, 211, 213,
   214
Assange, Julian   89n
Atkin, Hugh   89, 90, 128, 146
attention, economy of   14, 47–8, 49,
   91, 110, 112, 147
audience   3, 5–6, 7, 13, 16, 19, 23–4,
   41, 78, 80, 82, 87, 106, 118,
   119–21, 123, 125, 127–8, 141, 145,
   159–60, 163, 165, 167, 187
   active   5, 7–9, 26, 41, 57, 71, 143–4,
   181
   studies   5
Australian Research Council (ARC)
   12, 155, 236
Aynsley-Green, Sir Albert   148

Digital Futures for Cultural and Media Studies, First Edition. John Hartley.
© 2012 John Wiley & Sons, Ltd. Published 2012 by John Wiley & Sons, Ltd.

Bacall, Lauren (Betty Joan Perske)
23, 24
Bacon, Sir Francis 185
Baecque, Antoine de 61
Bagehot, Walter 59, 65, 66–9, 79
Bakhshi, Hasan 50
Banham, Reyner 124
Barabási, Albert-László 56, 188, 197,
204, 210
Baran, Paul 180
Barker, Chris 177
'Barlow, Ken' 117, 130
Barthes, Roland 34, 162, 194, 204,
207
Baudrillard, Jean 162
BBC (British Broadcasting
Corporation) 79, 115, 123, 165
Beaverbrook, Lord (Max Aitken) 65
Bednar, Jenna 39, 205, 206n
Beinhocker, Eric 110, 144, 196, 203,
210, 214
Bennett, Tony 28, 31, 162, 177
Bentley, R. Alex 48, 204, 236
Berlioz, Hector 183n
Bickerton, Derek 214
Big Brother 6, 122–3, 129
Bird, S. Elizabeth 77, 79
Blink (episode of *Dr Who*) 163–4,
166
Bliss 78
Bohr, Niels 162
'Bok' (moon rock) 170
'Bond, James' 20
Boyd, Brian 110, 147, 214
Boyle, Susan 148
'Boz' (Charles Dickens) 69
Brand, Stewart 105
Brangelina 20
Brazil 50, 133
Britain's Got Talent 148
Brooks, Cleanth 178
Bruns, Axel 77, 128

Brunsdon, Charlotte 34
Buckminster Fuller, R. 4–5, 178
Burgess, Jean 144, 166, 236

Camrose, Lord (William Ewart Berry)
65
Carlile, Richard 62, 69
Carr, Senator Kim 31
Caves, Richard 45
CBS 122
CCCS (Centre for Contemporary
Cultural Studies, UK) 30–1, 34,
44, 86, 87, 204
CCI (Centre of Excellence for Creative
Industries and Innovation,
Australia) 44–5, 203, 205–6
celebrity 3, 48, 56, 77, 78, 89, 91, 108,
110, 128, 129, 146, 149, 189, 196
culture 19, 22, 25, 67, 77
spectacle 19, 68–9
censorship 154
Chandler, David 170
Channel 4 (UK) 168
Chaplin, Charlie 24, 56
China 9, 12, 38, 50, 114, 127, 137
Cherry, Colin 180
children 4, 14, 40, 104, 133–5, 142,
143, 147–9, 200
childhood 134, 148, 151
sexualization of 154
Chomsky, Noam 35
citizenship 14, 16, 79, 84, 133–54
Classical 152–4
cultural 141–2, 150–2
discursive 147–8
DIY (productive) 143–5
history of 135–8
informed 64, 138–9, 191
media 143
silly 145–7
theory 134, 148
Cleese, John 23

CNN   122, 127, 129, 146
Cobbett, William   62
Colbert Report   127, 145
Colbert, Stephen   73
ColbertNation.com   127
Collini, Stefan   100–2, 105
comedy   41, 89, 119, 127, 143, 145, 146, 168
Comedy Central   127
communication, model of   2, 3, 4, 16, 70, 81, 84, 88, 189, 190
Communist Party of China   38
complex networks, systems   15, 26, 46, 54, 159, 167, 174, 194, 212
complexity science, studies and theory   9, 31, 37, 46, 51, 53, 184, 204, 213
Conboy, Martin   74, 76–7
consilience   16, 21, 22
Constantine, Susannah   194
consumer-created content   8, 25, 125
Coronation Street   117, 120, 124, 125, 126, 127, 130
Corrie   125, 126, 127
Courier Mail   97, 98, 99
creative agency, agent   41, 51
creative arts, artist   9, 47, 54, 192, 206, 207
creative citizens   51
creative clusters   49–50
creative content   91, 106
creative culture   45, 49, 55
creative destruction   5, 10, 15, 36, 43, 111, 115, 117, 199, 201, 202, 203, 213
creative economy   56 (fig.), 106
creative genius   169n
creative imagination   11, 71
creative industries   7, 42–5, 47–53, 193, 195, 196, 200, 206, 208
creative innovation   8, 44, 45, 49, 54, 114, 118, 198, 199, 207

creative inputs/outputs   50
creative occupations   24, 50
creative productivity   7, 45, 52, 208
creative services   50
creative work   11, 50
Creative Commons   145
cultural science   3, 15, 26, 58, 202–5, 213, 214
'cultural Science 1.0'   30–5
'cultural Science 2.0'   31, 32, 35, 36, 40, 46, 47, 54–7
Cultural Science (journal)   46
cultural studies   1–5, 10, 15–16, 19, 21, 22, 27–58, 60–1, 70, 74, 76, 80, 82–7, 91, 113, 130, 142, 181–3, 192, 199, 203–5, 206
Cyrus, Miley   129, 132, 146, 149, 150
Cyrus, Noah   153

Dahlgren, Peter   74
Dahrendorf, Ralf   184
Daily Herald   65
Daily Mail   65, 91
Daily Mirror   65
Daily Show   127, 145, 146
Dallas   121
dance   20, 89, 129, 149–50
   right to   144, 146, 154
   dance-off 14, 115, 129, 132, 134, 146, 150–1, 152–3
Darnton, Robert   62, 63
Darwin, Charles   1, 29
   Darwinism and neo-Darwinism   32, 33, 46n, 160, 203, 214
DCMS (Department for Culture Media and Sport, UK)   43, 44, 45, 50
deference   62, 66–7, 68, 138
   versus democracy   66
Democratic Unionist Party   214
Dennis, Felix   89

Derrida, Jacques 162, 190, 214
Deutscher, Guy 214
dialogic model of language 2–4, 8, 16, 22, 192, 194–5
  productivity 15
Diderot, Denis 63
Director's Guild of America 106
Disraeli, Benjamin 63
digerati 109
digital affordances 4
digital archives 160
digital creativity 12
digital communication 22
digital connectivity 144
digital content 8, 14n, 47
digital divide 152, 186
digital era 13, 150
digital information 14, 158
digital literacy 7, 93, 111, 113
'digital literati' 105, 109
digital media 2, 3, 4, 12, 16, 25–6, 47, 53, 76, 114, 144, 182
digital networks 205, 208, 210
digital rebel 105
digital revolution 52, 105, 106
digital rights management 131
digital social networks 182
digital technology 8, 14
Dilthey, Wilhelm 31
Dissanayake, Ellen 184
DIY (do it yourself) 8, 71, 76, 88, 92, 119, 124–32, 144–51, 171
DIWO (do it with others) 8, 124, 128, 144–51
Dobbs, Lou 146
Doctorow, Cory 105
Donsbach, Wolfgang 83
Dopfer, Kurt 184
Dyer, Richard 124

Eagleton, Terry 30
Eco, Umberto 169, 181, 204, 211, 212

economics
  evolutionary 5, 9, 15, 32, 35, 46, 53, 57, 199
  neoclassical 35, 37, 45, 46, 48, 55, 58, 189, 198, 205
Economist 63, 64, 66, 67
Ed Sullivan Show 121
Edge, The 95
Edgerton, David 203
eHow 109–10
Eliot, T. S. 182
emancipation 6–8, 10, 18, 24, 40, 55, 62, 70–3, 77, 83, 99, 105, 111, 124, 141, 182, 192
  of the sign 20, 22, 70
enabling social technology 7, 14, 17, 46–7, 72, 93
Enlightenment 6, 7, 18, 19, 62, 63, 74, 77, 136, 137, 140, 147, 161
'enterprise touch' content 8–9
entertainment 6, 7, 35, 41, 63, 66, 71–82, 91, 118, 121–2, 128, 134, 146, 163, 168
  media 25, 40, 113, 138
  platforms 15
entrepreneur(ship) 5, 7, 15, 51, 64, 75, 90, 197, 201–2, 206, 207, 209, 210, 212, 213
  'consumer entrepreneurship' 25, 48–9, 195, 198
Erni, John Nguyet 181
ethnicity 16, 72, 75, 84, 98, 142, 191
  ethnic others 143
  ethnic rights 147
Evans, Malcolm 176n
evolutionary theory 26, 46, 184, 203, 213
'Ewing, J. R.' (who shot?) 13, 121
expertise 9, 64, 70, 92, 103, 110, 114, 119, 130, 132, 152, 160, 170, 171, 207
  distributed 131, 152

Facebook   56, 93, 161, 193
fans   13, 24, 49, 115, 125–7, 143,
    149–50, 156, 164, 166
  fan studies   204
  fanzines   76
Faust(ian)   23, 177, 183
feminism   34, 41, 103, 137, 139, 204
Fiske, John   177, 181, 182
Flickr   52, 170
Flynt, Larry   89
Forgacs, David   76
Foucault, Michel   43, 137, 162
Fox News   91, 122, 127
Francis, Neil   214
Frankfurt School   23
Friends   122
Fry, Stephen   56

Galton, Sir Francis   174
Garnham, Nicholas   35, 45
Gates, Henry Louis   184
Gauntlett, David   82
Gay, Brigitte   210
Gibbon, Edward   134
Gibson, Mark   35, 84
Gillan, Karen   164
Gilroy, Paul   75
GLAM (galleries, libraries, archives,
    museums)   14, 157, 158, 162,
    163, 164, 165, 170
globalization   12, 55, 79, 125,
    182
  globalizing   157, 197
go-between   5, 15, 199, 200, 203, 206,
    210, 212, 214
Goel, Vinod Kumar   205n
Google (company)   9, 25, 115, 160,
    161, 172
Googling (search)   14, 98, 126
Gramsci, Antonio   34, 76
Gray, Jonathan   16, 127, 145, 236
Grayling, A. C.   63

Green, Joshua   144, 166
Greenfield, Susan   39, 192
Grossberg, Lawrence   41, 177
Gu, Xin   207

Haasler, Sue   125–6
Habermas, Jürgen   94
  Habermasianism   94, 151
  see also public sphere
Halavais, Alex   172
Hall, Stuart   32, 34, 35, 39, 43, 76, 84,
    85, 86, 180, 181, 182
  Hallism   87
Halloran, James   83
Harajuku (fashion)   48
Hardy, Thomas   211–12
Hargreaves, Ian   77, 78–9
Hartley, L. P.   199
Hawkes, Terence   184
Hawkins, Gay   53
Hayek, Friedrich von   35, 57
Haywood, Ian   64
Healy, Chris   155n
Hearst, William Randolph   65, 105
Hébert, Louis   112
Heisenberg, Werner   161, 162
Hermes (god)   185, 200–1, 202, 206n,
    211
  Logios   211
  see also Mercury (god)
Hermes, Joke   79
Herrmann-Pillath, Carsten   32, 49,
    53, 189, 192, 203, 214, 236
Hesmondhalgh, David   44
Hess, Charlotte   214
Hetherington, Henry   62
'Hey Clip'   129, 132, 146, 168
Higgs, Peter   50
Hilmes, Michele   185n
Hilton, Paris   56, 78, 128
Hobbes, Thomas   195
  Hobbesianism   189

Hoggart, Richard 30, 35, 74, 83, 86, 114, 124, 130, 178, 181
'Hoggartsborough' 124
hominin 162, 170, 184
Homo aestheticus 184
Homo cantans 184
Homo dicens 184
Homo ergaster 170
Homo habilis 162
Homo ludens 184, 193, 195, 198
Homo nuntius (*H. sapiens nuntius*) 4, 15, 16, 176, 184–7, 189, 192, 193, 194, 196, 198
Homo oeconomicus 184, 193, 195, 198
Homo sociologicus 184
Homo sapiens 4, 172, 184, 185, 193, 196
Howkins, John 50
Hrdy, Sarah Blaffer 214
Hughes, Robert 103–4
Huizinga, Johan 184
humanities 5, 9, 10, 15, 21, 22, 26, 31, 36, 38, 40, 52, 54, 83, 100–1, 102, 172–3, 190, 199, 202–6, 213
  harrumphing 103
  journals 46
  'new' 11, 205
  Queen of 30
Humanities and Creative Arts (HCA) 9–10, 11
Hurford, James 214
Hutter, Michael 214
Hyde, Lewis 169, 185n, 199–202, 210–11

ideology 7, 24, 33–4, 36, 38, 72, 79, 85–7, 91, 136, 137, 140, 166, 181, 204
Idle, Eric 172
Idol (TV franchise) 115, 121, 122
Illuminati 108, 109
Inglis, Fred 30

Ink 76
Iolanthe 63
innovation 3, 7, 27, 45–6, 47, 50–2, 54, 88, 131, 195–7, 205, 208, 213
  agents of 41
  anti- 30
  creative 8, 44, 49, 54, 114, 118, 198, 199, 207
  cultural 206–7
  distributed 7
  economics of 46, 210
  intellectual 31
  of knowledge 205
  open innovation networks 26
  system 205–6, 207
  user-led 25, 71, 114, 144, 192
International Communication Association 36, 177
International Data Corporation 8
Invisible College 95, 107, 108, 112
Iser, Wolfgang 178

Jacobs, Jane 155, 167, 203
Jarvis, Jeff 105
Jenkins, Henry 3, 130n, 144, 158, 182, 192
'JK [Jill and Kevin] Wedding Dance' 149, 150
Joannou, Maroula 124
Jones, Jeffrey 127, 145
Josipovici, Gabriel 99–102, 105
journalism studies 3, 60–1, 70, 76, 80, 82–3, 87, 92–3

Kagan, Jerome 203
Keating, Chris 156n
Keen, Andrew 77, 104–6, 107, 109
Kemsley, Lord (James Gomer Berry) 65
Kennedy, President John F. 121
Kennedy-Cuomo, Kerry 64
Kipling, Rudyard 103, 189

knowledge   7, 10, 20, 25–6, 33, 38–9,
41, 48, 53, 72–3, 77, 84, 85, 103,
110–13, 114–15, 127, 129–30, 144,
157–8, 160, 172, 173–4, 177, 185,
193, 196, 202–3, 205, 207, 209
  abstract, *see* abstraction
  democratization of   108
  disciplinary   9–11, 36, 46, 115, 135,
152, 159
  economy   205–6
  explicit, implicit, tacit   17, 135,
196
  growth of   7, 17, 32, 45–6, 47,
51–2, 54, 56 (fig.), 57, 113,
115–16, 135, 144, 175, 196, 198,
210n
  knowing subjects   24, 172
  'numbers' versus   66, 68, 69, 79
  objective/subjective   17, 41, 158,
159
  print and   18, 24
  professionals   139
  regimes of   137
  systems   10, 46, 53, 131, 135, 152,
202
Knowledge, Tree of   200
Kuhnian paradigm   27
kulturwissenschaft   31

Laclau, Ernesto   76, 141
Langer, John   77
Lanham, Richard   49, 91, 110, 147
Lasn, Kalle   57–8, 205
Latour, Bruno   53, 192, 214
Leadbeater, Charles   111, 161, 196
Leakey, Louis S. B.   162
Leakey, Louise   171
Lee, Richard E.   10, 29, 46, 84, 85, 87,
190, 203
leisure   18, 64, 119
  leisure-entertainment   73, 125, 143
Lessig, Lawrence   105

Lewis, Jeff   76
Life of Brian   23
linear causation   159, 162, 190
linear model of language   2–4, 80, 81,
189
literacy   55, 64, 71, 84, 113, 124, 196
  digital   7, 93, 111, 113
  print   17, 55
  publishing as   95, 108, 111
Lloyd's Weekly News   63
Loeb Classical Library   153
Loeffelholz, Martin   83
lonelygirl15 119
long tail   55–6, 111, 119, 125, 168,
188–9, 204n
Lotman, Yuri   15, 161, 181, 186n, 192,
198, 204, 212, 214
Love's Labour's Lost   17, 176
Luhmann, Niklas   204, 214
Lumby, Catharine   77, 78

Maccoby, S.   65
MacNeilage, Peter   214
Mad Men   179
Mao, Zedong   27
Marx, Karl   105
  Marxism   23, 31, 34, 38, 76, 83, 86,
137, 180, 181–2, 205
  Continental Marxism   34
  neo-Marxism   35
M*A*S*H   121, 123
Mason, Matt   105
Maxwell, Richard   182
Mayhew, Henry   64, 69
McCain, Senator John   122, 128, 146
  McCainiacs   146
McCalman, Iain   63
McCraw, Thomas   110, 201, 206
McGuigan, Jim   28n, 206
McKee, Alan   155n
McGregor of Durris, Lord Oliver Ross
68–9

McLuhan, Marshall   179–80, 182, 190
   McLuhanism   181
media effects   2, 7, 82
Media International Australia   61
media studies   1, 3, 5–9, 11, 12, 15,
      26, 82, 100–1, 131–2, 173, 176,
      177, 181, 182
memory
   archive of   158
   institutions of   157
   see also popular memory
Mercury (god)   176, 185, 200–1
   Mercuries (newspapers)   18, 200
   see also Hermes (god)
Mercury, Freddie   30
Metcalfe, J. Stan   198, 203, 210
Metropolis   25
micro-level analysis   21, 28, 34, 52,
      57, 83, 103, 152, 178, 181, 182,
      205, 210
micronations   142
microproductivity   52
Miller, Toby   35, 45–6, 141, 182n
Mirabeau, Honoré Gabriel Riqueti,
      Comte de   63
Mirror Group   65
'moments'
   Gutenberg   105
   in cultural studies   36, 43–5, 47
   of innovation   205
   of 'message'   181
   of television   121
   of the trickster   213
   YouTube   162
Monod, Jacques   211
Moore's Law   114
Montesquieu, Charles-Louis de
      Secondat, Baron de La Brède et
      de   63
Montgomery, Lucy   48, 195, 198, 236
Moss, Kate   196
Mouffe, Chantal   76, 141

MSNBC *see* NBC
Muecke, Stephen   204
Mulligan, Carey   163
Murdoch, Rupert   55, 65, 79, 99, 104
museums   12, 156, 158, 159, 160,
      163–6, 168, 169–70, 171
   American Natural History Museum,
      USA   170
   British Museum, UK   162, 165,
      169
   Museum of Anatolian Civilizations,
      Turkey   169
   National Museum of Denmark
      169
   National Museum of Photography,
      Film and Television, UK   65
   National Museum of Wales/
      Amgueddfa Genedlaethol Cymru
      169n
   see also GLAM
Mychonny (John Luc)   149–50, 168
Myspace   93, 98, 99, 112

NBC   122
Newcomb, Horace   177, 181
News Corp   50, 65
News of the World   62, 64–5
Northcliffe, Lord (Alfred Harmsworth)
      65
Northern Star   63

Oakley, Kate   208
Obama, Senator/President Barack   88,
      122, 128–9, 145, 146
   Obaminators   146
Obama Girl   88–9, 128
occupations   24, 50, 76, 80, 139
O'Connor, Justin   44, 57, 206, 207
Olduvai stone chopping tool   162,
      164, 166, 169, 170, 171
   Gorge, Tanzania   170
   'imperative'   171, 175

Olympic Games   121–2
Ong, Aihwa   135
Ong, Walter   17
Ormerod, Paul   204, 236
Orwell, George   94
Ostrom, Elinor   214
O'Sullivan, Tim   177
Oz (magazine)   76, 89

Packard, Vance   179
Page, Scott   39, 205, 206n
Paine, Thomas   62, 209–10, 213
Paisley, Ian   214
Panckoucke, Charles-Joseph   6–7
Panoramio   52
Pesce, Mark   90
Peterloo massacre   69
Peters, J. D.   195
Pettit, Tom   161
phatic   3, 14, 112, 113
Planck, Max   162
play, playful   3, 4, 14, 115–16, 148,
    150, 151, 153, 181, 184
  of signifiers   191
  players   22, 54
  plays   6, 7, 147, 153
  playwrights   44
Plunkett, John   67
political economy   23, 35, 45, 46, 55,
    82, 180,
Ponce de Leon, Charles Leonard   77
Poor Man's Guardian   63, 64
Popper, Karl   3, 17, 114
popular address   71
popular culture   1, 3, 5, 13, 34, 40, 41,
    59–93, 99, 103, 130, 148, 154, 179,
    191, 207
popular front   76
popular media   2, 6, 24, 40, 75, 76,
    99, 143, 145, 181
popular memory   155, 156, 175
popular, problem of   77, 79

'popular radical' versus 'popular
    commercial'   63–6, 70, 74–7, 79,
    86
Potts, Jason   46, 47, 48, 193, 195, 203,
    236
Poulantzas, Nicos   38
power law   16, 55–6, 111, 188
Pratt, Andy   44
probability theory   14, 159, 174
productivity   8, 9, 11 , 41, 207
  collective   16
  dialogic   2, 15
  entrepreneurial   49
  micro-   52
  networked, distributed   12, 47, 56,
    115
  participatory, democratized   130–1
  of the archive   160, 167
  of language, communication   2, 16
  of the sign, semiotic   20–1, 22,
    191–2
  of technologies   113
  of the user, consumer   20–1, 22, 48,
    54–5, 114, 143–4, 148, 152, 192,
    195
  versus representation   3, 25, 124–5,
    145
  see also creative productivity
Project Runway   197
public sphere   12, 13, 71, 94, 177
  Habermasianism   143, 147
pulpit   71, 72, 73

quantum theory   159, 160, 161–2,
    164n, 174
Quiller-Couch, Sir Arthur   30n, 103
Qvortrup, Jens   140, 147

race   31, 39, 142, 173
reading public   6, 18, 24, 60, 62, 64,
    71, 74, 84, 87, 91, 92–3, 138, 193
Rennie, Ellie   79

representation   3, 5, 17–26, 60, 63, 66,
  84–7, 91, 93, 124–5, 128, 131, 187
  expert/professional   24, 25
  political   6, 19, 22, 23, 24, 72, 77,
   119, 127, 138, 140, 147
  realist   19, 73, 159, 188, 190
  representative   20, 124
  self-representation   20, 60–1, 64–5,
   70, 74–7, 79, 83, 86, 88, 90–1, 135,
   154
  semiotic   19, 22–3, 24, 119, 127, 159
Republican   63, 69
revolution   62, 75, 76, 85–6, 209–10,
   213
  American   6, 18, 136, 209
  French   6–7, 18, 62, 70, 87, 136, 209
  industrial   6, 17, 18, 62, 87, 105
  Marxist   34, 105
  'rights'   139
  scientific   17
  'year of'   72
Reynold's News   63
Richards, I. A.   178
Rickert, Heinrich   31
Roache, William   117, 130
Robinson, Andrew   105
Rojek, Chris   67, 77
Rolling Stone   76
Romanticism   177, 183
Rosen, Jay   105
Ross, Andrew   180, 182
Rothermere, Lord (Harold Sidney
   Harmsworth)   65
Royal Society   17, 108, 204n
Rudd, Kevin   89
Runciman, W. G.   214
Rusbridger, Alan   79
Russell, Gilbert   186

Saussure, Ferdinand de   36, 181
Sawyer, Keith   212, 214
Schiller, Herbert   35, 180

Schrödinger's cat   161, 174n
Schudson, Michael   138–41, 191
Schumpeter, Joseph   10, 35, 57, 110,
   201–2, 206
  Schumpeterian   5, 10, 36, 111, 115,
   199, 201
semiotics   14, 15, 19, 22–4, 34, 36, 49,
   60, 119–21, 124, 125, 127, 142,
   169, 170, 174, 176, 181–2, 183,
   187, 188, 204, 211, 212
  semiotic excess   161, 176, 186,
   190–1
sexual awakening   62
sexual exclusionism   138
sexual gossip   62
sexual orientation   75, 142, 147, 191
sexuality   39, 84, 88, 173
  active   97
  adult   153
  heterosexual   141
sexualization of children *see* children,
   sexualization of   154
Shakespeare, William   5–6, 7, 41, 44,
   146, 179, 180
  Shakespearean   6, 18, 184
Shannon, Claude   2, 180
'Sharples, Ena'   120, 124, 126, 132
Shiny Media   125
Shirky, Clay   52, 94–6, 101–13, 208
Shklovsky, Victor   178
Shore, Joseph   184
Shuttleworth, Alan   31, 34
Simkin, John   62
Slockee, Tiani   98, 112
Smith, Adam   110
Smith, Chris   44
Smith, Matt   164
Sniffin' Glue   76
Snow, C. P.   203
social network markets   9, 25, 46,
   47–8, 49, 52, 56, 87, 131, 192, 193,
   195, 208

Sojka, Stefan   90
Sokal, Alan   40, 103, 191
Sonwalkar, Prasun   60, 83
South Bank Show   125
Spare Rib   76
Step Up 2: The Streets   129, 146
Stewart, John   127, 146
'Superman'   20
surveillance   134

taxonomy   28, 38, 39, 123, 131
TED.com   115, 168
teleology   42, 45, 140
Tennant, David   163–4
textual system   2, 3, 17, 21, 41, 59, 72,
    73, 84, 92, 178
The Australian   88, 90, 97, 153
The Sun   65, 79, 130
The Times   63, 64, 67, 68, 69, 88, 94
    Times Literary Supplement (TLS)
    99, 100
Thérèse philosophe   62
Thompson, Dorothy   69
Thompson, Ethan   127, 145
Thompson, E. P.   60, 74, 85
Thompson, Hunter S.   59
Thomson, Lord Roy   65
Thoth (god)   201
thought
    animistic   33, 173
    habitual   151, 174, 213
    materialistic   33, 173
    public   13, 15, 16, 18, 94–7, 99,
        102–4, 110, 112–13, 115–16, 208
    rational   14
    reflexive   41
    scientific   204
thought control   57–8
Throsby, David   45, 214
Today Tonight   149–50
Toilet Duck   120
Top Gear   123

translation   181, 200, 212
    untranslatability   181
trickster   5, 15, 185n, 199–202, 209,
    210–13
    trickster-entrepreneur   210, 212,
        213
truth   1, 21, 22, 33, 62, 73, 77, 78, 79,
    80, 169, 201, 211
    truth-claims   103
    truth-seeking   3
    (speaking) to power   64, 87, 127
    truthfulness   24
    truthiness   73
Tudou (China)   9
Turnbull, Sue   155n
Turner, G.   67, 77, 87, 103n, 124, 154,
    155
Turner, J. M. W.   38
Twitter   14n, 56, 115

US Magazine   153
user-created content   167, 176, 186
    see also consumer-created content
user-generated content   8, 13, 88,
    149

Vaidhyanathan, Siva   105
value chain   24, 47, 49, 82, 84
    model of communication   80–2,
        86
    of meaning   81
Veblen, Thorstein   27–8, 29, 32–3, 40,
    42, 43, 45, 54, 58, 60, 173–4, 203
Viacom   50, 127, 130
Vogue   197–8
Vološinov, Valentin   181
Voltaire (François-Marie Arouet)   63

Wales, princes of   68
Wallerstein, Immanuel   85, 135
Warren, Tony   124, 130
Watson, Emma   48

Web 2.0   6, 77, 115, 118, 125, 128, 131, 192
Webb, Robert   62, 63, 84
Weber, Max   31, 34
Weinberger, David   105
Wellcome Foundation   171
Westbury, Marcus   43, 208
Whiteley, Nigel   124
Wikipedia   25, 93, 115, 130, 161, 171, 175
Williams, Raymond   29–36, 39, 43, 74, 84, 86, 135, 177, 180, 181, 182
Wilson, E. O.   16, 21, 54
Wolfe, Cary   214
Wolfe, Tom   179
Wolframmathematica   161

Woodall, Trinny   194
Welch, Evelyn   197
Wright, Joseph (of Derby)   38

YouTube   9, 12, 25, 57, 60, 61, 88, 89, 92, 93, 97, 115, 118, 123, 126, 127, 128, 129, 146, 148–9, 150, 154, 155–6, 160, 161, 162, 166–7, 168, 171, 175

Zelizer, Barbie   80, 91, 177
zettabyte   9, 14
Zittrain, Jonathan   111, 118, 144, 167, 182
Žižek, Slavoj   195
Zoe, Rachel   194